Happiness
and Tears

LOUIS BARFE is an expert on all aspects of the
entertainment industry. He is the author of
*Where Have All The Good Times Gone? The
Rise and Fall of the Record Industry*, *Turned
Out Nice Again: The Story of British Light
Entertainment* and *The Trials and Triumphs
of Les Dawson*.

Happiness and Tears

The Ken Dodd Story

Louis Barfe

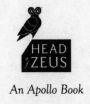

HEAD
of ZEUS

An Apollo Book

This is an Apollo book, first published in the UK in 2019 by Head of Zeus Ltd
This paperback edition first published in the UK in 2020 by Head of Zeus Ltd

9 7 5 3 1 2 4 6 8

A catalogue record for this book is available from
the British Library.

ISBN (PB): 9781788549547
ISBN (E): 9781788549523

Typeset by Adrian McLaughlin

Printed and bound in Great Britain by
CPI Group (UK) Ltd, Croydon CR0 4YY

MIX
Paper from
responsible sources
FSC
www.fsc.org   FSC® C020471

Head of Zeus Ltd
5–8 Hardwick Street
London EC1R 4RG

WWW.HEADOFZEUS.COM

IMAGE CREDITS
2, 8, 9, 11, 13, 14 Shutterstock Images;
5, 6, 10, 12 Alamy Stock Photo; 15 © Andy Hollingworth Archive

For Robert Forsyth Murray (1935–2014)

Contents

Contents

Introduction

'What a beautiful day for standing on the steps of the TUC headquarters and shouting a four-letter word. Work.'

The death of variety is traditionally assumed to have happened at some point in the mid-1950s, its demise hastened by the rise of television. Although the variety theatres were closing at an alarming rate in this era, the genre itself carried on for many more years through clubland and television itself. Variety didn't die in the 1950s. It was merely very unwell. Variety died on 11 March 2018, the day Sir Ken Dodd died.

Among the first to pay tribute was Sir Paul McCartney, who called Dodd 'a great champion of his home city and comedy' and recalled the occasions when the Beatles had worked with Dodd, which 'always ended up in tears of laughter'.[1] On Twitter, Sandi Toksvig called Sir Ken the 'best dinner companion I ever sat next to', remembering that she 'just laughed and laughed and tried not to drown in my soup. Thank you for the genius.'[2]

Sir Ken's wife, Anne, Lady Dodd, greeted the press and fans in the rain outside their home on Thomas Lane, Knotty

Ash, and said: 'I have lost a most wonderful husband. I've had the supreme joy and privilege of working and living with him as a partner for the past forty years. The world has lost a most life-enhancing, brilliant, creative comedian with an operatically trained voice, who just wanted to make people happy. He lived to perfect his art and entertain his live and adoring audiences.'[3]

Comedian Gary Delaney perhaps caught the mood best when he called Dodd 'one of the all-time greats' and announced that 'the funeral will be held on Wednesday, Thursday, Friday and most of Saturday'.[4] Dodd was not a man to whom the normal laws of time and space applied. When I finally saw him on stage, in March 2009 at the Marina Theatre in Lowestoft after years of wanting to, he finished around midnight, four and a half hours after curtain up.* His audiences loved him.

When Dodd died, social media seemed to be divided into two camps: those who wondered what all the fuss was about, and those who had seen him in live performance. Although Dodd made many decent television shows over his long career, the medium diminished his magic. If a person coming at the comedy of Ken Dodd cold, purely through his recorded legacy, fails to find any humour in it, the traditional response of 'You had to be there' applies several-hundred-fold. Once in the seat, it was easy to understand his popularity.

'The first time I went to see him live, it was a total revelation to me,' says Ashtar Al Khirsan, who spent several months with

---

* At the time, I lived ten minutes' walk from the theatre, for which I was grateful.

Dodd for a BBC documentary. 'He started singing a song that I didn't recognize, and every single person, it was a packed house, every single person in the audience started singing. I looked down the audience and God knows what the collective age of the audience, just that row of people I was sitting in, must have been. It was a really elderly audience but the joy on people's faces and the sense of communal enjoyment, the spirit of the whole thing. It was all about celebration and all about joy and pleasure.'[5]

One occasion when television did harness the magic of the man with the mad hair and the wayward teeth was in November 1963, when Granada producer Johnnie Hamp paired Doddy with The Beatles for a short feature on a regional news programme, *Scene at 6.30*. On one level, the only things connecting them were their common city of origin and their native Scouse humour.

However, at this early stage in the Fab Four's career, they were still very much a variety act themselves. Nobody could have quite foreseen the way in which they would change the landscape of entertainment, but Hamp knew that this was probably the last time The Beatles would deign to appear on a regional TV show. They were on the brink of conquering America. The survival of this piece of television captures a moment in time, a moment when the North of England was changing the world, and Ken Dodd was a part of it.

Most public figures have to die before they are celebrated in statue form. In 2009, Dodd was immortalized in bronze on the concourse at Liverpool Lime Street station, as part of a two-piece work by Tom Murphy called 'Chance Meeting'.

The counterpart to Dodd was a statue of Labour MP Bessie Braddock, with whom staunch Conservative* Dodd admitted he 'had many an argument about politics' on the train to London. Many people passing through the station stopped to have their picture taken with the statue. More than a few were surprised and delighted to be joined in the picture by the real-life Sir Ken.

At the time of Dodd's death, the statues had been removed temporarily while building work was being undertaken at the station. As a mark of respect, his effigy was restored to public view hurriedly and soon became a shrine for fans, as did his house in Knotty Ash, where tickling sticks and flowers built up around the gate. The public affection for Dodd was obvious wherever he went but nowhere more than his home city.

Although he stood up and told jokes, Dodd was never a stand-up comedian. To the very last, he was a music hall comic. His *Happiness Show*, which did the rounds of provincial theatres until his final illness, was an old-school variety show in every detail. Dodd's loyal partner, Anne, billed as Sybie Jones,† would provide musical interludes on piano, guitar and flute, and there was usually another act or two. Listing the bill for a Llandudno show on BBC Radio Wales in 2015, Dodd spoke particularly effusively of a musical act called Andante, consisting of 'a very beautiful lady and rather a plain man'.[6]

---

* Not a Tory, he always maintained. Tories came from the landed gentry and public school. He and Margaret Thatcher were Conservatives.
† Lady Dodd's full name before marriage was Sybil Anne Jones.

At his best, Dodd was a creator of superb absurd vulgarity. 'What a lovely day for sticking a cucumber through the vicar's letterbox and shouting "Cooee, Reverend, the Martians have landed."' While one of his best-loved jokes referred to alien beings, Bob Monkhouse thought he might well be one himself. 'Doddy is an oddity. The fact that he's a lovable oddity is kind of a plus, and we all feel very fond of Doddy, and audiences are devoted to him… I don't think that you can look at Ken Dodd and, however much you may laugh at him and enjoy him, you're always conscious of the fact that he's come from another planet. Ken apparently came from a loving home with a loving mother and a loving father, and had a very solid home in which he still lives, so he has a tremendous basis, but you're always aware of the fact that he's definitely of another species.'[7]

In an act running for several hours, it can't all be gold but Dodd had a winning way with corn. The key to his stage success was the rolling boil. Many of the individual jokes would raise barely a titter in isolation but delivered with Dodd's relentlessness and spiced with originals, audiences often found themselves still laughing at a tagline from three jokes earlier, and struggling to keep up. 'By relentlessly piling gag on gag instead of waiting for applause (the fatal Cleopatra of the modern telly-comic) Dodd keeps laughter going until it resembles Bergson's "successive rumblings like thunder in a mountain",' wrote the *Guardian*'s Michael Billington in 1973.[8] It was alchemy. It was a tsunami of cumulative humour. Those who left before the end to catch last buses usually did so very reluctantly.

From his childhood, Dodd was told by his father that to succeed in anything, you had to be different. Doddy was certainly that. Although he was in the very best traditions of variety and happily paid tribute to the turns who influenced him, Doddy was an original. It was a stroke of genius for the young man to work out that his distinctive features could be used to great comic effect. 'I'm going to say something now that you're going to be flabbergasted [by]. You're going to say "My my, we can hardly believe that." I wasn't a pretty baby. "My my... " Oh come on, be a bit more convincing, won't you? I was plain. I had it embroidered on my bib, "This way up". I was an ugly baby. I was the only baby in the street whose dummy had a 12-inch flange.'[9]

Dodd would take to the stage with the Great Drum of Knotty Ash, thumping it gleefully while shouting lullabies. That would be enough to make quite the entrance, but he added to the effect through his choice of clothing, described by Michael Billington as 'like something dreamed up by a colour-blind tailor on a weekend bender: a black cape with a lining striped like a liquorice allsort, a maroon maxie allegedly made out of 28 moggies, a mustard-yellow coat and a titfer that is eminently phallacious'. Dodd demanded attention. He was impossible to ignore. Nobody looked like him. Nobody sounded like him. Nobody thought like him. Nobody dressed like him.

In the old days of music hall, the big-name turns could tour with the same well-worn routines for decades, and often had their acts stolen wholesale by lesser performers. George Formby – the son of a legendary Lancashire comic with the same name – only got into show business because so many people were doing his late father's act word for word that he rationalized if anyone should be trading on the name, he should. Nobody could have copied Dodd. Not even himself. He never did the same show twice. Imitators could have done something resembling a Dodd act, and he was a gift to impressionists, but it would always be a snapshot of an ever-changing situation.

In cynical sales terms, and Dodd happily admitted he thought that way, he developed an irresistible product and marketed it brilliantly. What was the product, though? A big element was himself. He was lucky to be gifted with the raw materials. Dodd was born funny. He was born to do what he did and be who he was, he was clever enough to work on it and shrewd enough to take all the opportunities he could to make it happen.

However, the idea of Dodd as a salesman of jokes, one that he propagated himself, is an oversimplification. He was a craftsman and people paid willingly for that craftsmanship in the same way they'd pay for a handmade pair of shoes. Moreover, Doddy never took his audiences for granted. He was always genuinely thrilled that people wanted to buy his wares and his after-sales service was second to none, refusing to leave until the last autograph had been signed. He wouldn't just scribble a signature to get away. He'd take the time to talk to the punters. He always knew who paid his wages and treated those people with profound respect. As he noted in 2003:

It's eyeball to eyeball and you learn to love an audience, respect an audience and treat an audience as individuals.

It's terrible when you hear somebody in a theatre say 'What's that lot out there like tonight?' That lot. How dare you? That lot is an audience who have paid you the greatest compliment in the world by giving their time and their hard-earned money to see you perform.[10]

Sir Ken was highly protective of that audience. As the comedian and the fans got older, Dodd was quick to upbraid anybody inclined to sneer. 'He was very respectful of the people that would come and see him and follow him round,' says Ashtar Al Khirsan. 'He didn't want anybody taking the mickey out of anybody. He was very respectful of older people. He just didn't want people denigrating his audience in any way.'[11]

Dodd was a funny one, in both senses of the word. He was renowned for being 'close' with his money, and yet he never succumbed to the easy payday of a TV advert. He never wanted to make it in America. Indeed, he seemed fairly indifferent about making it anywhere other than his beloved Liverpool. He never craved film roles, even in the cheerfully cheap British comedies of the 1960s and 1970s. His career in television lasted for over sixty years and yet he seemed to hold the medium in contempt. He shunned show business parties.

Dodd was a driven man. All he ever really wanted to do with his life was to stand on a stage and make people laugh. Looking back on his life, speaking to those who worked with him, it becomes clear that this was his obsession, and his purpose, to which all else, even the women in his life – Anita Boutin and Anne Jones – came second. And yet, both women were integral to the development of that career and Dodd's success. Until she developed cancer, Boutin was Dodd's secretary, lover, constant companion and mother substitute, ready with a notebook to register the response given to each gag in each town. After Boutin's death, Jones took on a similar role but, as a trained dancer – indeed, a former Bluebell Girl – she took to the stage with her partner, her singing and piano playing becoming a vital part of Dodd's live shows.

His latter-day shows were billed as *The Ken Dodd Happiness Show*, incorporating the title of the 1964 single that became his signature tune. A year after 'Happiness', he scored his biggest chart hit with 'Tears', a million-seller that held the number one spot for five weeks and outstripped even The Beatles to be the biggest-selling single of the year.

Dodd knew both states of being. Happiness was his default setting. He was a self-described optimist, counselling regular use of the 'chuckle muscle'. When neglected, this vital organ was known to drop off. Some who worked closely with him have suggested that his happiness was largely contingent on getting his own way. He would have dismissed suggestions that he and his siblings were spoiled, but the impression one gets from his own memories of childhood was that he was indulged. The tears were rarer than the sunny hours, and were always related to loss. The deaths of his mother, father and his first fiancée, Anita Boutin, hit him hard. And then there was his tax trial.

Sir Ken Dodd was a difficult man who inspired love and loyalty. A cynical innocent, he knew how to operate in a business where sharks circle but he never lost his childlike outlook or fundamental kindness. He was always late for everything but he was more than tolerated because, when he finally arrived, he was well worth the angst. While many in show business affect to hate their fame, Dodd relished it. He loved being famous. He loved meeting his fans. 'I like to be Ken Dodd the comedian, the entertainer, the show business fella, yes,' he told Professor Anthony Clare on Radio 4's *In the Psychiatrist's Chair* in 1987.

Where others emerged from a run-in with the Inland Revenue with their reputations in tatters, Doddy came out of his tax trial beaten and bloodied, but still funny and still able to ply his trade. The normal rules don't apply to stars. They breathe a different air to the rest of us. The normal rules never applied to Doddy, even before he was a star. He was a one-off, and he knew it. He built a brilliant career on it. He died at a great age, albeit younger than he would have hoped ('I want to be shot by a jealous husband at the age of a hundred and twenty.'). This is his story.

1

Portrait of the artist
as a Diddyman

'Hands up all the mothers in the audience who've got
ugly children. Not many, is it?'

Every good comedian and comic writer knows the value of a funny place name. Some of them are made up. Doctor Evadne Hinge and Dame Hilda Bracket lived in the Suffolk village of Stackton Tressell. Don't look for it, it was never there. Some are based loosely on reality. In the Surrey and south London fringes, there is Cheam and there is North Cheam, but there is no officially recognized district called East Cheam. Ray Galton and Alan Simpson found the word funny and decided that its comic potential could be improved by a level of specificity that suggested that Anthony Aloysius St John Hancock couldn't quite afford to live in Cheam proper. Many, however, are taken straight from road signs and atlases. When naming the lead character in the brilliant, whimsical 1960 comedy series *The*

Strange World of Gurney Slade, writers Sid Green and Dick Hills, along with the show's star Anthony Newley, went to a real Somerset village for inspiration. The great Jimmy James named one of his stooges Hutton Conyers, after a village near Harrogate, and the other Bretton Woods, after the location of the Mount Washington Hotel in New Hampshire where the global monetary system was agreed in 1944.

Ken Dodd had the good fortune to be born in Knotty Ash. Many assume that the district is a figment of Dodd's considerable imagination, but it's real. For the removal of doubt, it's on the signs at Junction 5 of the M62 as you enter Liverpool from Manchester. Something about that 'Kn-' makes it irresistible. That's why Robert Wass became Bobby Knutt. Think of the Knorr adverts, where they claimed to have the 'k-nowhow'. Think of Cosmo Smallpiece's catchphrase, 'knickers, knackers, knockers'.

The area took its name from a gnarled, knobbly old ash tree on what's now the East Prescot Road. The former location of the tree was marked in Victorian times by the erection of the Knotty Ash Hotel. In its early years, it was a favoured stop-off for Lord Derby's farm labourers on their way to the market at Old Swan. Later it became a thriving boozer, one of the last to retain rooms solely for male drinkers. After a period when it was derelict and a stint as a discount bed emporium, the premises are now shared by a car rental firm and a restaurant.

From wherever it sprang, it's a funny name, and it's from where Kenneth Arthur Dodd sprang on 8 November 1927, born at 76 Empire Street to Arthur Dodd and his wife, Sarah (née Gray). Both born in 1896, Dodd's parents had married in 1922, with their first child, William, coming along in 1925, followed by Kenneth, and then in 1930, a baby sister, June.

On the day that Dodd was born, the attraction for the week at Liverpool's Royal Court Theatre was an 'important personal visit of the popular Liverpool favourites' Julia Neilson and Fred Terry in *The Wooing of Katherine Parr*. Over at the Shakespeare Theatre, *The Wrecker*, Arnold Ridley's follow-up to his hit play *The Ghost Train*, was on its out-of-town try-out run before taking up residence in London's West End at the New Theatre (now the Noël Coward). Meanwhile, moving away from the legitimate theatre towards variety, the Empire Theatre, a sumptuous barn opened just two years earlier by the Moss circuit, was featuring a musical version of *Peg O' My Heart* called *Peg O'Mine*. Ken Dodd would become intimately acquainted with all three venues, and would be instrumental in saving the Royal Court in 1970, but this was all a long way off on that winter Tuesday.[1]

The Knotty Ash into which Dodd emerged was a place transforming itself from a village to a suburb of Liverpool. Large houses previously occupied by moneyed families were being sold and torn down for new housing. There was an urgent need for accommodation after the First World War, with Lloyd George declaring that there should be 'homes fit for heroes'. In the short term, the huts formerly used as part of Unit W Camp Hospital 40, a facility for US Army personnel, were pressed into service for rehoming families.*

---

* The permanent buildings put up on the site towards the end of the war became the original Alder Hey hospital.

The conditions were less than ideal. One resident calling herself 'Mere Woman' wrote to the *Liverpool Echo* in the winter of 1925 to observe that 'all summer we are choked by clouds of dust, now we are ankle deep in mud'.[2]

The social house-building programmes of the 1920s and 1930s were the permanent answer, but they changed the character of Knotty Ash completely. It was the final stage in a process that had begun in the mid-eighteenth century when a new turnpike road was driven through the village. Prior to this, 'no stage coaches came nearer than Warrington, the roads from thence being impassable'.[3] Afterwards, the stage-coach service from London to Liverpool passed through the hamlet once a week, taking four days on the journey.

The next stage in the build-up of Knotty Ash had been the opening of the Liverpool and Manchester Railway in 1830, with a station at Broad Green, still in use today. Then came the electric Corporation trams, which began running in 1898. According to local historian Gordon Radley, right up until the Second World War, 'many people from the city would take a tram ride to Knotty Ash for the afternoon out in the country and some remember buying cut flowers at the cottages before their ride back to the hustle and bustle of the town'.[4]

Like anywhere, Knotty Ash had its share of eccentrics, fit to feed the mind of a growing surrealist. Chief among these was a man dubbed 'The Hermit of Knotty Ash' by the *Liverpool Echo*. His presence was noted and documented in the census year of 1931, when an enumerator called at 'a hollow, grass covered mound – formerly an "ice house" for storing game'[5] in what had been the grounds of Dovecot House, one of the grand houses of the district.

The man in the mound came to its muddy, sack-covered entrance and refused to give his name, age or any details to the enumerator, but when the *Echo* called to follow up on the discovery, he explained that he was an ex-soldier with a grievance. Born in Ireland, his name was William Cummings, although he was generally known as Paddy. He had been in the Connaught Rangers but 'after many years' service in the Army, I was shabbily treated, though I had a good record, and I refuse to appeal to the country that did me wrong'.[6]

He was a source of fascination to many, near and far. Indeed, Liverpudlians on their tram jaunts into the country used the hermit's mound as a landmark. Some local children took him scones and beer, but others were less kind. Many years later, an *Echo* reader recalled 'creeping up to the hermit's abode with his pals and being chased away by its irate occupier, armed with a stick'.[7] Given that Dodd described his childhood hobbies as 'digging holes, setting fire to my coat, falling out of trees, and sending away to this place in London for itching powder and stink bombs',[8] it's not too difficult to imagine him being chased away by Cummings, nor is it the biggest stretch for a whimsically minded boy from a real hermit in a hillock to jam butty mines and snuff quarries with tiny staff.

Many northern comedians have mined their poverty-stricken upbringings and the casual cruelty meted out by their families for humorous capital, but this was never an avenue open to Dodd. To his dying day, he idolized both of his parents. When asked by Roy Plomley on *Desert Island Discs* in 1963 to name his primary comic inspiration, Dodd replied 'my favourite comedian is my father. He always makes me laugh. I get a lot of material from him.'[9] Returning to the desert island twenty-seven years later with Sue Lawley, he picked up the subject again, calling his father 'a wonderful man... marvellous', and declaring with very obvious sincerity that his mother 'was only a little lady, but she had a heart as big as Knotty Ash'.[10]

Arthur Dodd was in trade as a coal merchant, running his business from the family home at Oak Cottage, 76 Thomas Lane, a house dating from 1782. It wasn't Dovecot House but, with a sizeable barn attached, it wasn't too shabby either. One journalist interviewing Dodd in 1989 claimed that his 'earliest memories are of a life of grinding poverty',[11] but this doesn't quite fit with the actual quote given by the comedian. 'I don't think I have ever seen anyone work as hard as my mother and father. Every Christmas Eve we would go to bed and my father was still out trying to sell coal until two or three in the morning.' The journalist noted that 'business was always in cash and Dodd senior had a deep distrust of banks'.

While Dodd's father clearly earned every penny, the fact is that there was money coming into the household, and they had somewhere to live, which was more than could be said for many in Liverpool at the time. Arthur Dodd might not have owned the means of production but he was a businessman rather than a wage slave. Nobody was forcing him to spend every hour God sent selling coal, just as years later, nobody forced his son to sell jokes for five hours a night. Certainly, by 1938, the Dodd family were doing well enough to have a telephone. How rare and special this was can be gauged from the fact that their number was Old Swan 10.

The Dodds might not have been poverty-stricken but they were not immune to suffering. When Kenneth was a toddler, he was hit with a bout of double pneumonia and 'nearly didn't make it'. Nearly sixty years later, he told Professor Anthony Clare on Radio 4's *In the Psychiatrist's Chair* that 'I know they had someone in to say prayers over me... they always regarded me as a miracle.'[12] For the rest of his life, Dodd had a weak chest, chronic asthma and emphysema. This could well have been related to the coal dust in and around the family home, as Arthur also suffered.

When he wasn't providing Knotty Ash with nutty slack, Arthur Dodd earned some extra money from music. Dodd told Roy Plomley in 1963 that his father 'came from a large family, they all played instruments';[13] in Arthur's case, the clarinet and saxophone. He led his own dance band and encouraged his son to take up the piano and cornet.* Meanwhile, Sarah gave her three children 'the most precious thing I think any parent can give any child, that was that she spoke to us'.[14] The idea of actually engaging with your children would have been anathema at that time to many parents, who preferred their offspring to be seen and not heard. 'We used to spend hours and hours just talking to my mum... about her childhood and schooling,' Dodd recalled, adding that 'she was quite a brainy lady'.[15]

---

* Dodd's teeth would have made the saxophone – 'an ill wind that nobody blows good' – problematic.

Dodd claimed to have got his first laugh in public inadvertently, aged two, when, during a duet by his aunt and uncle at a local amateur concert, he wandered on stage with no trousers. Despite being 'a shy youngster',[16] Dodd properly developed the urge to be a performer very early on and found his parents to be full of encouragement. For his seventh birthday, he received a Punch-and-Judy set from his father and began inviting his school friends around for concerts in the backyard.

In one version of the story, Dodd said he 'charged a penny and two pence for two grades of ground-floor seating',[17] but when speaking to Roy Plomley on *Desert Island Discs* in 1963, he said he 'used to charge two cigarette cards for admission'.[18] Later still, he would claim he accepted either, and noted his already robust attitude to audience disapproval: 'If anyone thought they had a criticism, you just used to hurl a clod of earth at the other person's head and this used to settle them.'[19]

The next step of his stagecraft development came in the post. Every week, he'd buy all of the boys' story papers and devour the tales of derring-do, but the advertisements were just as appealing as the yarns. 'I used to read this wonderful intellectual magazine, this paper called *The Wizard*,' he told Sue Lawley in 1990. 'I used to write away for these itching powders and things like a seebackroscope… a thing you put in your eye and you can see if an assassin is creeping up behind you, which is very important when you're eight years old. I read this advertisement one day, it said "Fool your teachers, amaze your friends, send sixpence in stamps, become a ventrilo-quist… and learn how to throw your voice." So this tickled me no end. I sent away for this little booklet and I became a ventriloquist.'[20]

Dodd told this story in just about every interview he gave. There is often a disparity between show business anecdotes and the truth of the matter, with stories becoming 'improved' beyond recognition. However, apart from a little polishing over the years, including a slight tightening up of the wording of the advertisement, a search through the back issues of *The Wizard* proves this one to be accurate.

Over several weeks in October and November 1937, Ellisdon and Son of 246 High Holborn, London, WC1, advertised their range of novelties, culminating in a full-page advertisement in the week of Dodd's tenth birthday. Alongside the Magic Nose Flute ('Produces very sweet music that somewhat resembles a flute'), Professor Goubert's course in hypnotism and the aforementioned Seebackroscope, there it is:

BOYS! Learn to throw your voice. This book by Prof. Foxton tells you how. Lots of fun fooling teacher, police-man or friends. THE VENTRILO. A little instrument fits in the mouth out of sight used with above for Bird Calls, etc. Anyone can use it. Never fails. A full course book on Ventriloquism, together with the Ventrilo. Price 6d. Postage 1½d.

Soon after the book arrived, Arthur Dodd was satisfied that his son was following Professor Foxton's advice sufficiently to warrant the acquisition of a dummy, or as Dodd preferred to call it 'a ventriloquial figure'.[21] The arrival of Charlie

Brown* inspired Dodd to practise the craft and he 'mastered the technique in a year'.[22]

A picture of Dodd and Charlie Brown shows the dummy wearing a sailor's suit, with the boy ventriloquist dressed as a senior officer. This could well have been the act with which Dodd made his debut outside the backyard of 76 Thomas Lane. The exact venue of Dodd's first gig was either his school or St Edward's Orphanage, located in Thingwall Hall, one of the few big houses of old Knotty Ash to survive.† The reason for the uncertainty is Dodd himself. In a 1956 *Liverpool Echo* profile, the school show comes first, with Dodd being paid a shilling for his efforts, and the charity show at St Edward's, for which he was paid half a crown, comes second. However, when talking about his formative years to Sue Lawley in 1990, he reversed the situation. 'I learned there, you see,' he explains. 'I had to learn a very, very important lesson in show business. You have to learn to take a cut gracefully.'[23]

Another lesson Dodd learned early on was the importance of good quality material. Luckily, he could call on the services of the man who he referred to frequently as 'my favourite comedian', his father. As he recalled:

---

* A name later made famous in ventriloquism by Arthur Worsley, while at the same time being very hard to say when throwing your voice – Dodd would later ask Dickie Mint if he wanted 'a big bottle of brown beer or a shandy'. Mint always went for shandy, Dodd's response being a very knowing 'Good'.

† Thingwall Hall had been bought in the early twentieth century by a Belgian religious group called the Brothers of Charity, who run it to this day under its original name as a home for vulnerable adults.

My father used to write my scripts for me. Charlie Brown resides now in the attic at Knotty Ash. He's only got one eye. Since then, of course, the Diddymen have come into being. The sort of act I used to do, I used to say:

'You're here?'
'Yes.'
'You've arrived.'
'Yes.'
'Can't you say anything but "yes"?'
'Yes.?'
'What?'
'No.'
'Your name is Dickie Mint.'
'Yes, cock.'
'When you talk to me you'll say "sir".'
'Sir.'
'Yes.'
'Yes, sir, cock.'[24]

As hard as they worked, the senior Dodds always knew the importance of fun. Dodd's nephew John Lewis described visits to Thomas Lane as an 'adventure'. Every time in adulthood when Dodd talked about his childhood, he talks of his parents almost as though he were an only child, rather than the middle of three. He says in passing how close he was to Bill and June, then speaks of his parents in idealized terms. His father was the funniest man he ever met, his mother was the kindest woman he'd ever known. It seems that Dodd

11

was very much indulged by Arthur and Sarah, and it raises a question as to whether Bill and June got the same treatment.

It was an impression picked up on by Professor Anthony Clare when he got Dodd *In the Psychiatrist's Chair* for Radio 4 in 1987. Responding to Dodd's claim that 'when you're a child sometimes you feel that you're special', Clare asks 'Were you treated special?' Dodd replies that all three Dodd children were. Clare presses the point, asking if his siblings would say he was special. 'I don't think so, no,' replies Dodd. 'I'm sure they wouldn't, no.'[25]

Dodd's birth as an entertainer was all happening in late 1938 and early 1939, and he already had one of the comic props for which he would become renowned. In later years, he described his younger self as a 'Just William' sort of figure, and one of the scrapes he got himself into had lasting consequences. 'I wanted to try and ride my bike with my eyes shut, and you can. For about six yards,' he told Lawley. 'Then boom, the kerb, over the handlebars,' and the most famous set of wayward choppers in show business came into being. 'I could have had them straightened. I asked all of my friends. My agent nearly had a heart attack.'[26]

When he was at infants' school, it had fallen to Miss Hill and Miss Sefton to keep the unruly young Dodd in line. He recalled Miss Hill as 'a nice plump lady [with] a very kind, rosy face'. One of her habits was 'to go round sniffing... a very matronly lady, she'd tower over the class of little tots and all of a sudden she'd say "Someone does not smell sweet in this room", and whoever the guilty party was had to leave immediately."[27]

When he ascended to the juniors, Dodd met the headmaster

who would later pay him a shilling for an exhibition of ventriloquism, William Powell, known to pupils as 'Bonky Bill'. Bonky wore a bowler hat, and pupils talked in hushed tones of the day it was knocked off when he wandered unwittingly into the middle of a snowball fight. Dodd was not one of the culprits that time but he was not unfamiliar with the concept of corporal punishment. 'That's when I was in trouble. Not with Bonky Bill, because he was a very nice man, but I always seemed to get the cane. A little tap. Talking, and I was quite good with an elastic band and ink pellets as well. Anything artistic like that.'

Dodd described his early school years as 'a very happy time', made undoubtedly more bearable by the fact that the school was mixed. 'Girls used to sit alongside boys, so I fell in love quite regularly.' When it came to secondary school, Dodd, being a bright lad, won a scholarship to Holt High School, the local grammar. Despite enjoying sport, a quality the school prized, the comedian found his new school far less agreeable. 'Knotty Ash [school] gave me confidence. I wasn't frightened of the world… it gave me the love and affection that children need. This lovely, cosy, warm village feeling. When I went to the Holt College, it was like being thrown into an icy bath. People didn't call you "Ken". It was "DODD". That was one of the things I objected to most of all. "DODD" [shudder]. It was like a slap in the face…'

The change of environment enhanced his rebellious streak and made him tend to concentrate only on the things that interested him. Anything else could fall by the wayside. This became Dodd's attitude throughout his life. He did best what he enjoyed most, so he chose to concentrate on that. 'I was always fond of English. I liked English, geography and history. I think I liked anything where, if I was ambitious or keen on the subject, I could make my own way. What I didn't take kindly to was discipline. I didn't like rules.' Dodd's most frequent breaches were related to punctuality, a theme that would recur throughout his life. 'I'm probably the worst timekeeper in the world,' he admitted in a 1973 television interview. 'My first billing was "Liverpool's latest comedian". It's probably because living so near the [Knotty Ash] school, I never really had to worry about the time.'

The Dodd family were regular visitors to Liverpool's variety halls, principally the Shakespeare Theatre on Fraser Street. Dodd noted with amusement in 1963 that 'they don't play Shakespeare' at the 'Shakey'.[28] However, the principal mode of entertainment even for avid theatregoers was the wireless. As he headed into his teens, Dodd, in his own words, 'fell in love with comedy', and with radio ventriloquism not yet a thing,* his new role models tended to be stand-up comedians. It just so happened that some of the biggest names in radio comedy were Liverpudlian too, and would make a big impression on Dodd.

Although the influence of the gentle, hapless, meandering Robb Wilton was not obvious in the adult Dodd, he was always very keen to cite him as an influence, as did so many others of the same generation, like Les Dawson. 'Every self-respecting

* Peter Brough did his first broadcast with Archie Andrews in 1943, with the series *Educating Archie* not beginning until 1950.

comedian can do a Robb Wilton,' Dodd told Ned Sherrin on Radio 4's *Loose Ends* in 2004, describing Wilton's beloved 'The Day War Broke Out' sketch as 'beautiful comedy... more acting than stand-up comedy... He was the absolute English droll.' Dodd would come to know Wilton well in his later years, as both men were vice-presidents of Liverpool FC.

In adulthood, Dodd adopted some of the speed and relentlessness of Tommy Handley, the dominant figure of wartime radio comedy in ITMA, and a native of Toxteth. He also spoke, awestruck, of the sheer professionalism of Ted Ray. However, the one who had the biggest influence on Dodd, the comedian he would describe as his 'idol', was the diminutive star of *Bandwaggon*, 'Big-Hearted' Arthur Askey.

The show had begun in January 1938, but got off to a shaky start, facing the axe after only three editions. Askey and his co-star, Richard 'Stinker' Murdoch, refused to accept defeat, arguing with producers Harry S. Pepper and Gordon Crier to let them take over writing the comedy side of the show. They invented a flat on the roof of Broadcasting House, filled it with a menagerie that included a goat called Lewis and a cockerel called Gerald, and moved into it once a week for the benefit of a growing and increasingly appreciative audience.

Both Askey and Murdoch came from a concert party background, the only difference being that Murdoch's concert party had been the Footlights at Cambridge University. The contrast – one tall and educated, the other short and instinctive – worked well. It's easy to see why this fantasy world appealed to the young Dodd. It was surreal and highly improbable, but at the same time it sounded not unlike the

15

backyard at Thomas Lane, where the horses that pulled the carts for the coal business, including the fondly remembered Duke, lived alongside domestic pets. Like his father, Dodd suffered throughout his life with asthma, possibly brought on by the proximity to coal dust, but he was an animal lover, with a particular fondness for dogs. In later life, he would be accompanied to his shows by one of a series of poodles, a favoured breed for dog lovers with allergies.

From a very early age, Dodd was addicted to laughter but he wanted to know how it worked. What made something or someone funny? He decided that he was most likely to find the answer in books. The bright young Dodd was a voracious reader, something he and his siblings got from Arthur and Sarah. To the end of his life, he told interviewers his favourite book was *The Wind in the Willows* by Kenneth Grahame. 'I was always proud of the fact that I could read when I was four. I've always loved books,' he explained in 1973, unable to resist making a joke of it. 'My father reads quite a lot. He used to take the *Manchester Guardian*. We found it was a very good paper, because it held the vinegar and the salt better.'[29]

Teasing about his teeth had made him a little withdrawn and he 'would sit in the Picton Reference Library opposite St George's Hall, finding solace in the works of such humorists as Stephen Leacock, Artimus Ward, P. G. Wodehouse and James Thurber. I made a study of their various techniques, trying to evolve a visual and oral style suited to my unorthodox appearance.'[30]

Revisiting the Picton reading room for a 2007 documentary in the BBC's *Arena* strand, Dodd outlined his young approach further. 'I started thinking about "what is a joke?",' he said.

I wanted to know why. Why does a human being laugh? Why do we make this funny noise? Your breath comes in short pants. Why don't your ears light up? Why doesn't your nose wiggle from side to side? Why this? What is a laugh? Why? What goes on in here? Why do human beings laugh when they're confronted with a funny situation, a funny picture or somebody tells them a funny joke? What is humour? What is a joke? How does one be a comedian? I used to come here every day of the week, for months on end. Just sit here and read. Look in the index. Look up the word 'laughter', look up the word 'humour', look up the word 'comedy'. Comedians, clowns, circus, music hall, variety, theatre, I just used to sit down there and read and read and read. And make notes, of course.[31]

Dodd undertook his researches because he couldn't find any existing studies that fitted his needs. In later life, he tended to romanticize the act of sitting in a library with his nose in a book, making it sound like the most exciting thing a 'shy... meek and mild' boy could do. 'I wanted life to be an adventure,' he told Professor Anthony Clare in 1987. 'I wanted to be an explorer, a pioneer. So, here was a land that was uncharted. Here was a land that had never been explained before. Aristotle, I think, said that the essence of the comic was a buckled mill-wheel and I can understand that now. I couldn't understand it then, but I can understand it now, meaning it's life a little bit wobbly.'

It's interesting that Dodd should turn to essayists and humorists like Thurber for inspiration, but never show any interest in developing his own skills on the printed page. From the start, Dodd's writing was intended to be spoken, hopefully for appreciative audiences. He needed the hit that a laugh provided, like an addict needing a fix. He wanted to hear the people enjoying his work. As a result, he spent a lot of his spare time looking for performance outlets where he could put all of his study into practice. Every year, in the run-up to Christmas, notices would appear in the small ads of local newspapers advertising auditions for pantomime dancers, and the *Liverpool Echo* in 1941 was no exception. Most of the ads specified that the dancers should be girls but when one failed to delineate, Dodd seized his chance. It could well have been the one on Thursday, 20 November 1941 requesting 'DANCERS, preferably 14, by Xmas, for Liverpool pantomime – Saturday 3.30–5pm, 26 Island Rd., Garston'.[32] Dodd had just turned fourteen, so would have regarded himself as ideal for the job.

Unfortunately, the ad had been placed by the producers of the Pavilion Theatre's production of *Cinderella* with certain assumptions. 'The producer looked puzzled when I lined up with a bevy of beauties,' he said fifteen years later. 'I had not realized the audition was for girls. He drew his stage manager aside and they conversed in whispers, every now and then glancing at me oddly.'[33] Sensing the boy's enthusiasm, the producer offered Dodd a few weeks' work over the Christmas holidays as props boy and general dogsbody. The work wasn't just behind the scenes. When Cinderella's coach took to the stage, it was Dodd's responsibility to lead the ponies. On one occasion, Dodd found himself adding an unplanned extra scene to the production:

For the transformation scene, I had to rush onto the blacked-out stage and remove the pumpkins and rat-traps. One night the lights went on too soon. I was left standing in the centre of the stage – with the pumpkins, rat-traps and the galloping ponies. Embarrassed, I looked from one rat-trap to another, feeling a fellow sympathy for Britain's rodent population – and wishing a pumpkin would open up and swallow me. The audience roared.[34]

The lad's calm under pressure impressed Albert Burdon, the South Shields-born comedian who was playing Buttons. Now largely a forgotten figure, Burdon was, in his day, loved by audiences and respected hugely by his fellow professionals. If his name is obscure, his work remains highly visible. Burdon was the originator and master practitioner of a scene that remains a pantomime staple – the wallpaper routine. When, in 1961, Bruce Forsyth and Norman Wisdom had to fill a whole edition of ATV's *Sunday Night at the London Palladium* themselves because of an Equity strike, they borrowed Burdon's masterpiece. This timeless silent slapstick scene involves two workers attempting and failing to wallpaper a room, with the stage becoming thick with paste (in reality, shaving soap in water). Eventually, they attempt and fail to remain upright because of the slick of slippery foam. Dodd was in the privileged position of being paid 15 shillings a week to watch Burdon at work, an experience that he filed away as a masterclass in stagecraft.

Soon after his first taste of work experience in a proper theatre, Dodd met Hilda Fallon, a vivacious and talented young singer, actress and dancer from the nearby district of West Derby. Only four years older than Dodd, she was nonetheless already an accomplished dance teacher in her late teens, providing her troupe of pupils for charity shows around the Liverpool area. This would become Fallon's life's work, and her Roadshow of young talent became well-known on Merseyside. Meanwhile, many of the performers she trained, like Keith Chegwin, Freddie Starr and singer Tommy Blaize, would go on to achieve national fame. Dodd was one of Fallon's earliest protégés, brought in to provide comic relief among the balletics, and he was always keen to stress how much she had taught him.

With the Second World War ongoing, Fallon toured the hospitals of Merseyside with shows for convalescing troops. 'We were awful [but] God loves a trier,' he admitted to Ned Sherrin in 2004. 'We all tried very hard, and we were kids as well, you see. I think the soldiers and the airmen we were playing to had children themselves. I think it didn't really matter what we did. We were children and we reminded them of home.'[35]

As well as giving Dodd vital performing experience, being part of Fallon's concert party brought home the realities of the conflict to the young comedian. 'Up til then,' he explained, 'it was a bit like the football league table, you know, we'd sink one of theirs and they'd sink one of ours. One day, in this concert party, we did a show at what was then the Royal Southern Hospital. [...] That's when war really came home to me. I knew what war was then, it wasn't an adventure anymore, it wasn't fun. It was very, very tragic.'

Dodd left school at sixteen and began working for his

father, delivering coal with his brother Bill. 'They were very happy times,' he told Sue Lawley, recalling that he and Bill made the journeys between deliveries pass with humour: 'We used to write jokes and make up songs.' He stayed with the family firm until he was twenty, when he felt the urge to strike out on his own. This he did by purchasing a furniture van and fitting it out with shelves so it could serve as a mobile shop. His plan was to become 'a travelling tinker', selling household products to the housewives of 'the new estates, such as West Derby, Huyton and Dovecot, which had no shops'.[36]

With an investment of £4 10s from his mother, he went to buy stock and came back with a job lot of boot polish. On his return, Sarah told her son that he might need to carry a greater range of items and sent him back with some more money to diversify. He returned with soap and bleach, which he combined to make 'my own soap preparation, "Kaydee"'. The mixing of the ingredients was, he later admitted, an inexact science and some bleach-heavy batches caused havoc with the laundry of Liverpool: 'One of my best customers said delightedly, "Grand stuff, your Kaydee. Made the sleeves of my hubbie's shirt fall off!" Her attitude puzzled me. I concluded she was not her husband's best friend. I kept my eye open for an irate docker with bulging muscles and no shirt sleeves.'[37]

Full-time work had not curtailed Dodd's show business activities and he spent his evenings performing at clubs and masonic functions. He had matured into a decent baritone but rather than try his hand as a straight singer, he decided his voice was best used in the service of comedy. 'My idea of being funny was to take one of the classics and burlesque it,' he explained in his 1982 BBC television series, *Ken Dodd's Showbiz*.[38] Putting Charlie Brown to one side after a decade, he donned a tailcoat, greased his hair into a centre parting, stuck on a fake moustache, picked up a battered euphonium which he never played, and billed himself as 'Professor Yaffle Chuckabutty, operatic tenor and sausage knotter'.

Reprising the act for posterity* in that 1982 series, Dodd performed 'an haria from the opera *If She Wants to Wriggle, Let Her*. This is "La donna e mobile", translated means "Does anybody want to buy a lady's bike?"' After tackling the piece in the original Italian, he continues in English with spoof lyrics:

> Woman is fickle,
> Give her a tickle.
> Hold her waist tightly,
> Do it twice nightly.

> All over Italy,
> Birds sing so prettily.
> To keep a tidy town,
> They all fly upside down.

> My auntie Nelly,
> Has a big... telly,
> But me auntie Lil,
> Has a bigger one still.[39]

---

* Doubtless at the prompting of producer John Fisher, a keen historian of comedy himself.

A booking at the Vaudeville Club on Tweed Street in the early 1950s introduced Dodd to a young nurse called Anita Boutin. Boutin and Dodd were from the same part of town, Anita being a West Derby girl, and they seemed to hit it off. Already making a name for himself, Dodd struggled to keep up with the correspondence involved, particularly with fans. Anita began helping him with the fan mail in her spare time. This grew into a full-time job and, at the same time, a romance developed. According to her brother Bill, speaking to *The People* in 1965, Boutin would be a vital catalyst in Dodd's career. She was the one who persuaded him to do less straight singing and more comedy.

In December 1952, Dodd returned to his family's favourite variety hall, the 'Shakey', this time as a performer, not an audience member. He had been booked for a week on the bill supporting a live action transfer of 'The Back Entry Diddlers', a popular *Liverpool Echo* comic strip about a football team of Scouse urchins. George Green had been providing cartoons for the *Echo*'s sports pages since the 1930s and had begun by including the Diddlers as background colour. They proved so popular that in February 1951, they were given their own full-page strip every Saturday, and less than two years later were on stage.

The show sounds fairly gruelling, showcasing 'local juvenile talent who sing, dance, whistle and play the piano',[40] so it's unsurprising that Dodd's act shone out like a shaft of gold. One gentleman who went to see the show, a Mr W. Barber of Maghull, was moved to write to Ronnie Waldman, head of light entertainment at BBC Television, to alert him to Dodd's existence. Referring to him as 'Ken Dodds', a common mistake in his early billings and notices, Barber informed Waldman that Dodd was funnier than Norman Wisdom. Waldman passed the note on to the auditions department, who replied to Mr Barber, suggesting that 'Dodds' [sic] should apply for an audition in the conventional manner. Either Mr Barber did not pass on the advice or Dodd felt that he was not yet ready for radio, as there is no trace of an audition in the BBC files.

Dodd might have been a 'shy youngster' but he never lacked self-belief. His early story is short of tales of woe. The overall impression gained is of a young man who knew what he was good at and how to make it work for him. He had enjoyed a relatively comfortable upbringing in a house full of love and laughter. His was never the comedy of adversity. He used bathos skilfully but his humour was fundamentally upbeat. He liked to suggest this was down to a combination of the place where he was born and the time in which his comic mind was formed.

Liverpool people are, he told Sue Lawley in 1990, 'supreme optimists [seeing] humour and laughter in every situation… Everything's a joke.'[41] From this default position, he added the influence of wartime comedians. 'People needed their spirits lifting,' he said to Ned Sherrin in 2004, 'and that is why, I think, when we started winning… the comedians were all jolly… Very optimistic comedy. I suppose I was born and bred in that era, therefore my comedy is "By Jove, what a beautiful day, ha ha, what a beautiful day for putting your kilt on upside down and shouting 'How's that for a shuttlecock?'".'

The importance of Dodd's day job in honing the comedy cannot be underestimated. As noted by Michael Billington in

1977, Dodd addressing audience members as 'Missus' was a hangover from the door-to-door days. Over in Manchester, Les Dawson would hone his people skills in similar circumstances, working as a Hoover salesman and a hawker of plastic utensils. Dawson, however, would experience numerous setbacks on his way to the top. Dodd's trajectory was steady and seemingly inexorable. The only question was what he wanted to be: a businessman or a comedian? The answer came in September 1954.

2

The road to Mandalay and fame

'What a beautiful day for a new adventure said the termite as he crawled into the wooden leg factory.'

Ken Dodd always cited his week at the Nottingham Empire in September 1954 as the start of his professional career. In truth, the transition had been more gradual. Being his own boss meant that he could take time off from the day job when a lucrative or interesting booking came in, and this was increasingly the situation. Over the summer of 1954, it was becoming clear to Dodd and those around him that he was becoming a full-time entertainer with a sideline selling household goods. He was faced with a choice: develop Kaydee or go professional on the boards.

The Nottingham Empire engagement was the prompt he needed but it wasn't in isolation. It was the start of a two-month run of almost continuous weekly bookings arranged by agent Dave Forrester, who had taken Dodd on. He was almost a caricature of a showbiz agent, described in *The Stage* after his death in 1988 as 'the personification of the dour, growling hard-as-nails ten-per-center who won't relinquish a penny of his commission under any circumstances'.[1] Born and brought up in Wigan, the son of a furniture store proprietor, Forrester began his show business career as a drummer but soon realized there was more money in booking bands than playing in them. This agency business proved lucrative throughout the 1920s and 1930s as dance bands grew in popularity.

By 1937, Forrester felt ready to diversify and ploughed some of his capital into building a super-cinema in Chorley, the Plaza. A 1300-seater with full stage facilities, the Plaza was able to supplement the films with dance band shows by the big broadcasting names like Joe Loss, as well as variety shows and a pantomime. In April 1938, David Forrester Theatres Ltd was founded and he began building up a small circuit, including the Plaza in Batley and the Belfast Hippodrome. But Forrester's seemingly unstoppable business development was checked somewhat by the Second World War, and by 1944, Forrester was out of the cinema business.

By 1951, Forrester was filing for bankruptcy, after which he left Manchester with his wife, Rose, to make a fresh start in the south, settling in the Sussex resort of Hove. He returned to agenting and in July 1954, with Forrester barred temporarily from being a company director, Rose applied, along with Forrester's assistant Nancy George, to the London County Council for a licence to operate an agency to be known as Forrester George. Forrester was a keen talent scout, priding himself on the great distances he would travel to catch promising new acts, and Dodd became one of the new agency's very first clients.

Forrester came up from London to meet Dodd at the Adelphi Hotel in Liverpool with a view to signing him. While many would have torn Forrester's arm off, Dodd had questions and when the answers weren't quite to his liking, he acted boldly. 'He showed me this contract, and it was very good,' said Dodd in a 2016 radio interview with Russell Davies. 'A good contract. Good starting wage. I said, "Well, Mr Forrester, what sort of a chance do you think I stand, then?" and he said "I've no idea, son. I've never seen you work." So, I just took the contract and I tore it into little pieces, and he went "What?" I said "If you haven't got enough confidence, enough faith in me to come and watch me work, then obviously I don't feel like putting my whole life into your hands."'[2] Initially shocked but then impressed, Forrester asked when Dodd was next working so he could come and see him. The pair would be together for thirty-four years until Forrester's death, and for much of that time, they didn't bother with a contract.

Peter Pilbeam, who worked on many of Dodd's radio shows, first as a studio manager at the BBC in Manchester and then as a producer, recalls: 'Dave was always an awkward so-and-so to deal with. Ken was never available when you wanted him, or if he was it was going to cost you. As far as Ken was concerned, though, Dave was a good agent. He got him the right jobs and the right money.'[3] The bookings were mostly at theatres controlled by the Moss Empires circuit or its nominally separate sister company, the Stoll Theatre Corporation. The Moss and Stoll tours were regarded in the business as the 'number one' halls, and some variety turns went through their entire careers without ever getting above the 'number two' and 'number three' halls, even briefly. Dodd was starting his professional career at the top instead of working his way up. Admittedly, changing tastes had resulted in quite a few of the twos and threes closing by 1954, but it was still a notable measure of Dodd's promise as a performer and an indication that Forrester could take him places. His potential was noted with great enthusiasm along the way. When Dodd arrived at the Ardwick Hippodrome in Manchester with jazz trumpeter Kenny Baker, in November 1954, Dodd dominated the *Manchester Guardian*'s write-up, with the big name on the bill being almost an afterthought.

The trammels of gentility still cling to the splendid madness of the down-at-heel comic figure created by Ken Dodd... last night, but the bow-tie is awry, the boots are laceless, and the morning-suit has lost its glory. We have only a man with rabbit-teeth, lank descending hair, and a lank descending sense of humour, perpetually seeking to escape from a conscience that seeks to put him in the strait-jacket of convention. This warfare is very funny, for Mr Dodd has that glorious gift of comic insanity which is given only to the few. With him on a good bill, there is Kenny Baker, who, with rather less inspiration, performs some flashing pyrotechnics on the trumpet and flugelhorn.[4]

Writing about the same opening night, the *Manchester Evening News* critic called Dodd's performance 'a diverting mixture of clowning, comedy and song' and noted prophetically that 'his spike hair and dishevelled appearance are likely to be about for a long time'.[5]

During this run of engagements, Dodd had two fateful encounters with other turns. The week at the Sunderland Empire saw Dodd sharing the bill with Jimmy James and his stooges, Bretton Woods and Hutton Conyers. Born James Casey in Stockton-on-Tees in 1892, Jimmy James had been in show business from childhood, turning professional at the age of twelve when he joined a troupe called Will Netta's Singing Jockeys. Wily even then, he won a singing contest at the Stockton Hippodrome by abandoning the smart velvet suit his mother had bought him, dirtying his face and hands, and taking to the stage barefoot after being introduced as the paperboy from around the corner.

He served in the Northumberland Fusiliers in the First World War until he was invalided out in a gas attack. The post-war years were hellishly lean, James working as a labourer and busking at racecourses, but by 1925, he was a star comedian and singer in revue, with the *Hull Daily Mail* reporting that he received £75 a week for appearing in *Ten to One On* at the Tivoli Theatre. Even then, the journalist was 'struck by the force of his personality', which had 'a magnetic quality that commands attention throughout his performance, and makes an audience all the more susceptible to the droll humour which he imparts into all that he does... his voice, gesture and facial expression combining to make all his work thoroughly convincing'.[6]

James's star continued to rise as he developed an idiosyncratic, surreal, rambling style that endeared him to fellow

31

comedians, who all watched him avidly. Once, in a cafe frequented by professionals on the Charing Cross Road, Tommy Trinder loudly and eloquently declared James to be the comedians' comedian, and nobody in the room could disagree. For many years a solo performer, it wasn't until a musical in 1944 called *Jenny Jones* that James began to develop the act for which he's best remembered. The show was going down so badly that James was positively encouraged by producers to ad-lib. One night he greeted the entry of another character with 'Oh come in, love. Are you an actress?' Her baffled response was all James needed to spark off a monologue:

> No, y'see, it was the red on your lips. Cos I used to be an actor meself, y'know. You may have seen me. It ran three nights. It would have gone four, only the vicar wanted the hall for the Harvest Festival. Y'see, I'd be sitting on this settee with the lighthouse keeper's daughter when he'd start to come down the steps from the top of the lighthouse. He'd been up there trimming the wick. Anyway, he had a wooden leg, y'see, so there was a clonk and then a soft one, so that gave me plenty of time to get down to the other end of the settee.

The audience's wild response to James's flight of fancy coupled with the actress's befuddled reactions convinced James that he should stop addressing audiences directly and work with a stooge. In the end, he had two. His brother-in-law, Jack Darby, was the first to play the long-coated lunatic called Hutton Conyers, while James's nephew, Jack Casey –

a tall, lugubrious string bean of a man – became Bretton Woods then Eli Woods. By 1954, the act was well established. James would take the stage to the strains of 'Liebestraum' and introduce his new protégé. Some nights he was 'The Singing Skunk Trapper', others 'the next heavyweight hope'. However he was introduced, it was always Woods that came on next. Straight away, James would try to throw Woods off course with an unplanned line but Woods always managed to keep up. His stammer was undoubtedly to his advantage. Woods had already mastered it as a comic timing device. The lines were good enough as they were, but the time Woods took to say them increased the anticipation and made them funnier. The forced extensions also bought him time to think. Then the act would be interrupted by Conyers, most famously with the line 'Are you putting it about that I'm barmy?', claiming to have two man-eating lions in a shoebox.

Dodd watched James from the wings avidly, keen to learn the secret of how he mastered an audience. However, it was the star's son, born James Casey like his father but known professionally as Cass James, who would have the greatest effect on Dodd's career. Working at this time in the Hutton Conyers role, Jim Casey would, the following summer, leave the act to become a full-time scriptwriter. Living in Liverpool and working regularly for the BBC in Manchester, Casey was in pole position when a job came up as a producer in the North Region variety department. When Dodd was ready for his own show, Casey wrote and produced it for his friend.

The other important encounter on that first tranche of bookings came during Dodd's week at the Empire in Leeds, when he worked with Suzette Tarri. Born Ada Tarry in Shoreditch, east London, in 1881, Suzette Tarri first came to public notice in her thirties, working as a contralto and 'soubrette', the term in music hall for a young woman specializing in coquettish but saucy songs. In 1912, she was working on the Wirral Peninsula in West Kirby as part of Wilson James's concert party, The Revellers. By the following year, she was working in a double-act with her husband, Tom Copeland, a basso singer and 'Scottish humorist' as well as being Tarri's accompanist. The pair began broadcasting in 1923.

As Tarri got older, she realized her soubrette days were numbered and so she developed a new character, a Cockney charwoman. Adopting 'Red Sails in the Sunset' as her signature tune, this began the period of Tarri's greatest success, leaving a legacy that includes film roles, records and short movies of her act made for the British Pathé company. Dodd's friend and TV producer, John Fisher, is sure that Tarri's duster was the inspiration for Dodd's tickling stick. 'She had been giving him advice,' said Fisher in 2006. 'This is how you play the business. It wasn't necessarily telling him how to develop his style. I never saw Suzette Tarri live, but I found some pictures of her on stage. And she had on the charwoman's outfit, what's she holding in her hand? A feather duster.'[7]

For a young comedian watching the old pros he found himself working with and soaking it all up, the duster must have been the perfect answer to the problem of what to do with his hands. Although he never mentioned the connection explicitly, he did say that Tarri had taught him to take a bow properly at the end of his act, going off-stage and waiting for a precise amount of time before going back to accept the applause. Tarri was seriously ill at the time of her week with Dodd and she retired two months later, dying the following October.

Dodd's first run as a professional variety performer had been an education in lots of ways, not least in the matter of theatrical digs. For the first week in Nottingham, all he could find was a bed-and-breakfast for commercial travellers with a landlady who insisted on the house being cleared by 9 a.m. With no chance of a lie-in, Dodd would head to the theatre. 'It was unheard of to be in there before 10 at least – *at least*,' he remembered in 1972. 'Anyway, I'd go up to my tiny dressing room right at the top of the theatre, more or less a bare room with no bed, no chairs, and have a quick sleep. "'Ere" – I used to hear the cleaners whispering outside the door – "'e's in there again, lying asleep on his dressing table. D'you think 'e's barmy?"'[8]

After a week at the Palace in Hull at the cusp of November and December, Dodd went into rehearsals for his first panto-mime as a performer. Fittingly, he was making his debut at the Pavilion, known locally as the 'Pivvy', where he had been props boy thirteen years earlier. This time, working for Manchester-based producer Jack Gillam, he was Wishee-Washee in *Aladdin*, with Jim Couton, who some years later would find fame with a superb droll act incorporating his singing dog Rex, as Widow Twankey.

The *Liverpool Echo* noted before the run began that Dodd couldn't fail, given that he was on home turf, and confirmed this hunch the morning after the first night by declaring that he was already 'a master of his new medium', hoiking volun-teers out of the audience to sing 'There's a worm at the bottom of the garden' and receiving a 'vociferous reception' from the children in the audience at the finale.[9] Taking stock at the end of the run, though, the *Echo*'s critic wondered if Dodd wouldn't have been better suited to the Dame role. 'He looks like a "natural" to me,' he wrote. In fact, Dodd was never to play the Dame, rationalizing in 1983 that 'I haven't really got the legs for that, I'm much more your hero type'.[10]

During these first few months as a professional, Dodd was making progress at a startling rate. On Thursday, 23 December, four days before he started the pantomime run, he had made his first radio broadcast, for a fee of 15 guineas, on a *Workers' Playtime** from Barton power station on the Bridgewater Canal near Eccles. On his debut, broadcast live 'from a canteen at Barton, Eccles' between 12.25 and 12.55 p.m., following a rehearsal at 10 a.m., Dodd was allotted five and a half minutes by producer Geoffrey Wheeler,† which he seems to have kept to.

Doddy admitted to being very nervous before that first broadcast but got a boost from the senior comic hosting the show, Charlie Chester. 'I was terrified, I don't know why... absolutely terribly nervous. I went outside. It was done from a works canteen. I went outside, I was shaking like a leaf, and Charlie, I don't know whether he'd seen me, when he came out, he said, "You alright, son?" I said, "No not really, Mr Chester".

---

* *Workers' Playtime* had begun in 1941, transmitted live from factories 'somewhere in Britain', and was intended as a boost to morale. The show would run until 1964, and after the war, listings could be a bit less coy about the location of the factories, while being careful never to advertise.
† Later the inventor of the game show *Winner Takes All*, providing the voiceover and eventually taking over as the show's host.

He said, "Why?" I said, "I'm so afraid. I'm so frightened." He said, "What are you frightened about?" I said, "Well, you know, doing this. This is my first radio show." He said, "Is that your script? Let's have a look. Gor blimey, you've got a better script than I've got, boy. Get on there and do it, you'll be fine."[11]

Between 1954 and 1964, Dodd would appear on the show over twenty times. As his fame grew, his fee rose and by the time of his final appearance, from 'a heavy chemical works in Avonmouth' near Bristol, in May 1964, he was receiving 45 guineas a show. As good as the money might have been, the show had other fringe benefits, according to producer Peter Pilbeam:

There were quite a lot of freebies that came along with some of the shows. Go to the decent places. I did a couple of *Workers' Playtime*s. One was a nut and bolt factory, and the other one was Belling's electric fires, neither of which provided much. A biscuit factory, chocolate factory or materials, clothing mill or something, they were quite nice. Geoff Lawrence and Jim Casey cornered that market. There were several that they always used to vie with each other over who would get it. Strictly illegal of course, but there it is, those things happened.[12]

Dodd was already well known to producers at the BBC in Manchester, then based over a bank facing Piccadilly Gardens. A Mr Bower of Northenden had written to senior variety producer Ronnie Taylor, recommending Dodd after booking him for a club function, while in July 1954 a Mr H. H. Chapman of Warrington had done similarly. Taylor had followed up on the leads and concluded by September 1954 that 'he has a good deal to offer, although at present he works with little finesse'. Some gentle prodding from Forrester led to that first radio engagement and a call from Barney Colehan in Leeds offering Dodd his television debut, on *The Good Old Days* the following March.

When Dodd started in variety in the early 1950s, summer season and pantomime could account for half of a performer's year. It wasn't uncommon for a successful pantomime to run into April, and some exceptional shows only came off because the venue was needed for the summer season in June. His first pantomime season at the Pavilion had only been two weeks long but this was because it was a second-tier hall and the Empire had the season sewn up. It was the last time Dodd would be playing second-tier halls.

Blackpool's Central Pier wasn't the most prestigious date in town, with the North Pier and the Opera House vying for that position, but it was pretty good going for someone who'd only done their first *Workers' Playtime* the previous December to make his summer show debut in Blackpool rather than in a lesser resort. So it was in May 1955 that Dodd took his place in *Let's Have Fun*, alongside bill-toppers Morecambe and Wise – then just in the process of re-establishing their reputation after their disastrous television series *Running Wild** – the sinister man-child Jimmy Clitheroe and the jazz

---

* The show that elicited Kenneth Baily's infamous review in *The People*, 25 April 1954: 'Definition: – TV set: the box in which they buried Morecambe and Wise.'

trumpeter Kenny Baker, a regular on the Light Programme with his *Baker's Dozen*.

Dodd's contribution to the show was 'a single 22-minute spot'.[13] In those days, it was the norm for the bill-toppers to be the penultimate act in a show, with a lesser-known act bringing the audience down from a state of high excitement before they went back to their digs. Unsurprisingly, it didn't quite work like this with Dodd. If anything, audiences went home in an even greater frenzy. Dodd, it was noted early in the Blackpool run by *The Stage*'s James Hartley, 'excels in popular forms of affected insanity' and 'owns a set of tantalizing features, expressive eyes, teeth like kerbstones and a shock of black, unruly hair... he possesses a likeable voice... [but] could not maintain sincerity in songs... [and] found his metier, the brand of inane gags, corny choruses and face-play that is proving so happy now in Blackpool's bright summer season'.[14]

His act went down so well that by August, Dodd had been booked by the Pier's manager, John Capstack, and the show's producer, Peter Webster, for the following year's show, as well as being spotted and signed by producer John Beaumont for that year's pantomime at the Sheffield Lyceum, playing Jolly Jenkins in *Red Riding Hood* with the bawdy drag comedian Rex Jamieson, aka Mrs Shufflewick. That first season also brought Dodd some more valuable broadcasting experience, recording three editions of *Blackpool Night* for the BBC Light Programme in the Jubilee Theatre on the top floor of the Co-op Emporium department store on Sheppard Street, and taking part in a shortened version of *Let's Have Fun* for television, live from the Central Pier.

It transpired that *Let's Have Fun* would keep Dodd busy right up until he was due in Sheffield. The Illuminations meant that Blackpool's summer season was longer than anywhere else. After the show closed on Saturday, 15 October, Dodd, Baker and Clitheroe began a variety tour also called *Let's Have Fun*, starting at the Ardwick Hippodrome, Manchester, on Monday, 24 October, then calling at the Chiswick Empire, Belfast Opera House, Nottingham Empire and Sunderland Empire before closing with a week at the Glasgow Empire.

Described by Stanley Baxter as the place where 'English comedians came to die quietly',[15] the Glasgow Empire was the venue where Morecambe and Wise left the stage to the sound of their own footsteps, where Des O'Connor faked a faint to get off stage early and where Mike and Bernie Winters, infamously, were greeted with a pained shout of 'Fuck, there's two of them.' Somehow, though, Dodd bucked the trend. During the week at the Empire, *The Stage*'s Scottish correspondent, Gordon Irving, called in for a chat, noting that Dodd, 'for an English comedian, had one of the warmest receptions yet in Glasgow variety'.[16] Everything's relative. As warm a reception as it was, Dodd claimed it still involved an audience member shouting 'Christ, what a horrible sight' before collapsing.

A review of the Chiswick Empire show sets out its stall in the headline 'Ken Dodd Is Tops', stating that Dodd 'left the stage on Monday first house to more enthusiastic applause than heard for a long time'.[17] 'With a "mountain" of hair, buck teeth, a crazy laugh, big eyes and a quiet, reposed style, he is of star quality,' the reviewer continued. 'He goofs his way through a routine of patter and song parodies which builds up to encore applause. In ill-fitting shoes, tails, striped pants, and a yellow sunflower in his lapel, he does a singing burlesque of [Josef] Locke, a Frenchman and Johnnie Ray; then in a huge stetson hat, decorated with ping-pong balls, he chants a parody on "Granada" and finally, in a good singing voice, does a hilarious version of "The Floral Dance".'[18]

The reviewer ends by declaring that Dodd is already worthy of his own television show, but omits to mention the temperature. In a TV interview over thirty years later, Dodd recalled that it was a testing week. 'It was freezing cold and the boiler had bust, so there was no heat on. It was freezing, and I remember a little lady called Eva May Wong. She was a Chinese contortionist/juggler, and she should have been yellow, but she was blue. Every bit of her was blue.'[19] The Chiswick week was also memorable for the landlady at Dodd's digs, who confided in him that her husband loved eels but that she'd stopped giving them to him because 'when he's 'ad eels, he starts making a nuisance of 'imself in the middle of the night'.

Most other contemporary write-ups tend not to let light in on magic, registering merely whether an act was a hit or a miss, with Dodd always proving to be the former. A more detailed flavour of his act around this time can be gained from Bob Monkhouse, writing many years later about the night he had to follow Dodd on a corporate cabaret gig. The agent told Monkhouse that Dodd was to be a warm-up act, having been booked by the managing director's wife. Retelling the story, Monkhouse claimed to have been unaware of Dodd before this night, asking what sort of turn he was. The agent reassured Monkhouse, already a big star, that he had nothing to fear. Dodd would do fifteen or twenty minutes at most, 'a bit of nonsense with a big bass drum'.[20] The immaculate Monkhouse was also informed that Dodd was 'a mess' with 'hair sticking up like a fright wig' and a 'dress suit stolen off a scarecrow'.[21] Monkhouse's claim of innocence and ignorance has to be taken with more than a pinch of salt, given that he and his then partner, Denis Goodwin, had already worked with Dodd on one of the *Blackpool Night* radio shows during the 1955 summer season, but his vivid description of Dodd's act rings fundamentally true.

As Monkhouse told the story, the first indication of difficulty was as he waited to go on, already ten minutes later than planned. 'Up until now I have never heard such screams of joy from any crowd anywhere,' he wrote. 'The cause of the hysteria is this creature from another planet, a clown escaped from some circus asylum... His behaviour is a mad mix of mischief and baby innocence.'[22] Monkhouse cited the clear phallic imagery of the tickling stick and recalled a suggestive line. 'This is me knocker's-up pole. If I can get this through your bedroom window, I'll send you to work with a twinkle in your eye.'

Dodd's act consisted of exploding guitars, errant accordions and Turkish baths that turn out to be fish-and-chip shops, 'piling absurdity upon absurdity'. For his grand finale, he put on 'an outsize pith helmet and strap[s] on an army belt decorated with dangling pots, pans and the leg of a shop-window mannequin to sing a bizarrely comical version of

"The Road to Mandalay"',[23] followed by a straight song that brought the crowd to a standing ovation. The twenty-minute act had stretched to an hour and a half, the audience were wrung out and Monkhouse knew he didn't stand a chance. He spent fifteen minutes 'getting no laughs at all with my best material'.[24] Like Dodd, a keen student of comedy and comedians, Monkhouse knew better than to bear a grudge against this force of nature, instead recalling his humiliation with awe and admiration. Small wonder that even Glasgow couldn't resist him.

Indeed, Dodd had, from the outset, applied serious thought to how different jokes were received in different parts of the country. Anita travelled with him and was there at each show with a notebook, grading the audience responses to the gags 'from VG to what happened to that one?'[25] Speaking in a 2012 radio interview, he said: 'I was a salesman beforehand and I wanted to know what I was selling. You've got to have confidence in your product. The art of salesmanship is to find something that people want and supply it... It's eye-to-eye contact. You learn how to talk to people and try to sell them something. So, it seemed common sense to me, this notebook I used to keep as to how many buckets I'd sold per day, to [record] how the jokes went.'[26] Dodd called the findings of his survey his 'Giggle Map of Britain'.

The *Guardian*, reporting on the phenomenon in 1960, noted that 'thumbing through the dog-eared notebooks, which now number about forty, you can with patience pin down an old Dodd joke like a butterfly, and trace its birth, life and eventual death with an occasional resurrection. You can tell for instance that at 8.10 p.m. on a certain night at, say, Leicester four years ago a joke went mysteriously against the grain. Yet at Wigan a month later it was received as profoundly comic.'[27] Naturally, Dodd turned even this into a joke. 'I've always said you can tell a joke in Manchester and it won't get a laugh in London. They can't hear you,' he told Roy Plomley in 1963, a very early outing for what would become a Dodd favourite in interviews. Amusingly, Plomley takes the first part of the statement at face value and treads on the tag by asking, 'And vice versa?' When Dodd reveals the punchline, Plomley insists on repeating his question for a serious answer.

Almost chastened, Dodd replies: 'I would say that a West End audience, a London audience, they find humour in the comedy of manners, topicalities, name-dropping, things like that. Rural areas would find humour in basic things. Things that touch them, like living, and dying and you know, planting things. Lancashire, for instance, Lancashire humour is a little bit aggressive. Yorkshire humour is very, very friendly. They like softy comedians. Scots people, well, Glasgow, anyway, they like the American style wisecrack.'[28]

In Glasgow, an English accent was a significant handicap and football jokes were *verboten* on Friday and Saturday. Glaswegians also didn't go a bundle on jokes about sex, with the same applying in Wigan. 'Plumbing jokes and a little hearty vulgarity, yes,' said the *Guardian* digest of Dodd's findings. 'But no sex.'[29] The converse was true on the south coast, which liked 'a bit of spice' and an authoritative comedian. In this summary, Dodd was almost certainly invoking Max Miller, a Brighton lad who stayed there until his death in 1963.

In Birmingham, it was a matter of pace. In the city, a slow approach was preferred, with things decelerating the further into the Black Country you went. For a relentless comedian like Dodd, this must have been a considerable test of technique. In contrast, Coventry liked quicker delivery, while Nottingham went for 'picture gags', as did Belfast. Of course, other imponderable variables meant that geography wasn't always a guarantee. The joke 'I'm not married really, I've always been round-shouldered' went reasonably well at first house, stormed it in the second house and then died at a matinee. Perhaps the lateness of the hour and the likely quantities of alcohol consumed lowered inhibitions – earlier in the day, husbands feared a handbagging for laughing too loud at that particular gag.

Dodd noted early on that 'death, religion and coloured people are potentially bad subjects for strolling jesters'. This has the pleasing result that very little of his material is racially dubious, at least before the 1970s. As for religion, Dodd managed to find a way through the pitfalls. 'I won't attack any belief,' he said in a 1977 John Pitman BBC documentary on comedy and religion. 'I won't tell a joke that even could be construed as a criticism, or taking away anybody's belief. I won't tell crucifixion jokes. I won't tell any jokes about the religious belief itself, but the people who administer religion? Oh yes.' Dodd found humour in what he called 'the trappings of religion' and expanded on the point in 2004. 'The man-made fashions, you know. Wearing sort of white nighties and party hats and swinging cans of smoke, yes, I think you can do as many of those as you like. I'm sure God wants us to laugh. We are the only animal that laughs… It's a release, it's a strength, it's a weapon, it's balm to a hurt mind.'[30]

As an example, Dodd gave the story of a dour Scottish minister, 'one of these hellfire and brimstone characters… really laying it on. "Ye've all been sinning. I'm sure as heaven's above, ye'll all die [corrects self], dee and descend into the fiery pit. Ye'll all descend into the bowels of hell and och, it'll be terrible. Ye'll be up to here in sulphur and brimstone. There'll be smoke and fire and fumes everywhere and the smell will be terrible. The Lord, in his mercy, will gaze down on you, and you'll gaze up to God and say 'Oh Lord, we didnae ken, we didnae ken'. The Lord, in his infinite mercy, will gaze down on you and say 'Aye, well, you KEN NOO.'"'[31]

The joke works well because of the obvious gleeful malice of the minister and the punchline being delivered in an accent that gives a faint impression that the preacher is convinced that God is a Scot. Dodd was less convincing when questioned by Pitman on how a Gentile could tell Jewish jokes without coming across as anti-Semitic. 'Being an entertainer, if we have a gift at all… it's the gift of empathy and sympathy. The good entertainer is able to actually sit in the audience and watch himself, so therefore I would think like a Jewish person. First and foremost, really, I would think like a human being and think "Would that joke offend me?"'

Dodd was also fine sending up the bigotry of sectarianism. 'A comedian went to Heaven and they said he could only go in if he'd done something really brave. He said "I stood up in Belfast and said 'To hell with all the Protestants and the Catholics'." They said "When did you do this?" He said

"About ten seconds ago." Despite his core of faith, Dodd was never pious or prudish. His fruitier jokes always suggested that sex was a gleeful exercise and something to be celebrated, not swept under the carpet. He always seemed particularly supportive of older people – particularly when it involved older, more portly people still enjoying themselves fully: 'It was your birthday last week and all your friends clubbed together and bought you an old-fashioned bedwarmer. A sixty-eight-year-old chorus girl.'[32]

Having proven himself so thoroughly in guest spots over the previous three years and a one-off radio special in the *Northern Variety Parade* series in April 1957, it was no surprise when Dodd landed his first radio series in October 1958. Producer James Casey had begun in June that year by offering the Light Programme in London a pilot show at a cost of no more than £300, including the whole BBC Northern Dance Orchestra. Cautious agreement was forthcoming but by August, the North Region executives had decided to make a series of six shows, entitled *It's Great to Be Young*, and send the tapes to London for evaluation.

Dodd was very lucky to have Casey as his producer. Like many producers of the era, Casey was also a prolific script-writer, bringing a wealth of experience from working on stage with his father, Jimmy James. He knew where all the old gags were buried and generated a few new ones himself, along with Frank Roscoe, who was used extensively on BBC shows from Manchester in the 1950s and 1960s, including Morecambe and Wise's *You're Only Young Once* and *The Clitheroe Kid*. In those days, radio comedy shows usually had an announcer on duty to open the show, read the credits at the end and announce the musical guests in between, while frequently being dragged into the comedy with feigned reluctance. *The Goon Show* without Wallace Greenslade is unthinkable. For *It's Great to Be Young*, the role was filled by Judith Chalmers, already a vastly experienced broadcaster at twenty-three, having begun her career on *Children's Hour* at the age of thirteen. 'Jim Casey asked me,' Chalmers recalls. 'He said to Ken "You've got to have an announcer." I was quite terrified really because I'd never done anything like that, at that stage.' Chalmers' terror soon evaporated and she became a vital part of Dodd's radio repertory company for a decade.

Dodd's rise to prominence had been meteoric. By November 1958, just four years after he had turned professional, BBC executives were sensing that it might be prudent to get Dodd tied into an exclusive contract with the Corporation. ITV had nabbed some of the BBC's biggest stars, including Arthur Askey, and many of the brightest producers, including Bill Ward and Brian Tesler. There was a growing perception that the BBC had to try harder to develop and retain talent. Dodd's agent Dave Forrester may have been bluffing but he had convinced Grahame Miller, the acting head of programmes for the BBC's North Region, that ATV were ready to offer Dodd regular spots on *Sunday Night at the London Palladium* and a tour of variety theatres controlled by Moss Empires, which was the majority shareholder in ATV. In addition, Forrester suggested that Moss Empires were ready to pay him a retainer for finding and suggesting Dodd's support acts.

The response was a proposal to give Dodd his own BBC

television series and a lot of special treatment. In the theatre, Dodd would close the first half and reappear in the second half, preceded by some supporting acts. Grahame Miller noted that, as a result of the supporting turns, the audience 'is "keyed up", expectant and ready' for Dodd.[33] As such, the suggestion was that the shows should be transmitted from a theatre, not a studio, and that the programme should be the second half of a full variety bill, including turns in the first half who would not appear in the transmitted show. Moreover, the show would be pre-recorded on Sundays but transmitted on Saturdays, to make the most of Dodd's availability. Miller also proposed paying Forrester 100 guineas a show for providing the supporting cast.

The full proposal was dismissed by the head of programme contracts, W. L. Streeton, who felt there could be no justification for booking acts who wouldn't appear on screen. He also anticipated objections from rival theatre and cinema proprietors regarding the provision of free entertainment, and had a problem with the idea that Forrester should receive a retainer. If he represented the acts he was booking for the TV shows, would he not already be receiving commission? He also feared 'moral blackmail, such as refusal to deal, as agent, with us over a particular artist unless we also agree to insert some other artist in the programme as well'.[34] Having asked around, Streeton reported that he had been assured that Forrester was eminently capable of pulling that sort of stunt. Both Streeton and Miller agreed that Forrester was difficult to deal with, but Miller thought that if a personal deal with the agent sealed the deal, it was a price worth paying.

Miller's compromise position was to use some of the acts
that were booked for the televised show for a thirty-minute
warm-up before the recording, in an attempt to replicate the
theatrical experience. Streeton appreciated the concession
but noted that most warm-ups were five or ten minutes long,
and that even ATV's *Sunday Night at the London Palladium*
managed with less than a quarter of an hour.

The one-year contract that was agreed and signed in May
1959 – presumably backdated to March so it covered the
extra editions of *It's Great To Be Young* recorded especially
for the Light Programme network run – was as suggested in
November 1958 in every detail but one. As laid out in the
original draft, Dodd was to star in at least four television shows
at £500 a show, receiving 40 guineas for every radio show he
starred in and 30 guineas for shows where he was a turn or
a guest. The contract guaranteed that Dodd would receive at
least £3000 from the BBC, with the shortfall being made up
if he did not receive sufficient bookings, so the onus was on
producers to use him as much as possible. It also included an
option on a second year, with Dodd's TV fee rising to £750 a
show and the guarantee going up to £4000 a year.

Although Dodd's television series was to be made in his
northern heartland, the light entertainment department in
London, under Eric Maschwitz, opted to take direct control
of production. Aptly for a theatre-based show, Dodd was
allocated a producer steeped in stage variety. Albert Stevenson
had begun his show business career as a call boy at the
Alhambra on Leicester Square in 1930, rising to become a stage
manager. Wartime RAF service saw Stevenson being captured

and enduring several hard years as a Japanese prisoner of war. After his release, he joined Stoll variety theatres as stage director of the whole circuit, which included the Wood Green and Shepherd's Bush Empires. After a brief diversion into the film industry with MGM at their UK studios in Borehamwood, Stevenson joined the BBC in 1953, initially as a floor manager, but soon being promoted to producer.

Stevenson soon became well-known at the BBC for his irreverence and humour, which sometimes got him into trouble. Early in his television career, when floor managing *Panorama*, he was asked to sit in for United Nations secretary general Dag Hammarskjöld during a rehearsal. The interviewer, Francis Williams, asked Stevenson how he'd come to be appointed. Stevenson replied, 'Well, I was unemployed at the time, and as I was walking down the road one day this geezer comes up to me and says, "How'd you like to be Secretary-General of the United Nations, mate?"'[35] Despite presaging Pete and Dud by a clear decade, Stevenson's levity was not appreciated and producer Grace Wyndham Goldie came through from the gallery to the studio to give Stevenson a dressing-down, unaware that Hammarskjöld had already arrived. When his presence was noted, he was invited to take part in the rehearsal himself. Williams repeated the question, to which Hammarskjöld replied in a Swedish Cockney accent, 'Well, I was walking down the road...'

The second show, to be recorded as live at the Hippodrome, Ardwick on 25 October 1959 (for transmission on 9 January 1960), hit technical trouble and forced Stevenson to draw upon all of his wit and experience as he filled with a thirty-eight-minute warm-up while the problem was being fixed. After the show, the BBC Northern Dance Orchestra clubbed together to buy him a tankard, which they had engraved as the 'BBC TV Longest Warm-Up Award'. Paul Kay, one of the cameramen on the show, recalls: 'The trouble was caused by a fault at the BBC Birmingham switching centre.'[36]

The response to those early TV shows, none of which survive, show the beginning of a recurring theme throughout Dodd's career in television. While he was a compelling performer, all too often the shows fell flat. Mr C. J. Dunn of Liverpool 11, one of the *Echo*'s Telepanel viewers, said of Dodd's BBC TV show on 9 January 1960 that 'I thought Ken Dodd was far better when appearing alone'. Dunn said Dodd 'suffered through a very bad first sketch', as well as expressing disappointment with The Raindrops ('a very ordinary quartet') and ventriloquist Dennis Spicer ('didn't seem... up to his usual standard'). Dodd was far more happy and effective on the wireless, and the BBC contract made provision for the comedian getting his own radio series. 'Radio's such a wonderful medium for comedy, because it all takes place in the mind. On radio you can be in Hong Kong one minute, then London, then Berlin, all with a flick of the brain,' he said in 1992.[37] Despite his obvious aptitude and love for the medium he'd grown up with, Corporation executives felt that Dodd and Forrester were deliberately avoiding radio bookings.

Television made the need for a constant supply of new material even more pressing. Thankfully, the answer was only a mile or so from Thomas Lane in West Derby. Eddie Braben was a couple of years younger than Dodd, having been born in the Dingle on 31 October 1930. Braben always preferred to refer to the festival with which he shared his birthday as 'Duck apple day', rather than the Americanized Hallowe'en. The gap, however, was close enough for the pair to share many of the same influences and reference points. Like Dodd, Braben and his family were regulars at Liverpool's variety theatres. Braben's father, also called Edwin but known to his friends as Ted, was a butcher with a stall in the city's St John's market, and would sometimes send his son on errands. The boy once found himself delivering a chicken to Wilfred Pickles in his dressing room at the Empire. Scouse comedian Billy Matchett was a distant relative of Braben's grandmother, but both Braben senior and junior claimed him as an uncle, and Matchett indulged young Eddie when he visited, asking for tips on comedy.

Just as with the Dodd household, there was a lot of love and laughter at the Brabens. Braben remembered his father declaring proudly that the family's Marconi wireless set was the best you could buy, and that 'on a clear night, you can get Birkenhead'.[38] Another line of Ted's that stuck with his son came when his mum, Kathleen, was standing looking out of the front parlour window. Ted told his wife, 'Come away from there; people outside will think it's a pet shop.'[39] On the basis that nothing in a comedy writer's life is ever wasted, Eddie used his dad's gag with great pride many years later.

Also like Dodd, Braben was an avid *Bandwaggon* fan, and visiting Broadcasting House on business as an adult, he made his way up to the roof to pay homage to Big, Stinker,

Mrs Bagwash and her daughter Nausea. Being evacuated to Gaerwen on the Isle of Anglesey was a wonderful opportunity for the young, comedy-obsessed, radio-mad Braben. The BBC variety department had been evacuated too, to Bangor on the mainland, and he regularly took the train there to hang around the Penrhyn Hall studio, where shows like *ITMA* and *Happidrome* were made, with his autograph book.

On leaving school, Braben went to work in Ogden's tobacco factory on Boundary Lane. He stayed there for four years, in his own words 'completely and totally void of all ambition',[40] unable to work out what he really wanted to do with his life. His father forced the issue by setting him up with a fruit and veg stall in the market. So, like Dodd, Braben was a self-employed salesman. The main difference was that he hated it. 'A lady bought a pound of tomatoes from me,' he later recalled. 'Sticking to the unwritten rule "Thou shall always give them at least one bad one", I placed a rotten one at the bottom of the bag. I hadn't got the knack right... You're supposed to place the rotten one halfway up the bag... "What do you call this?" I looked at the tomato for a couple of seconds and said "Norman"... Like me, it may have dawned on you that I wasn't cut out for this job.'[41]

It was while reluctantly serving the people of Liverpool with mostly fresh produce that ambition struck Braben at last. He found he could make fellow stallholders (one of whom was George Jamieson, who would, in 1960, undergo sex reassignment surgery and become famous as April Ashley) and customers laugh, and decided that he wanted to make a professional go of comedy. A disastrous appearance on a radio talent show confirmed to Braben that he was meant to be a writer and he began jotting down jokes as they came to him on the brown paper bags.

Despite persistence, success was slow to arrive. 'The breakthrough would have to come soon because I was running out of brown paper bags and all the fruit was going rotten,' he later wrote.[42] It came when Charlie Chester was playing the Empire and Braben sent him some gags on spec. 'When Hopalong Cassidy was a baby, his mother knew that he was going to be a cowboy because he always wore a ten-gallon nappy' tickled Chester so much that he paid Braben 30 shillings and promptly added it to his act. When he returned to London, Chester told Bob Monkhouse and Denis Goodwin about this promising lad on Merseyside and, through their agency, Braben began to pick up regular commissions. Some went better than others, with Braben recalling a radio routine he wrote for Peter Sellers receiving no laughs whatsoever.

The next breakthrough was when he began working for the dour Lancastrian comic Ken Platt, whose catchphrase was 'I'll not take me coat off, I'm not stopping'. Platt was a regular at the BBC in Manchester, and Braben soon came to the attention of producers like Jim Casey and Peter Pilbeam. Dodd asked Braben to provide a few jokes for his new television series, and instantly, the comedian knew he was on to a winner.

Much is written about the magic and chemistry that Braben had with Morecambe and Wise later on, but the same happened with Dodd. The relationship was more than just that of a writer and a comic. For the best part of a decade, Braben was Dodd was Braben. The pair shared a love of innuendo and

archaic references. Both believed passionately that Liverpool
was the funniest and best place on Earth. The similarity of their
backgrounds enabled Braben to imbue his material for Dodd
with a level of richness that other writers would have struggled
to provide. Braben and Dodd understood each other. Judith
Chalmers observed their relationship closely at the recording
sessions for Dodd's radio shows. 'They were a couple,' she says.
'They enjoyed working together. I think that was a huge part
of it. You always felt that they were working, both of them, the
way they wanted and enjoyed each other's work. Eddie was a
lovely man. He was so much quieter.'[43]

As Dodd's stage act expanded and lengthened, and his
broadcasting appearances grew in number, he began to include
more straight songs, partly because it made the comic material
go further and partly because the shrewd Anita encouraged
him to diversify. At first, these sober interludes must have
come as a surprise to audiences used to his burlesquing. However, music publishers soon cottoned on to the fact that Dodd
had considerable appeal as a sentimental singer and began
offering him songs to use on broadcasts. Dodd developed a
particularly strong relationship with Jimmy Phillips of the
Keith Prowse company, and took a particular shine to a
French song that Phillips offered him. Dating from the later
years of the war, 'Mon coeur est un violon' had been popu-
larized by Lucienne Boyer and even recorded by Bing Crosby.
With new English lyrics by Jimmy Kennedy, a Tin Pan Alley
stalwart with 'South of the Border' and 'Teddy Bear's Picnic'
among his credits, 'Love Is Like a Violin' seemed ideal for a
Workers' Playtime.

It appears that Dodd hoped to include the song when he did the show from a police training centre at Pannal Ash near Harrogate on 25 February. However, a thank-you letter from producer Geoff Lawrence sent the following week apologizes for having to 'carve up your script quite so much' and says he was 'sorry about the Violin',[44] suggesting that the song was cut or curtailed. Lawrence tells the comedian that 'you can reassure your song-plugging friends at Keith Prowse' that the Northern Dance Orchestra would be featuring the tune on their own *Make Way for Music* show.

Phillips was pushing the song aggressively, with violinist Max Jaffa recording an instrumental version for Columbia Records, but he wanted a vocal version out there too. Dodd's next *Workers' Playtime* booking was in late April at a spinning mill in Nottingham, and it seems likely that he finally got to sing the song on this one. In early June, Dodd went into the Decca studios at Broadhurst Gardens, West Hampstead with producer Alex Wharton to record the song commercially. The original broadcast version had only a trio for accompaniment but the Decca recording had full orchestral backing, arranged and conducted by Eric 'Carry On' Rogers. It reached number eight in the charts and, suddenly, Dodd was a hit pop singer.

While Dodd's music career took off seemingly effortlessly, producers and executives continued to struggle with how best to present him on television. His growing box office appeal meant that both the BBC and ITV were keen to feature him but the results always seemed disappointing. Tom Sloan, BBC television's head of light entertainment, was very clear about the situation. Although the plan had always been to present

Dodd in an approximation of his stage variety shows, he didn't need turns and sketches of variable quality to pad out the show. Writing to Dave Forrester in 1963, Sloan said 'the real strength of Ken Dodd is his ability as a stand-up comic – he is probably the greatest in the country – but we have never exploited his talents enough in this way. Instead he has been buried in some of the dreariest unfunniest sketches it has been my misfortune to watch for many a long day.'[45]

However, while Sloan was effusive in his praise of Dodd in communications with Forrester, in internal correspondence, he and his colleagues knew that a significant proportion of the blame for the creative failure of the shows had to be shouldered by Dodd himself. For one *Ken Dodd Show* recording at Blackpool's Winter Gardens in March 1962, Dodd turned up three hours late for the 3pm Friday band call, and on the day of the show, he arrived at noon for a 10.30 a.m. camera rehearsal, reducing the time available for preparation considerably. Having arrived late, Dodd's inability to be concise meant the rehearsals ran longer than planned, and on the recording, Dodd would extemporize and 'spread' the material further. On this occasion, a planned nineteen minutes of comedy material became thirty-one minutes, including one six-minute sketch – entitled 'Mainly for Women' – doubling in length. Great fun for the audience but not so much for producer/director Barney Colehan, who had to hack the recording to pieces for transmission. Colehan was continually up against it with Dodd and the results showed all too clearly.

Reviewing a later show in the series, *The Stage* declared that 'the lighting was of amateur dramatic society standard and when the director was unable to resist the urge to throw in audience shots, these were almost completely in the dark'.[46] Blaming the 'severe restrictions' of the theatre stage for television, the reviewer also noted sound problems, with singer Hazel Scott suffering 'a loose connection in her microphone' and Les Franky Babusio's 'act involving an ancient automobile… had no sound at all which may have been the cause of an off-beat idea falling flat'. Oddly, the review makes no specific mention of Dodd himself or his material, which included a parody of BBC television's *Farming* programme and an appearance as an Indian chief in the finale, but the anonymous critic stated that the show overall was 'tame and weak'.[47]

The March show was the first of a new exclusive one-year BBC contract. The hassle of dealing with Dodd and the frequently obstructive Forrester had resulted in doubts that it was worth taking up the option. P. Thurstan Holland, assistant head of North Region programmes, advised against it in July 1961, noting that 'Dodd himself has made little effort over his previous programmes and I do not think we would have any difficulty in booking him ad hoc'.[48] In October, however, a contract was back on the cards, seemingly at the prompting of Tom Sloan in London. Colehan, despite everything, was arguably Dodd's strongest supporter within the BBC, having been the man who first put him on television. In a 1983 documentary made to mark the end of *The Good Old Days*, a framed picture of Dodd is clearly visible on the otherwise bare window ledge by the producer's desk.

Colehan wrote a memo noting the good reception that Dodd's flawed shows received and observing that 'in spite of his bad habits (and these also apply to his theatre appearances), it is an accepted fact that Ken Dodd is one of the very few comedians who can fill a theatre to capacity at both first and second houses. If the enthusiasm which he puts into a stage appearance could be captured on television, then the programme would be an undoubted success.'[49] The producer noted that one recent show had been a roaring success despite having the benefit of only one day's rehearsal. It became a central point of the contract negotiations that Dodd would have to commit to a week's rehearsal for each show.

What Colehan might not have realized is that, from Sloan's point of view, there were question marks over his own suitability. Although Colehan's contacts in the industry were second to none, his technical skills left something to be desired. 'He was a lovely guy,' Peter Pilbeam recalls, '[but he] was notorious for shooting the faces of the dancers and the feet of comedians. If you ever saw a shot of a dancer that was from the waist up, you'd say, "That's a Barney Colehan shot." Especially if they were a tap dancer.'[50] So, while Dodd was contracted through Manchester, Sloan very much had a London takeover in mind.

During talks, Forrester took issue with the BBC's interpretation of the contract's exclusivity. He had become used to receiving letters from the BBC contracts department asking why he'd allowed Dodd to appear on commercial television promoting his records, and arguing that it represented a breach of contract. Forrester was willing to let the BBC have complete exclusivity as long as all of Dodd's single releases were featured on *Juke Box Jury*, BBC television's only regular pop showcase at the time. This, however, would have created issues of undue prominence. Unlike the contracts staff, the pragmatic Tom Sloan had no problem with Dodd promoting his records elsewhere, as long as the appearances didn't spill over into a comedy routine, an ever-present risk with Dodd.

The rehearsal stipulation was another matter, and any lateness or absence was very much to be regarded as a breach. All went quiet and seemingly everybody was satisfied. Dodd was to receive £850 for a TV show and 52 guineas for his radio appearances. Throughout 1962, Dodd fulfilled his contractual obligations to the letter, with the freedom to promote his discs wherever he liked. It wasn't until January 1963 that a member of staff in the contracts department noticed that neither Dodd nor Forrester had ever signed the agreement. Thus, if the BBC had tried to invoke breach of contract, there was no valid contract to be breached.

Dodd was firmly but subtly in charge and Dave Dutton, one of Dodd's writers through the 1970s, suggests that this was a recurring theme throughout his career. 'Control. That's the thing with Doddy, as he admitted to me when I asked him what the best part of the job was, he said "the control it gives me over people". And he did, he manipulated people. He manipulated the audience. He manipulated the writers. He controlled the audience on stage, you know what I mean? That was wonderful to see. I think he continued it off because he studied psychology. And that enabled him to inflict his personality on people. I asked him "What are you studying?" And he said "It's called Gestalt psychology." I looked it up. And I still don't know what it was all about. He must have been into it in a really big way to give him the edge.'[51]

Dodd always maintained that he had thirty seconds to get an audience on his side. While this was undoubtedly true when he was establishing himself, in later years the adoring crowds who came to see him were already on his side. Nonetheless, the ever-competitive comedian stuck to his policy. 'Actors from the other side of show business, they're called legitimate. I'm not sure what that makes us. They call it rapport. They have to establish rapport,' he said in 2003. 'I call it building a bridge. Your first words are very important when you go on stage. You have to try and make them like you, try and make them love you.'[52]

He was always keen to make sure everybody felt included. 'It's always a big temptation to play to the first two or three rows. Always play upstairs. Always play upstairs. You've got to make them feel that they're part of the show, you've got to try and bring them all... hug them all and bring them all to you.' However, the affection had a purpose. He wanted to 'get them':

> To go out to a giant audience it is a wonderful, wonderful feeling when you've got them. There comes time when you go on stage and you do all the nonsense, please love me, please like me, and all that, and then suddenly you tell one or two really good ones, and that's it. Got 'em. And then you can relax and do any sort of joke you like [...] I think you have to make the audience trust you. For a time it's a partnership, I think, but gradually you get the upper hand.[53]

This approach to contracts and control perhaps shines some light on many of Dodd's relationships, not least those with women. He was engaged to Anita Boutin for twenty-two years until her death in 1977 without ever marrying her, and his engagement to Anne Jones lasted until he finally married her two days before he died. Dodd needed the security of those loving relationships, just as he felt he needed the security of the BBC in an insecure business, but at the same time, he seemingly felt the need to regard himself as free from commitments on paper.

In 1987, he told Professor Anthony Clare that he had never married because he'd been too busy, just as he claimed his trademark of sticking his hair up on end had been a by-product of being too busy to get his hair cut. Clare found these claims 'somewhat unconvincing to say the least', suggesting to the comedian that he always seemed to find the time for things he really wanted to do. Clare concluded that his 'desire to retain control of his life and circumstances proved too strong'.[54] 'In some ways, he was a selfish person,' says Dutton.[55]

And yet within that power imbalance, on his own terms, he displayed enormous loyalty towards Boutin, Jones and the BBC. The majority of his broadcast output was done for the Corporation, and for most of it, the contractual side went through Manchester, where he felt most at home. Angela Wilson, who would go on to become a distinguished vision mixer at the BBC in London, began her Corporation career in radio as an eighteen-year-old agency secretary, working with producer Geoff Lawrence. Dodd was a great one for bestowing nicknames on people, and instantly dubbed Wilson 'Miss Temp'. He also noted that, at 5 feet 10 inches, she was considerably taller than the BBC secretaries he was used to.

'He didn't say hello, but instead made a big show of eyeing me up and down from top to toe,' Wilson recalls. 'With perfect comic timing, he said "By-y Jo-ove, they hire 'em by the yard at the BBC don't they?"'[56] Dodd was always looking for the joke in every situation and Wilson remembers an example of the constant ticking of the comic brain with great fondness. Peter Pilbeam's regular secretary was away and her work was being covered by a woman called Gay Granger. 'It's always stuck in my mind,' says Wilson. 'Ken saying to Gay, "Ooh, so when Peter's out of the office you can sign his letters 'GG, pp PP'."'

3

The Liverpool explosion

'We're City of Culture in 2008. We're going to have night classes in graffiti.'

Throughout his life, Dodd was a proud Liverpudlian and one of the few entertainers from the city who didn't move away when the money started coming in. His pride in his birthplace overflowed when four young men became the most famous band in the land, and then the most famous band in the world, making Merseyside suddenly the centre of the musical world.

'You're always proud of whichever city you belong to, you know, your hometown,' he said in May 1964 when he was appearing at the ABC in Gloucester. 'I always think it might get on people's wick a little bit if we're always shouting about the Mersey Sound and all that at the moment, but I think it's only because we're proud of our city... of course we've got all the groups now. We have Percy and the Jerrywalkers and all these people... Everybody's group mad in Liverpool. On the

65

way home from work a few months ago, I used to have to pass this big block of shops, and one night in a shop doorway, there was this courting couple. I'm not nosy, missus, but you can learn from anybody. As I passed, I heard a girl singing away to her boyfriend... "How do you do what you do to me, I wish I knew, if I knew what you're doing to me, oooh". Next night I passed, she was singing "I like it, I like it". I passed there last Saturday night and she was singing "Listen, do you want to know a secret?"'[1]

Dodd observed that, wherever he went, Scousers abounded. 'You can always tell somebody from Liverpool, wherever you are. They're usually between two policemen... Liverpool people are dotted all around the country and I usually shout "Is anybody from Liverpool?", and they all shout "Yes". I say "It's nice of you to take the blame"... They've emigrated to Tewkesbury, somewhere around there, they ran away when we had the black pudding famine in Liverpool.'[2]

With Dodd's exclusive BBC contract having lapsed, he was now free to appear wherever he liked, doing whatever he liked. Whenever he had a single or a show to promote, he was always happy, for a very modest fee, to make the trip from Knotty Ash to Quay Street in Manchester, where Granada Television was based, to make an appearance on the regional news show *Scene at 6.30*. Referring to *Scene at 6.30* as a news programme does it a significant disservice. First transmitted on Monday, 28 January 1963, the new show, usually hosted by Mike Scott or Irish broadcaster Gay Byrne, and featuring a young reporter from Barnsley called Michael Parkinson, replaced the more sedate *People and Places*. The North of

England was, as now, a major contributor to British cultural life and *Scene* aimed to reflect this fully as well as reporting on drain trouble in Altrincham. Liverpool and Manchester had always been disproportionately represented in entertainment, with the former making an ultimately successful bid for world domination.

Moreover, until a shake-up of ITV contracts in 1968, 'Granadaland' covered both Lancashire and Yorkshire, with Granada providing the weekday service and ABC providing weekends. This meant it had the largest potential audience in the whole network, covering a population of 14.6m compared to the 13.5m covered by Rediffusion and ATV in London. Granada was in the right place at the right time, capitalizing on its cultural riches and displaying them to a massive audience.

Also in the right place at the right time was Johnnie Hamp, who had been booking acts for the live shows at Granada's theatre circuit as well as producing game shows like *Spot the Tune* and *Take a Letter* for the TV side of the business. In the run-up to the launch of *Scene at 6.30*, Granada's chairman, Sidney Bernstein, decided that Hamp was the ideal person to oversee the light entertainment side of the show, and asked him to move up to Manchester permanently. By this time, Dodd and Hamp were already firm friends, having met during the 1958 summer season in Blackpool, where the comedian was appearing at the Central Pier in *Let's Have Fun*.

'A great friend of mine was Peter Webster,' Hamp explains. 'He was such a big Blackpool character. He ran the Central Pier, and I was booking Granada Theatres at the time. That was where I first saw Doddy. When I came up to do *Scene at*

6.30, he almost became our resident comedian. We always had a musical spot, and every time he had a tour or a record out, he'd give me a ring and say "I want to come in and do this." He hadn't really made it that big in London yet but he never got too starry. He always appreciated the plug for the records. It was the biggest record plug, really, apart from the national ones.'

Dodd wasn't content to just sing a song and have a chat, though. As on stage, he always aimed to give good value for the modest Granada fee, and the relatively low pressure of the environment enabled him to try out new ideas. 'The best thing, the funniest thing about those visits was his prop list. He'd ring me probably in the morning, when he was due that evening, and ask for things like two pounds of exploding sausages and a life-size cut-out of Adolf Hitler. Of course, the props boys loved doing it. I remember one time, and this was Eddie Braben's idea, he had a piano accordion that stretched out gradually as far as his arms could take it, and then Bill Grundy and Gay Byrne had to go and take the other end and it stretched right across the studio. Such a funny prop. The prop boys loved making it for Doddy. A cut out of Queen Victoria in polystyrene and all that sort of thing. And we always used to wonder how he was going to work these props.'

Sometimes, the budget allowed for Dodd to venture outside the studio. One such case was when he was promoting the single 'Happiness' in the summer of 1964. 'We did one on location at Capesthorne Hall for that, and I wish I'd kept that tape, because my son and daughter, Christopher and Merry, were in it with him. They were young, only 10 and 8 at the time I suppose. They were fishing in the river at Capesthorne Hall, and the gag was that they pulled out a boot or something. That's one tape I really wish I'd kept.'[3]

Only one of Dodd's *Scene at 6.30* appearances survives and that's largely because of the other guests on the show. 'The Beatles were almost our resident group as well at that time,' says Hamp. 'They came in every single, to plug their record, but they were getting enormous by then. Doddy was never too big to appear on local programmes, but I'd got a suspicion that this would be The Beatles' last time.'

The Beatles were only available on the afternoon of 25 November 1963, this being a day off between appearing at the ABC in Hull the night before and the Regal in Cambridge the night after. As a result, pre-recording was vital and Hamp decided to stockpile material for future use. 'They wanted to come in to do "I Want to Hold Your Hand",' he recalls. 'I said to them, "Well, while you're here, let's just turn the record over and do 'This Boy'." They said, "Yeah fine," because they were good friends. I also had a 16mm camera for the whole afternoon following them, so I got about an hour and a half's worth of Beatles material.'

It was a coincidence that Dodd was booked to appear on the same show. Hamp hadn't planned to make the show a big Scouse summit. 'It only struck me on the day. Doddy was going live in the evening, doing one of his daft props things. He came in early, which was a change for him. So I said "How do you fancy doing a two-minute interview with Ken Dodd?" They said, "Yeah, that's great." You know, great fun. And of course, Doddy was happy to do that, and Gay Byrne conducted it, and this two-minute interview stretched to eighteen minutes. That was very Ken.'

The recording took place in studio 4 at Granada, the smallest of the five studios on site.* 'I think the Beatles probably came about two o'clock,' Hamp recalls. 'It sounds like there's an audience there, but it's just the crew and a bunch of nurses that were doing a tour around the studio, with maybe a few office staff. Studio 4 was tiny, but it sounded like a full audience, so that was great.' The nurses had plenty to laugh at:

Gay Byrne: We have always thought that it might be a good question to put to Mr Kenneth Dodd and the members of The Beatles, to what extent do they attribute their success to their hairstyles, and we'll start by asking that question now of Mr Ken Dodd.

Dodd: Hairstyles? Well I think it has a great deal to do with my, with me what? Success?

Byrne: Hairstyle.

Dodd: Well, I think so, yes. I like to keep it in trim. I eat a lot of Shredded Wheat because it's good for the hair. I have it cut twice a year whether I need it or not. Short back and sides and a bit off the shoulders.

Byrne: What do you feel about the boys?

Dodd: I think there's a remarkable... it's a wonderful style, of course they're different than me, with them being

---

* The Granada studios were all given even numbers, to make it sound as though the company had twice as many as it really had. Studio 4 closed in the early 1970s and was redeveloped to form part of the reception.

Martians. A professor of archaeology at Knotty Ash University discovered some tablets which say 'The Beatles are definitely Martians. Grundy's their leader.'*

Byrne: How long have you known this, Ken?

Dodd: Bill Grundy? Well I've known he was out of this world for a long time.

[...]

Byrne: Do you think their hairstyles are the things that caught on, Ken? Do you think that's why they're so successful?

Dodd: Oh no, no, I think these boys have a very nice gimmick. Talent. I think they would have gone, with or without hairstyles. Who actually designed it, boys, is it Cammell Laird?

John Lennon: Disraeli.

Dodd dominates proceedings at first, but gradually Byrne opens the chat up so that The Beatles can start to get a few words in edgeways.

Byrne: Now let's turn the tables, boys. What do you think of Ken Dodd?

Ringo: He's great.

Lennon: He's marvellous.

Paul McCartney: He's a good'un.

---

* A reference to Bill Grundy (1923–93), a Granada presenter with a pugnacious manner. Later he would become notorious for his interview with the Sex Pistols on Thames Television's evening magazine show, *Today*.

Lennon: His hair is lovely.

McCartney: Yeah.

Dodd: We call it hurr in Liverpool, you see, we always say 'The Judy with the furr hurr'.

[…]

Byrne: Do you think he owes a lot of his success to his hairstyle, fellas?

Lennon: No, I don't think it helped at all.

George Harrison: It would have been better if he was bald.

[…]

Byrne: Have you no ambitions to form a group yourself?

Dodd: Love to. With the boys. Kenny and the Cockroaches. Or Doddy and the Diddymen. Or Ringo and the Layabouts.

Byrne: Would you not form one yourself, Ken?

Dodd: Yes, I'd like to. The only thing is I'd have to change my name, you see. I'd have to have a name like Cliff or Rock. Something earthy.

Harrison (quietly): Sod.

McCartney: Cliff Dodd.

Dodd: No.

McCartney: Rock Dodd.

Dodd: You'll have to invite suggestions for an earthy name for me.

Harrison [louder]: Sod.

Dodd: [laughing] Follow that.[4]

Over twenty years later, Hamp, by then Granada's head of entertainment, called up all the Beatles material in the archive.

'It was all on two-inch tape or 16mm film, and I thought "This is obsolete or going to be obsolete, and the film disintegrates. Let's put it on the new one-inch tape",' he explains. 'I got all the material, and I made a documentary called *The Early Beatles*. I included a clip of that interview. I got a phone call from Doddy. "I'm in this film," he said. "I'm due for some spondulicks." So I said, "What I've done, I just sent a copy to the three remaining Beatles saying that I didn't know what to pay them." Megastars, weren't they? They said "We don't want payment." That was George, Paul and Ringo, and they didn't want any payment. I didn't think about Doddy. So, he rang me and said, "I want some cash." I said, "Yeah, OK, you do. I'll sort it out for you." I rang him back and said, "I've looked up your old contract. You got twelve quid. So repeat fee, you're due for six quid." I sent a hundred actually. So sharp, though.'

In late 1963, as wild as The Beatles' success had been, the Fab Four were looking nervously ahead. How far would it all go, and what would they do when their moment had passed? Paul and John mused about becoming full-time songwriters, while Ringo joked about wanting to own a chain of hairdressers' shops after the bubble had burst. Nobody, least of all The Beatles themselves, could have realized that the bubble would remain robustly inflated fifty years after their final album. So, at this time, The Beatles still had one foot in the variety camp with Doddy. Cliff Richard was already well on the road to becoming an all-round family entertainer, increasingly dropping rock and roll rebellion for ballads and pantomime. Panto was a bridge too far for The Beatles but they pitched up at the Astoria, Finsbury Park, London for a sixteen-night run of their own Christmas Show. This was a light workload compared to Doddy's festive commitment: a ten-week run at the Royal Court Theatre in Liverpool for the Howard and Wyndham circuit beginning on Friday, 13 December 1963.

Variety theatres had been moving away from week-long runs to longer seasons in an effort to stave off the threat of television. Dodd had been Moss Empires' first choice in 1960 when they had decided to try out extended runs at their major locations. Dodd's *Startime* show ran at the Manchester Palace for a month from 24 October 1960 rather than the standard week, followed by another month at the Liverpool Empire before Dodd returned to Manchester in triumph with a Christmas show. Having proven adept at pulling in the punters for an extended period, managements merrily decided to keep extending Dodd's runs longer and longer with each booking.

On this production, Dodd was joined by a bizarrely unvaried variety bill consisting of singers Barbara Law, Barbara Simpson and Brian Budge, and his old friend, ventriloquist Dennis Spicer. Thankfully, Dodd had the benefit of director Dick Hurran to make it all work. Like Dodd's agent Dave Forrester, Hurran had begun his career as a dance band drummer, but instead of moving into the back room, he became a song and dance man in revue, joining the company of London's Windmill Theatre in 1937. After wartime service in the RAF, he joined Moss Empires, directing shows at the London Palladium, before moving to Howard and Wyndham's circuit in 1958, where he took over the legendary *Five Past Eight* shows at the Alhambra, Glasgow.

At this stage, Dodd was giving the audience more of himself than most bill-toppers, although the shows weren't quite the tests of endurance and bladder control they later became. 'There can surely never have been a more zany comic – or a more generous one – than Ken Dodd, judging by his contribution to the show that bears his name,' noted the reviewer in *The Stage*'s round-up of 1963's Christmas shows, noting that his final spot 'lasted forty-five minutes as he gagged and clowned in his own irrepressible way, bringing howls of laughter from every part of the house'.[5] However, it's worth noting that the Royal Court run was twice-nightly and while his timing was always excellent, his on-stage timekeeping was already heading adrift. 'The first house performance of the *Ken Dodd Show* – superslick though it was – overran its time last night because a responsive audience was loth [sic] to part with the comedian with the electric hair,' noted the critic of the *Liverpool Echo*, the paper being always a sturdy supporter of Dodd.[6]

One of the items for the Liverpool Christmas show hit a snag before the first night. It was a comment on the Mersey-beat boom, with some new lyrics for The Beatles' hit, 'She Loves You'.

If you want to be a star,
Make a thousand pounds a day-e-ay.
Buy a second-hand guitar,
Cut your hair a funny way-e-ay.
Look like a Beatle, and you know that can't be bad,
When you're a Beatle, everyone goes raving mad.[7]

An Anfield-based band called Bobby and the Cannons were enlisted to record an authentic Mersey-style backing track for the spoof, but the Musicians' Union intervened because the band were non-union. Dodd admitted to being disappointed but said the song would be in the show, with accompaniment from the pit orchestra, directed by veteran bandleader Geraldo.

As Dodd's stage career gathered astonishing momentum, so did his broadcasting work. Television was still a problem but he finally hit his stride on radio after a shaky start. *It's Great to Be Young* had been a disappointment nationally and caused the radio light entertainment management in London to exercise a degree of caution. In September 1961, Dodd had Eric Miller, a North Region producer who had moved to London, fighting his corner, but there seemed no urgency at Aeolian Hall* other than for assistant head of radio light entertainment Jim Davidson to offer Miller 'the possibility of a trial script and maybe a trial recording'.[8] Dodd's exclusive contract meant that he had to be offered radio work to a certain annual value but this was achieved through regular star guest bookings on *Midday Music Hall* and *Workers' Playtime*.

The mood changed in December 1962 when Miller booked Dodd for *Carnival*, a special Christmas co-production between the Home Service and the General Overseas Service of the BBC, showcasing stars from the Commonwealth. On a bill alongside singer Edmund Hockridge representing Canada

---

* The former Grosvenor Gallery at 135–137 Bond Street, occupied by the BBC from 1943 and home to the radio light entertainment department until 1975.

with Bernard Braden and Barbara Kelly, and Trinidadian pianist Winifred Atwell representing the West Indies, Dodd – aided by old chum Peter Goodwright – stole the show. Speaking to Davidson and fellow assistant head of light entertainment, Con Mahoney, afterwards, Dodd said that he'd like to have a go at doing a radio series from London. The waters were tested with a one-off in the Light Programme's *Star Parade* series in April 1963, and soon after Dodd was offered another series.

This put backs up in Manchester, with the North Region's head of programmes, Grahame Miller, calling it a 'volte face' on the part of the Light Programme, noting a lack of enthusiasm for *It's Great to Be Young*, and suggesting that the orthodox view from London was that Dodd had 'no national appeal'.[9] When Con Mahoney replied to Miller that Manchester hadn't offered Dodd any shows, he replied that 'we had understood from Light Programme that they were no longer interested'.[10] Miller was hurt not to be informed of the change of heart and suspicious that the London series would be given a fairer chance on the network than North Region's efforts had been. When the North Region had a success, London often tried to kill it 'or took it over', says Peter Pilbeam.

It's understandable that the Manchester executives were unhappy to see Dodd being poached but listening back to the surviving shows, it's clear that London had a point. Compare an opening monologue from a 1960 edition of *It's Great to Be Young*, written by Casey and Roscoe with contributions from Braben, with the start of the 1963 *Star Parade* that convinced Aeolian Hall that Dodd was worth the effort.

From 1960:

First of all ladies and gentlemen, I would like to say how tickled I am. How tickled I am, at the kick-off. Have you ever been tickled at the kick-off, missus? You shouldn't play rugby. They're always having a try. By Jove, I'm full of bounce tonight. I've had budgie seed for my tea. In this show, we're going to do all sorts of experiments. I'm always experimenting. I once put sunglasses on a hen. It was three weeks trying to hatch out a black pudding.[11]

Then 1963:

Dodd: Well, ladies and gentlemen, first of all, I would just like to say how highly honoured high ham to have been chosen by the BBC to take part in this programme, which celebrates the 125th anniversary of the birth of Frankenstein.

Voice off mic: Many happy returns of the day.

Dodd: Pull that man's beard off and shove it down his earhole. Here are just a few of the magnificent prizes that can be won here. A year's supply of fluff. One Crippen set. A grandad cosy. A fur-lined thingy. A mechanical cabbage. A dwarf remover. And tonight's star prize, an unmentionable object.[12]

The earlier monologue is serviceable but frequently obvious. Moreover, Dodd sounds slightly uncomfortable, as though he's reading someone else's words. Only the hen in sunglasses joke sounds like authentic Dodd. Three years later, Dodd opens confidently with a freewheeling surreal list, clearly written by someone in love with the rhythm of words, always keeping the comedian's voice in mind. What is a 'Crippen set'? Braben seems happier with selling the concept of mechanical cabbages than he ever was with selling the real thing.

A series was commissioned to go out on the Light Programme in autumn 1963, with Bill Worsley – erstwhile husband of the glorious Beryl Reid – taking over from Eric Miller as producer. For *Star Parade*, Miller had retained Judith Chalmers from the Manchester shows and, in a masterstroke of casting, added Scottish actor John Laurie – later known as Private Frazer in *Dad's Army* – to the ensemble. Worsley knew that the combination was a winner and booked Chalmers and Laurie for the series, to begin on Sunday afternoons from late September.

Early on in their working relationship, Braben realized that working with Dodd would be a highly pressurized job. 'There's the world we live in and there's the other very secret world Doddy inhabits,' Braben explained in his memoirs. 'I shared it with him... [and] it's the planet frenzy at a thousand miles an hour. The ratio was five gags per minute, probably more. I was writing one-liners that didn't even take up one line: "Literature killed him. He was run over by a mobile library"... It was one hell of a lick and well worth an ulcer, a relentless pace.'[13] Their relationship set a pattern that would be emulated with Dodd's other writers later on. They were on call at all hours, and with Dodd's idiosyncratic work and sleep patterns, that could mean a phone call in the middle of the night. One of

Braben's successors, David McKellar, recalls just such a communication:

> He never used to go to bed until about four because he was still so hyper after. He used to do the shows until about midnight, didn't he? So, he rang me up, three o'clock one morning it was, with a show the next day, and said, 'I've got an idea for a sketch.' So, I wrote this sketch idea down and thought, 'Fucking hell.' I put the phone down and then the phone rang again. I picked it up and he went [sings] 'There's no business like show business...' OK, you win. It was complimentary. He knew when he rang me and woke me up, he wanted this sketch to be done by morning, and I'm working for him, so that's, you know. You're honoured to be on call, aren't you?[14]

Judith Chalmers remembers the recordings with great fondness but notes that there was no messing about. 'As soon as you got into the studio there was no easy little tittle-tattle chatter. When we got to the studio, and it was a recording day, we just got on with rehearsing. The thing with Doddy was that he wasn't a social animal. He was lovely and we had laughs, but he was absolutely single-mindedly on his comedy and his fun, and of course his songs. He was very dedicated to what he did. So brilliant. You always knew he'd arrived and gone into his dressing room. It was quite strict in a way, but that's good. No time for laughter and chatter, and then the rehearsal. On rehearsals it was always great fun, because we were all laughing with him, if you like, and fortunate enough to be sharing the fun of what he was saying, in very close contact.'[15]

Hearing those shows, it's clear that Dodd spent an awful lot of time and effort trying to put Chalmers off her stroke and make her laugh, and equally clear that he nearly succeeded quite a few times. She recalls the cheerful conspiracy between Dodd and Braben to test her professionalism and trip her up:

> Obviously they wrote the intros and out cues on most of the things I did do, but as time went on, I remember this was in the Paris studio,* the [announcements] were made longer and longer, but they didn't make the music longer and longer, so I had to go hell for leather to get the announcements done in the time. They were devils and I'm sure they did it deliberately. I was determined, ever so determined, not to make a fluff of anything. They gave me more words to say in the same length of music. I thought 'I'm not going to make a muck of it', and of course, it was in front of live audiences. Touch wood, thank goodness, I managed to get through, but it was quite a nerve-wracking thing when they began to do that.[16]

It is a testament to Chalmers' skill that she managed to negotiate tongue-twisters like the opening of the 2 May 1965 show at breakneck speed. 'Let's cast off and set sail with the Ken Dodd Show. Here he comes with his blooming big baggy

---

* The former Paris cinema on Lower Regent Street, London, used as a BBC radio light entertainment studio between the 1940s and 1995.

blue bell bottoms, blowing in the balmy breeze, as he bounds aboard his British-built battleship, swaying slightly, smiling stupidly, and singing snatches of saucy sailors' songs of the sea, the Navy's number one nut, Rear Admiral Nelson Dodd.'[17]

During the years when Braben was Dodd's writing collaborator, they made great use of recurring sketches. Among the most memorable were the two-handers featuring Dodd and John Laurie discussing a particular subject, the conversation heavy with innuendo and wilful misunderstanding. The setting varied. It could be in a hospital, with Dodd and Laurie as patients assessing the doctors and nurses (Ken: 'His wife told me that she thinks in time he'll become an FRCS.' John: 'Will he? The swine.'[18]). Or it might be two gentlemen in a box at the theatre, surveying the action on the stage. Or, as introduced by Chalmers on the *Ken Dodd Show* that went out on the Light Programme on 4 July 1965, 'two friends sitting on the yacht club balcony, watching the annual yacht race':

Ken: [breathily] He's a magnificent yachtsman.

John: Quite brilliant.

Ken. It's amazing when you realize when he was nineteen, he had a catamaran.

John: The poor chap. I didn't know that.

Ken: The whole family is keenly interested in boats. Have you seen his wife's dinghy?

John: Once. Quite by accident.

Ken: I'm told that his sister's got two men going over her jolly boat with a tar brush.

John: Nasty. I don't know what pleasure they get out of it.

Ken: Can you see him from here?

John: I've lost sight of him.

Ken: He's on the poop with his brother.

John: The two of them? They don't care what they do. Foreigners. Yes.

Ken: Oh, he's struck the buoy.

John: The swine. I can't sit here and admire his seamanship after what you've just told me. I must leave.

Ken: I'll come with you, Margot.[19]

Although, as Chalmers says, Dodd was not a social animal, bosses noted very clearly that he needed to be surrounded by people he liked, trusted and respected. Laurie had been unavailable for most of the second series, transmitted in the summer of 1964, and his place was taken by fellow Scot Duncan Macrae or bloodhound-faced Cockney John Slater. Macrae is a superb replacement, especially in the two-hander sketches. However, at the end of the run, Dodd insisted to Worsley that he needed Laurie and Patricia Hayes, and asked him to plan the recordings around their availability.

This sort of loyal insistence was pre-empted when the bookings department suggested the unthinkable act of ditching Chalmers. Dodd's radio show was often preceded by *Two-Way Family Favourites*, a request show intended to link up British forces personnel overseas with their loved ones at home. Chalmers was a regular presenter of the show and there were occasions where she would do the closing announcement of one then open the Dodd show immediately after. Assistant head of radio light entertainment Con Mahoney noted gently:

'Judy is very much one of Doddy's favourites… [and] in the absence of Bill Worsley I can only say that he and Dodd would be very alarmed if she was unable to take part.'[20] Relaying Mahoney's concerns to the Light Programme management, Rich was rather more colourful: 'She is a definite asset to the Dodd show, and I think Doddy himself would moan to high heaven if we lowered the boom on her.' Chalmers was reprieved and the show could go on.

The BBC got its money's worth out of Dodd's radio shows, with Sunday afternoon transmission on the Light Programme being followed in the middle of the week by an evening repeat. Then, a few months later, the whole series would be given an outing on the Home Service, on Saturday afternoons. These 'delayed repeats' were common policy for radio light entertainment shows but were not without their pitfalls. While Dodd was never in the vanguard of satire, he and Braben poked fun at contemporary phenomena and had a particular fondness for gags about Richard Dimbleby. One of these appeared in the fourth show of the 1965 series, transmitted originally on the Light Programme on Sunday, 2 May. By the time of its contracted Home Service repeat on Saturday, 13 November, the rotund broadcaster was seriously ill in London's St Thomas' Hospital. The official reason, reported dutifully in the *Daily Mirror* on Saturday, 30 October, was the draining of a pelvic abscess but the reality was that Dimbleby was dying of cancer.

The standard practice was for programme producers to check their old shows before repeats for material rendered dubious by events. Unfortunately, on this occasion Bill Worsley failed to make the necessary checks and the gag went out once again. This prompted head of radio light entertainment Roy Rich to write to all of his producers. 'We dropped a major clanger last week,' he observed. 'It would be invidious to name names, but you have my word for it that it was a beauty.'[21] Rich reminded the producers that it was their responsibility to check these things. However, taking a belt and braces approach, Rich's deputy, Con Mahoney, had already sent a memo to the department's script editor to give delayed repeats the once-over just in case producers forgot or couldn't be bothered.

Although Rich spared Worsley's blushes officially, everyone would have known precisely what he was referring to. Aeolian Hall may have lacked Television Centre's circular corridors, built to allow rumours to travel faster, but its gossip mill was well oiled in all senses. On this basis, it's highly likely that Rich and Worsley had an idea of the true gravity of Dimbleby's condition.

Worsley undertook some damage limitation by writing a letter of apology to Dimbleby's wife, Dilys, eliciting a gracious handwritten reply from her husband's bedside telling the producer not to worry and that she was sure no harm had been done. Certainly, the incident went unremarked in the papers but Rich noted that luck had been on their side. 'I think it's only due to the kindly intervention of one Mr Kenneth Tynan that we didn't make the press ourselves,' he noted, referring to the *Observer*'s drama critic saying the word 'fuck' on the BBC2 satire show *BBC3* the same evening as the offending Dodd repeat.

*

For any turn, the London Palladium is the pinnacle of achievement. Ken Dodd could almost certainly have added a season at the world's premier variety theatre to his CV way before 1965 but he seemed to fight shy of it. Even invitations to appear on ATV's *Sunday Night at the London Palladium* had to be rebuffed due to the exclusive nature of Dodd's BBC contract. It's suggested that he and Dave Forrester wanted to ensure that his appeal was national rather than regional before mounting their assault. Through the early 1960s, even though his TV shows were networked, Dodd's pulling power was still strongest in the north west. 'He hadn't really made it that big in London at that time,' says Johnnie Hamp.[22]

By the spring of 1965, however, the time was right. Having seen how he could pull in the crowds for weeks on end at the Royal Court in Liverpool in the winter of 1963/1964 and again in 1964/1965, Bernard Delfont and Leslie Macdonnell were certain that he could pull off the same trick at the Palladium – but this time for thirty-four weeks.* With his material extensively tested, graded and marked up on the Giggle Map, Dodd felt ready for the Palladium too.

With vocal group The Kaye Sisters and comedy group The Barron Knights on the bill, the show opened on Saturday, 17 April and ran for thirty-five weeks, only finishing on 11 December to make way for Arthur Askey in *Babes in the*

---

* Dodd would later claim the show ran for forty-two weeks.

*Wood** It was twice-nightly variety, with shows at 6.15 and 8.45, and an additional 2.40 p.m. matinee on Saturdays. To ensure the best possible result, Delfont and Macdonnell assigned Robert Nesbitt to stage and direct the show. Nesbitt had begun his West End career in the 1930s, working extensively with the French impresario André Charlot on revues and, later, at the Palladium with the Crazy Gang. It was Nesbitt who, after a trip to Las Vegas, visualized the re-modelling of the Hippodrome on Charing Cross Road into a cabaret restaurant called The Talk of the Town, which opened in 1958.

The Times was decidedly unconvinced by the whole exercise, in a review that suggested the writer had no concept of the comedian or his stamina. 'It used to be a golden rule of variety to keep the top of the bill until last, and ration the length of the star's appearance in strict relation to his public standing... Leslie Macdonnell and Bernard Delfont have lost all sense of proportion and exposed Mr Ken Dodd to an ordeal that must be as exhausting for him as it is boring for all but the most indiscriminate fans... He is on stage alone for over fifty minutes in a two-hour show.'[23]

The anonymous reviewer had some faint praise for Dodd's technique, calling him 'engaging... swift and sly when he is not being self-indulgent', but called a lot of the material 'the corniest patter' and 'the usual string of second-rate jokes'. As might be expected, the assessment given by Clifford Davis in

* Two of the children performing in Askey's panto were Elaine Paige and Sharon Arden, now better known as Sharon Osbourne.

the *Daily Mirror* was rather warmer, calling it 'the greatest one-man comedy performance London has seen since the heyday of Max Miller and Tommy Trinder'.[24] Michael Walsh in the *Express* noted that while it took the London punters 'a time to warm to his regionalized talk of diddy folk and jam butties... soon it was evident that... the Palladium has found the finest patter comic since Max Miller'.[25] The box office receipts throughout the run tended to support the popular papers' view rather than the broadsheet opinion.

Although Dodd had spent many weeks in digs away from the family home as he traversed the British Isles in the pursuit of humour, the Palladium run required him to take up residence in the capital for several months. 'I lived in London. I couldn't commute back to Knotty Ash, even if I'd wanted to,' he explained in a 2007 documentary. 'I lived in a hotel in Jermyn Street, and then an apartment in Kensington.' Asked if he missed Knotty Ash, he replied, with a look of real glee on his face: 'Not really. It was too exciting here. I was having a whale of a time here... Don't forget, this was... the swinging sixties... Everywhere was wonderful. London was the most exciting place in the world.'[26]

It didn't get much more exciting for Dodd than on Saturday, 1 May 1965, when Liverpool played Leeds United at Wembley in the FA Cup Final, winning 2–1. Instead of relaxing the night before the game, manager Bill Shankly had taken the whole team to the Palladium. Doddy was scheduled to be on stage throughout the game but the show finished as the match was going into extra time. 'The show had just come down on a Saturday afternoon, so we were all looking at the television set,' he recalled. 'First time Liverpool had ever won the cup final. That was the year they won it, '65. And in the evening, all the fans were all round the Palladium, shouting "We want Doddy." I don't know what they were going to do to me if they got me. But they were all round, all cheering, that was very exciting. I was probably the most well-known of all the "wackers".'*[27]

Later in his life, when asked if he'd ever craved transatlantic success, Dodd always demurred but added that he'd played to a lot of Americans during his seasons at the Palladium, having become one of the must-see sights of London. He joked that you could always tell when they were in because all of them wore glasses and the bright lights used to reflect off them. The show was also a must-see for Prime Minister Harold Wilson, who attended the show on Tuesday, 14 September 1965 with his wife, Mary, and their son, Giles. Wilson claimed it was his first night out since becoming PM.

Dodd was already known for his support for the Conservative Party but he enjoyed a cordial association with Bessie Braddock, MP for Liverpool Exchange, who conveyed the invitation to Wilson. The exercise had an obvious mutual publicity benefit. The comedian had the leader of the country in the audience, and the PM got to align himself with the hottest ticket in town, as well as showing he could take a joke.

Indeed, there were more than a few jokes about Wilson in Dodd's act and on the night he was in the house, the band began to laugh when they knew they were approaching.

---

*   A Scouse slang word for Liverpudlians.

Acknowledging the situation, Dodd asked Wilson if he minded. Wilson replied that he didn't. The gags began: 'Harold's gone into hospital for a little operation. He's going to have his raincoat removed... He says "Vote for me, I'll let you out of the mess the country's in. I've got to – I've got another one round the corner waiting to take its place."'[28]

The visit was a triumph for Dodd's press agent, George Bartram, who had set it all up. Described by *Tatler* as 'a tireless worker with a sharp eye for an exploitable situation', the Birmingham-based Bartram counted numerous top comedians among his clients, including Harry Secombe. One of Bartram's favourite tricks was to ghostwrite mildly amusing letters on civic issues to local papers the week before his client was due to play the town. Parish pumps all over the land appeared to contain the wisdom of the biggest names in entertainment on bin collections, blocked drains and dog mess, followed by a plug for the show. Bartram's manoeuvring in getting Wilson to the Palladium was rather more subtle. Knowing her friendship with Dodd, he approached Braddock months before and wrote twice directly to Wilson. Bartram also ensured that the press got to know all about it when John Osborne took the cast of his latest play to see Dodd in action so they could 'see a real comedian'.

Dodd's first Palladium season coincided with the irresistible rise of the Diddymen. Dodd liked to mythologize slightly about his diminutive co-stars in interviews, talking of them as though they had been in his act from very near the start. As in a 2006 radio interview with Ed Doolan: 'Somebody said to me once about 1954, 1955, he said, "You know Doddy, you get on very well with children." "Yeah, I went to school with them." He said, "You ought to find a point of contact." Lo and behold, I went right down the bottom of our garden, to think. I often do that. I often go to the bottom of the garden, wait until the tortoise gets down there and turn it round the other way. All of a sudden I saw these little men, these little diddy men and that's where it came from.'[29] One particular inspiration was his Uncle Jack, a gentleman of restricted height given to wearing bowler hats.

However, there is no mention of the Diddymen in reviews, billings or listings before 1964, and they make no appearance in Dodd's 1963 radio series or the surviving edition of *It's Great to Be Young*. Dodd made a passing reference to them in his encounter at Granada with the Beatles in November 1963, when trying to invent Merseybeat band names, which seems to be the earliest surviving citation. He gave himself away slightly by explaining that they made their debut when he was presenting *Housewives' Choice*, which he did for the first time of several over a week in April 1964. What seems most likely is that Dickie Mint was a fixture in Dodd's stage act before the other Diddymen came into being, and that the rest were developed by Dodd and *Housewives' Choice* producer Teddy Warrick, with their high voices created using speeded-up tapes in the style of David Seville and the Chipmunks. In 1966, Warrick told the *Observer* that the programme 'becomes a Ken Dodd show with records',[30] adding that the BBC had a collection of one hundred sounds especially made for Dodd, and that Eddie Braben was on call throughout each show. This involved a lot of work and preparation on the part of the rehearsal-averse Dodd but he clearly saw the comic value in the extra effort, and was richly rewarded when the Diddymen became an instant hit.

'I realized I'd have to get an Englishman, an Irishman, a Scotsman and a Welshman,' he explained.[31] So Mint was joined by Mick the Marmaliser from Ireland, Wee Hamish from Scotland, Little Evan from Llantickelellan and, residing at 140 Park Lane, London, Nigel Ponsonby-Smallpiece.* The Diddymen were soon making records for EMI's Columbia label, to which the comedian had transferred from Decca in 1962 under the guidance of songwriter and producer Norman Newell. The first releases were the single 'Song of the Diddymen' and an accompanying EP, 'Doddy and the Diddymen', both released in October 1965. The EP opened with a spoken word track, 'Doddy and the Diddymen make a record', where Dodd visits each of his tiny protégés to sound them out about making a 'diddy disc'. At 1½ Titchy Terrace, Mick is happy to join in as long as he can play the drums: 'Let me bang the big drum, Doddy, or I'll marmalise ya.' A similarly positive response comes from Hamish, in his little cottage 'with a wisp of tartan smoke curling from the chimbley', Little Evan and Nigel.

The star of the show, though, is obviously Dickie Mint, always Dodd's favourite, to the point where he said he regarded him as a real person. On the EP's sole original composition,

* The choice of address for Ponsonby-Smallpiece was a little in-joke for those in show business, being a block of luxury flats that had long since been converted to suites of offices, one of which was occupied by Dodd's agents Forrester George.

'Where's Me Shirt' (a collaboration between Dodd and actor/ songwriter Max Diamond),* figures throughout history find themselves bare-chested at a critical juncture – Adam in the Garden of Eden, Napoleon Bonaparte in Moscow, Wyatt Earp in a shoot-out. In each case, their frustrations are expressed sweetly in the chorus through a catarrhal yell of the song's title followed by a character study by Mint, like this one of Napoleon:

Where's me shirt? Ooh, sacre blue. Sacre-flippin'-blue. Where's me shaaairt? By Jove, it isn't 'alf frosty. Oooh this tent isn't half draughty. I don't know where the draught's coming from, but I know where it's going to.[32]

The other tracks on the record were lively cover versions of the traditional tunes 'Old Macdonald had a Farm' and 'The Wee Cooper of Fife'. Although the orchestral arrangements were by Brian Fahey,† his contribution on the label was credited as 'Orchestration and musical direction', with Dodd claiming arrangement credits on the older numbers. This was a shrewd ruse to claim the composition royalties for Dodd, as an arrangement of a traditional piece is treated as a fresh composition in copyright law.

Dodd wasn't able to try the same trick with his latest straight single, as, although it was an old song, it was still

* Diamond had previously co-written 'My Boomerang Won't Come Back' with Charlie Drake.
† To this day, Fahey's 'At the Sign of the Swinging Cymbal' is the theme tune for Radio 2's *Pick of the Pops*.

in copyright. None of his other releases since 'Love Is Like a Violin' had made the top twenty, let alone the top ten. Even 'Happiness', released in July 1964, only reached number thirty-one, although it would be guaranteed a long and happy life after its chart run by becoming Dodd's signature tune. So, when Dodd came out of EMI's studios at Abbey Road, St John's Wood, with a recording of a song made popular by Rudy Vallée in 1929, it was expected to sell respectably but not spectacularly. Indeed, the *Melody Maker*'s reviewer said of 'Tears' that 'his many fans will no doubt be queuing outside the record shops, but probably not enough to get it up much beyond the 40s'.[33] To apparent surprise, 'Tears' entered the chart on 8 September at number thirty-seven, rising to number sixteen the following week, then number seven a week later. The *Melody Maker* had to report that it could get 'possibly even as high as "Love Is Like a Violin"', which went to number three. Dodd told the paper that 'I'd been looking for a song for some time' and that 'Jimmy Phillips of KPM Music, who has found a lot of hits for me, rang me and said he'd dreamed about this old song which he'd managed to dig out… I liked it, the melody was good and it had a lyric which I could put over with sincerity. It was an obvious choice.'

Obvious as it might have been, even Dodd was 'surprised that it's taken off so quickly. After all, it's a sentimental ballad and it's hardly Sonny and Cher's cup of tea, is it? More Doctor Chuckabutty's!' Was it as big a surprise as all that, though? Dodd had been featuring the song on his radio show as early as July 1964, so by the time it came out as a single, it was already well-established with his fans. Furthermore, the comedian had recorded two potential A-sides at the session, and decided to use the acetate test discs he'd been given afterwards for a touch of market research. 'When you used to do recordings in those days, you'd do three in an afternoon at Abbey Road, and I remember one was "Tears", one was "The River", and I can't remember what the other one was,' he said in a 2006 radio interview. 'I was at the Palladium at the time... and I played it to visitors that came in. People said "Oh I like that one", "The River" because it was a beautiful melody. Then suddenly one day, somebody said "That Tears one, that's a real back of the chara [charabanc] song, real back of the coach song." So I said "Right, that's the one we'll do, then."'[34]

The single achieved its predicted third place in its fourth week on the chart, then, the following week, it clambered to number one, knocking the Walker Brothers' 'Make It Easy On Yourself' off the peak. In all, the song would spend five weeks at the top of the chart and seventeen weeks in the top ten, only dropping out of the top forty in early February 1966. It had sold a million copies by Christmas and brought Dodd a gold disc. Only The Beatles achieved the same level of sales but Dodd pipped them to claiming the best-selling single of 1965, indeed one of the five best-selling singles of the whole decade, with his hometown chums bagging the other four.

Most of Dodd's musical repertoire was at odds with his comic persona. 'Happiness' was his only upbeat hit single. The rest were sentimental ballads, with lost love being a recurring theme. His records are notable for the absence of songs for swinging lovers. In 'Eight by Ten', his beloved has left him for another man and all he has left is a framed picture of her. In the case of 'Tears', he hasn't even got a photograph, only moist eyes. With the same self-knowledge that pervaded his choices in comedy, he was never persuaded to tackle repertoire with which he didn't feel comfortable. 'I was very lucky,' he said in 2006. 'In those days, in the 1960s, most entertainers were given a song by the music publisher or the record company. "Make a disc of that," and you have to do it. I was able to choose my songs, because I was given lots of songs. Half a dozen songs a year, and I'd pick a couple out. I picked some marvellous songs, but I wasn't... right all the time.'[35] For example, he rejected Jim Reeves' 'I Love You Because', a number that would have sat very neatly in his comfort zone, because he felt it was too similar to 'Down by the Old Mill Stream'.

At this time, The Beatles were using the same Abbey Road studios to revolutionize recording but Dodd preferred the traditional methods to the end, with a three-hour session intended to produce an A-side and a B-side at the very least. 'In the old days, you went to the studio,' he explained fifty years after the runaway success of 'Tears'. 'The orchestra was there, about forty or fifty people, you stood in a little glass box like a telephone box, and that was it, you did it there, live. Now, you take, oh it might be a couple of weeks. First of all they put the drum track down, then they put the strings track down, then they do the brass. It takes a long time, and it's all time-consuming.'[36]

Broadcasters were understandably keen to capitalize on Dodd's invasion of London and his chart success. Although

Dodd's exclusive contract with the BBC had lapsed, the Corporation seemed to command his loyalty. He told Barney Colehan that he had refused an offer of a series from ATV. Understandably, Tom Sloan was eager to exploit Dodd's successful season at the Palladium, and approached Dave Forrester directly with a proposal in June, just over six weeks into the run of *Doddy's Here*. He knew that the busy Dodd would be likely either to say no flat out or play extremely hard to get. However, Sloan had an ace to play. BBC2 had launched in April 1964, broadcasting only to London and the south east of England. Transmissions were extended to the Midlands in December 1964, and the North of England was due to get the new service in October 1965. For the opening night, a schedule of distinctly northern programmes was planned and Sloan thought Dodd was the perfect choice for the comedy element.

Sloan broached two possibilities with Forrester. His preference was for outside broadcast cameras to visit the Palladium for a heavily abridged version of *Doddy's Here*. This, he suggested, 'would be the finest possible way of showing the North how completely Ken Dodd has conquered the South!'[37] The sticking point would be whether Moss Empires, proprietors of the Palladium, would permit such a venture, given that they were owned by Lew Grade, who also owned ATV. The alternative was for a special to be made at the BBC Television Theatre, with a performance fee of £1000 and a script fee to be negotiated on top.

Dodd agreed to Sloan's blandishments and a recording date of Sunday, 5 September was set, this being the only date on which both the TV Theatre and the star were available. Sloan had tried to persuade Forrester to release Dodd for a two-day rehearsal and recording stand over the weekend, but this proved impossible as Dodd had two performances at the Palladium on the Saturday. Sloan had long regarded Dodd as needing a tougher producer than the affable Colehan, and suggested Bill Lyon-Shaw for the job. A seasoned pro, Lyon-Shaw had run his own touring repertory company before joining BBC Television in 1950. Headhunted to join ATV at the start in 1955, he had later moved on to be the programme controller at Tyne Tees in Newcastle when it opened in 1959.

Sadly, the show no longer exists, but the *Liverpool Echo*'s reviewer, while admitting to being 'no fan of Doddy's patter' and regarding 'Tears' as 'the sort of maudlin mush that makes me want to crawl quietly under the carpet', was full of 'admiration of the way he handled the visual humour in last night's filmed sequences'. Noting that these elements were somewhat 'derivative' of Michael Bentine's *It's a Square World*, it was nonetheless a fresh direction for the comedian, suggesting 'an ability and apparent willingness to undergo some tailoring for television'.[38]

In contrast, Kenneth Eastaugh in the *Daily Mirror* called the show 'unspectacular', which he regarded as a surprise for 'a mature performer of integrity to the tips of his flowing locks... With Dodd you do not see the unsightly seam where his TV personality and smile don't quite cover his performance.' Working here with 'weak' material, Eastaugh worried that 'perhaps this muted Dodd is the new Dodd... I wish he'd get back to the old'.

Doddy got a far better response for his first Royal Variety Performance, with his beloved parents in the audience. This was the pinnacle of an extraordinary year for the comedian, and the first of six appearances at the gala show between 1965 and 2006. The venue for the show on Monday, 8 November was the Palladium, so while he was sharing the comic duties on the bill with Spike Milligan, Peter Cook and Dudley Moore, he had the home advantage. *The Times*, which had given *Doddy's Here* that drubbing, was far more favourable about his Royal debut: 'It is Mr Ken Dodd, who is funny by nature rather than art who deservedly won most laughter. He made lively, silly, naive little jokes which somehow, by virtue of skilfully casual timing and his own fantastic personality, involved his audience at once in his quaintly zany world.'[39] The *Guardian* agreed that Dodd had the audience from the start: 'The generally high standard of performance from the twenty British, American and French stars could not conceal the fact that Ken Dodd is a man in form. His fantasy, humour, intelligence, and speed conquered the audience in a matter of seconds.'[40]

Dodd capped off a whirlwind of a year, including 1.5 million record sales, with a BBC1 special on Christmas Day, the earliest of his own shows to survive. Interestingly, the copy in the archive is not the completed show as transmitted, but two hours of studio recording, beginning with Dodd warming up the party-hat-wearing audience by asking them to pretend that it's Christmas Day:

You're all sitting there now, you're all full of pudden, you've got the Wills' Whiffs out. We're going to have a bash.

We're going to have a few dirty jokes and some charades, and then we'll all adjourn down to the local and have a few drops of, er, thingy there. OK? So, we want to hear you laugh as loud as you possibly can, really get your chuckle muscles working, and I ought to tell you... that the lad upstairs who does the sound here, he has a nasty habit of not turning the laughs up. I don't know whether you notice that on my shows. It's funny that, the laughs are always down. I've found out who he is. His name's Mr Moore, so whenever we come to any part, the last gag of anything, you shout 'MORE, MORE' and then he knows that's his chance to turn the sound up. Don't forget that it's Christmas Day, everybody's watching us, millions. Far more than will be watching the commercial lot, so you're all on telly.[41]

Eddie Braben makes an appearance on screen in a sketch about a 'Grandad bowling' contest, where he plays Dodd's opponent in a lawn game that involves pushing old men in bath chairs into a large hole. Then from Knotty Ash Baths comes an underwater ballroom dancing contest, and a visit to a pantomime horse stud, a sketch stuffed with pantomime producer in-jokes. 'This magnificent beast here, by Tom Arnold out of Emile Littler,' Dodd announces, 'is called Nesbitt's Choice. This wonderful animal is called Freddie Carpenter. A chip off the old block, by Howard out of Wyndham.'[42]

Andy Mann, the DIY expert made popular in Dodd's radio series, pops up in vision. As on radio, very little DIY is undertaken, the character being primarily a vehicle for wife and mother-in-law jokes. 'At the moment, my dear lady wife, she's in bed actually with a slipped disc. She was going upstairs last night and suddenly it went. Oooh, it gave me a terrible shock because she nearly dropped me.'[43] What becomes more obvious in vision is how much the character owes to Robb Wilton, with Dodd, perhaps unconsciously, using a lot of Wilton's mannerisms.

The recording also features early, wordless appearances from two future comedy giants in a sketch about Christmas Day in the workhouse. As the inmates pull wishbones, they wish to be young and smart again. Suddenly one turns into Michael Palin, and another into Terry Jones, both almost fresh out of Oxford.* At the time, they were jobbing gag writers and one of their regular duties was writing links for the *Billy Cotton Band Show*, produced, like Dodd's special, by Michael Hurll.

There's also a telling insight into Dodd's impatience with the mechanics of television, when a technical hitch causes a brief break in the recording. When the halt is called, Dodd says 'Oh, that's charming', puts his head in his hands, exclaims 'Thanks for nothing' and then rolls his eyes. The recording runs for over twice the scheduled length and there is no repeated material, so there is a lot here that didn't go out that Christmas Day.

The summer after the Palladium season, the BBC had another crack at televising Dodd, pairing him this time with Duncan

---

* There is a third transformation but the young man involved is unidentifiable, although he bears a slight resemblance to John Fortune.

Wood, producer of *Hancock's Half Hour* and *Steptoe and Son*. With Dodd in residence at the Opera House in Blackpool, it made sense logistically to make the shows there too on his nights off. Unfortunately, yet again, the artistic side suffered. Wood, a director who had made his reputation capturing Tony Hancock's facial mobility to supreme effect, was hampered by the location. He simply couldn't get cameras close enough to Dodd – a mid-shot* being the best achievable with the early zoom lenses available. One prime camera position was at the front of the balcony, almost looking down on the top of Dodd's head, enough to give viewers vertigo.

The shows are not without their highlights, though. They are notable for the television debut of the Diddymen, brought to corporeal form and given life by master puppeteer Roger Stevenson. Also, the first show of the series sees Braben being joined on the writing side by Ray Galton and Alan Simpson, who provide a long sketch pitting Doddy against Harold and Albert Steptoe on their holidays:

Dodd [dressed in caricature golfing garb]: Is this your father? What? This little diddyman? Hello, Pop. I've got one just like you sitting in our front garden by the pond on a little concrete...

Albert [in an Edwardian bathing suit]: Who's this great hairy twit then?

Harold: Don't be rude, pater. This hairy twit is Mr Ken

---

* TV term for a shot where the whole upper body is in view, halfway between a wide shot and a close-up.

> Dodds and we're going to play golf with him. Now
> go and get changed.
> *Dodd*: Yes, go and get changed. You can't go wandering
> around the golf course in ridiculous clothes like that.[44]

Not that television mattered to Dodd as much as it did to other performers. Benny Hill was a giant on television, but a reluctant stage performer. Dodd was the opposite. He always held to the view that comedians had to 'pass an exam' with the public every decade or so. Television was all part of the process of reminding the public that he existed but the theatre was where he wanted them. However, taking Christmas 1966 off meant that Doddy was ready to take his first set of exams for commercial television.

4

Doddy at the top

'I went to the Army and Navy stores. Asked where the camouflage jackets were. "Good, aren't they?"'

Nineteen sixty-seven was a big year for Doddy. He was on TV more regularly than at any point in his career and he was set to spend the summer of love basking in the audience's love at the London Palladium with a mammoth run for *Doddy's Here Again.*

The end of Dodd's exclusive BBC contract meant that he could run his TV career much more along the lines of his stage career: turning up, eventually, for whoever had booked him. After his 1966 Christmas show for BBC1, he began work straight away on a new Saturday night series for the ITV company that served the Midlands and North at weekends, ABC Television. Then at the end of the year, he would return to the BBC for another Christmas show, then back to ABC again.

Beginning on 7 January 1967, *Doddy's Music Box* was billed by the comedian himself (or possibly a publicist speaking on his behalf) as a 'very slick, punchy mixture of comedy and music, featuring people in the charts'.[1] As well as the guests, who included Tom Jones, Cat Stevens, Dusty Springfield, Sandie Shaw and Adam Faith, Dodd contributed to the musical side, both in straight songs and comedy numbers. His new Columbia EP, *Diddyness*, provided four of the latter to promote, including 'The Nikky-Nokky-Noo Song' and 'Diddycombe Fair':

> Dickie Mint, Dickie Mint, what have you got there?
> A diddy red Mini of vintage so rare,
> To take diddy people to Diddycombe Fair…

It was decided that the comedy element would work best if he had a foil. Dodd, Braben and producer Peter Frazer-Jones didn't have far to look for the answer. Upstairs from ABC's main studio in the former Capitol cinema in Didsbury was the small room where in-vision continuity announcers linked the programmes and covered for the technical faults that occurred in those days of live television. One of the announcers was David Hamilton, still in his twenties and a regular presence on pop music radio. As Hamilton explains: 'He'd had a straight man or interviewer, or however you like to put it, called David Mahlowe, when he worked for the BBC, but David Mahlowe was under contract to the BBC, and couldn't do it. It was Ken who said, "What about that one that does the announcing in between the programmes?" We'd never met but he saw something in me that he thought could be something to work with.'[2]

They might not have met, but they had a lot of mutual friends at the BBC in Manchester, Hamilton having made his British broadcasting debut with Bernard Herrmann and the Northern Dance Orchestra ('The band with the beat that's reet') on *The Beat Show* in 1962. The producer who gave Hamilton that first break, Geoff Lawrence, had worked extensively with Dodd over the years. For Hamilton, working with Dodd was a perfect combination of time, place and people. 'The Didsbury studio was a very happy studio,' says Hamilton. 'Quite small. They did other things up there, like *Opportunity Knocks* and *Variety Bandbox* and programmes like that. It was just one of those magical places. Of course, it was a great time as well, the 1960s. You had a combination of things, really. The Beatles and the Mersey Sound, the Manchester bands too, those two cities together.'[3]

It was while working on the pilot show that Dodd gave Hamilton a nickname that would endure. 'During the rehearsals at "Diddy Didsbury", as Ken inevitably called it, he called me "Diddy David" for the first time. The people who were there, the cameramen, the make-up girls, the props boys, they chuckled. In fairness to him, he took me to one side afterwards and said, "Do you mind me calling you that, because if you mind, I won't do it anymore, but if you don't mind, I think it will stick." I said, "I don't mind," and I've been stuck with it for fifty years.'[4]

The dominance of the music content meant that the show could be done without the week's preparation stipulated by the BBC, which obviously appealed to the rehearsal-averse star. 'We were given the scripts on Tuesday afternoon,' says Hamilton, 'and then we rehearsed with the scripts in our hands on Wednesday, recorded on Thursday, the show was edited on Friday, and it went out on Saturday night on the ITV network. For the programme finale, each of us walked on, and Ken gave us a ha'penny, and our name came up. You walk on, he gives you a ha'penny.'

Mostly serious-minded in rehearsal, Dodd would sometimes send himself up for the benefit of the cast and crew. Hamilton remembers one occasion with particular glee:

We were doing rehearsals one day, and he did 'Happiness', this is just for the studio staff, he wouldn't do this in public, he wouldn't do this on stage, but he did it as 'A penis'. The whole thing. 'A penis, a penis, the greatest gift that I possess. I thank the Lord that I've been blessed with more than my share of a penis. A wise old man said to me one time a penis is a state of mind. You see it in the sunshine, feel it in the air...' The whole bloody thing. The studio – the make-up girls, the props boys – they were in stitches. Peter Frazer-Jones, everybody, were on the floor. He said to me after 'That was funny, wasn't it? Of course, I'd never do that in public.'[5]

At ABC, Dodd was able to exercise a degree of editorial control that he was unlikely to be permitted at the BBC, with taskmasters like Barney Colehan and Michael Hurll. Although a highly skilled director who would later become renowned as one of the best situation comedy practitioners in the business, Peter Frazer-Jones found it hard to assert his authority with Dodd. According to Hamilton:

Ken's way of working was to record twice as much as there was time for. He would then look at it and decide what he thought worked and what didn't work. He only kept the best sketches in. Nobody knew, until Saturday night, what they did if anything was going to be in the show or not. I knew that I would always be on the show because I was the interviewer. Sometimes there were really good sketches that I did that didn't get in. With the others, with the actors, they never knew if they were going to be in or not. They had a day of waiting and wondering, then they'd watch the show and find out.

Normally, it's the producer who calls the shots, but Ken's way of controlling it was to say 'I think that goes, and that'll go, but we'll keep that', and I think Peter was quite long-suffering. At the end of the recordings, Ken would go into the VT room, he'd have a couple of lagers with him, he'd sit there with Peter and he'd pretty well tell Peter what stayed in and what didn't. At the beginning of the series, Peter had a thick head of red hair. By the end of the series, he was grey. He went grey in a few weeks.[6]

Writing about the show in the *Observer*, George Melly would probably have preferred the private, profane, rehearsal-mode Dodd. 'His stage image suggests an adulterous milkman who, despite his homely appearance, can make the housewives of Knotty Ash laugh so much that they finish up on their backs on the kitchen sofa,' the flamboyant jazzer said of his fellow Scouser. 'He is a comparatively suggestive comedian when live, but his TV show *Doddy's Music Box* is as clean as a whistle, with the result that his Diddy-ridden side, which in my view needs some innuendo to make it work, becomes rather twee.'[7]

Others disagreed. Reviewing the series in *The Stage*, Marjorie Norris said that 'at last' here was 'a show which carries this artist's very personal appeal into the home instead of squandering it in the auditorium'.[8] Past Dodd shows had 'left me admiring his skill and his complete control over his live audience but unmoved by his style of comedy'. *Doddy's Music Box*, she said, benefited from 'the more intimate style' adopted by Frazer-Jones, and the presence of Patricia Hayes, one of Dodd's favourite sidekicks.

Norris wrote: 'Without stealing any of Dodd's own laughs, this versatile comedienne ensured that the fun was kept going and proved the perfect foil as "Monica" in a send-up of *Double Your Money* and as the laboratory assistant in a jelly-testing factory sketch in which inventiveness and slapstick were irresistibly blended.'[9]

Dodd used his editorial control on one occasion to remind a supporting player precisely whose name was over the door, as David Hamilton recalls. 'Rita Webb, who was a little fat Cockney woman, talked to him one day and she said "Here, Ken, I'm an actress, why don't you give me some decent lines? All I am in this is a little fat cow. I'm an actress, give me some decent lines." She was the only one who gave him a hard time. Everyone else took what they were given.'[10] Dodd decided to give Webb what she wanted, resulting in an increased workload for the already overstretched Eddie Braben. 'The next week, we all turned up, and she had so much material. There was one solo sketch, with her reading the *News at Ten*. "Right, here's the bleedin' News at Ten, innit. And I'm bleedin' giving it to you." It was hilarious. It was wonderful. And then there was a two-hander with her and Ken, then other sketches. She had so much to learn and so much to do.'

Although Webb had dominated the recording session, the transmitted version was very different. 'This particular night, no *News at Ten* sketch. No double-hander with Ken. Nothing of Rita Webb's appeared at all. All she did was, she walked on and got her ha'penny.' Hamilton was booked for every show but the other supporting players were booked on a weekly basis. 'Rita gets the call, says yes, turns up and he never had another dickie bird out of her. After that, she never said "No, I'm a bleedin' actress, I am."'

This was Dodd's manipulative, controlling side at play. Webb had been made to work extra hard, then humiliated in front of her colleagues. The message was not lost on them either, with Hamilton taking particular note: 'I think that was his way of saying "I call the shots. Don't give me a hard time. I'm the star of the show." I listened and learned, and I thought "Keep your mouth shut, learn your lines, don't rock the boat, he's the star of the show."'

Thankfully, Hamilton was able to learn from Dodd in other, more positive ways, not least in terms of how to deal with fame and the demands of fans:

He was wonderful with the public. He was very flattering to people. He'd say, 'How are you, Commander?' He'd call them by names that made them feel important. I've known well-known names being asked for autographs and telling people to fuck off, even children. Dreadful. I never once saw Ken being rude to anybody.

All those people had a little bit of Ken Dodd, a slice of him, and they went away thinking, 'What a funny man, what a lovely bloke, he had time for us, and he spoke to us.' His PR with the public was second to none. It was fantastic. My mother came up to Manchester for the recording of one of the shows, and my mother up until that point had not been a particular Ken Dodd fan, but he was so charming to her, that after that she was absolutely his biggest fan. She was totally disarmed by him.[11]

Many years later, entertainer Andy Eastwood had a similar experience observing Dodd's way with people when he joined the *Happiness Show* company:

He didn't really have time but he made time when there wasn't time. He was there half the night. There wasn't really time for it but he just did it anyway. Incredible. He took a real liking to my father, because he used to come along to the shows sometimes, and he made pals. He was pallier with my dad than he was with me, because he looked at me as working for him, whereas my dad he could just chat with. He had a lot of respect for families. I remember him talking to journalists sometimes and he was very, very curt with them, and then suddenly they'd mention their family or their children or whatever and he'd become a different character, taking an interest in people's families.[12]

As a result of their television partnership, Dodd began to be asked if Diddy David was joining him on his lucrative personal appearances, such as opening bingo halls and super-markets. This gave Hamilton a privileged glimpse of the private man behind the public persona, and an insight into his timekeeping. In many cases, Dodd's lateness wasn't caused by disorganization. It was a deliberate policy to build up demand. Hamilton remembers:

> People could see Ken in Liverpool any day of the week, but even in his home patch, enormous crowds turned up. I think we were opening a Fine Fare supermarket, and I went to his house in Thomas Lane, Knotty Ash. Somebody opened the door and let me in, and there was a kind of waiting room. In this waiting room was memorabilia like Diddymen and tickling sticks and everything. Finally, he came down, and I said to him 'Ken, it's eleven o'clock, we're due there now to open the supermarket.' 'Don't worry about that,' he said. 'A crowd will get a crowd.' By which I think he meant that these people who didn't know it was on might turn up, see a crowd, wonder what the crowd was and it would be an even bigger crowd.[13]

While playing for time, Dodd offered Hamilton a tour of his home: 'We walked into one room, and he showed me a suite of furniture and he pointed at it and he went "Lewis's, Liverpool". So, we went into another room, another suite of furniture, he pointed at it, he went "Paulden's, Sheffield", then we went into another room and he went "Lewis's, Manchester". These were all suites of furniture that he got in lieu of payment. As we left the house, he looked over his shoulder and said "Listen and learn."'

One of the most valuable pieces of education that Dodd passed on to Hamilton came during the disc jockey's first season in pantomime, playing Buttons in *Cinderella* at the Bradford Alhambra in 1971:

One day, turned up at the matinee. I didn't know he was in. He came down to the dressing room afterwards and he said, 'Come on, I'll take you out for dinner.' So, knowing that Ken was known to be a little, shall we say, careful, I thought, 'Well, that's nice.' Anyway, we went across the road to the fish and chip shop. We walked into the back parlour, which was unlicensed, he took two lagers out of his overcoat pocket, and he put them down on the counter, and he said to the woman behind the counter 'Cod and chips twice, love.'

So we sat there, eating our cod and chips, drinking our lager, this was before the evening show, and I thought to myself, 'My God, I'm here with a man who is undoubtedly a huge star' – he was the Variety Club entertainer of the year, he'd been number one in the charts with 'Tears', he'd just done a long sell-out season at the Palladium – 'and we're sitting here eating fish and chips and drinking lager.' But at this dinner that we had, he gave me wonderful advice about how to play Buttons and Ken had been a wonderful Buttons. He said to me, 'You've got the bubbly effervescent bit. What you've got to do is you've got to work on the pathos.' I remember his words. He said, 'You've got to remember Cinderella is a cow. She is only after the prince because he's wealthy. The person she really loves is you, the little page boy, and you've got to work on that pathos,' and he gave me some advice on how I might do that.

A couple of days later in the kitchen scene, when I sung 'Smile' to Cinderella, I looked off to the wings and a little boy in the front row shouted out, 'Cinders, marry Buttons.' So, I rang Ken and told him the good news, and he said, 'Well done, son, you're on your way.' So, I thought about it afterwards and I thought would I really have preferred to go to the best hotel, let's say Yates's Wine Lodge, and had an absolute slap-up dinner and talked about football and holidays or whatever, or had fish and chips and lager and advice that money couldn't buy? It was a no-brainer, wasn't it?[14]

Doddy's Music Box marked the beginning of the end of the relationship between Dodd and Braben. The writer got wind of a pay rise for the comedian that was not being reflected in the remuneration for his creative partner. Dodd refused to budge and, after a final BBC Christmas special, Braben walked away. This was short-sighted and selfish of Dodd, sacrificing a friendship and a close professional association for the sake of a few quid. Just how much of a misjudgement it was became apparent in Dodd's subsequent TV work. He employed some very good writers but very little of the material came close to Dodd and Braben at their height. Other writers wrote for Dodd. Braben knew Dodd inside out, and wrote with him.

Some years after the split, Anthony Wall, later to become

an arts documentary maker of distinction, but then a fresh-out-of-university radio producer on secondment to BBC Manchester, eavesdropped on a conversation at the Playhouse Theatre in Hulme, where Braben was recording one of his Radio 2 shows with Jim Casey:

> I was at the back, in the cubicle, where you recorded the stuff, and it was a dinner break. I was twenty-three or whatever. Everybody had gone. Eddie Braben, who was completely and utterly brilliant, and Eli Woods were on the stage. Who walks in, just because he was in town, but Max Wall? So stupid of me just not to turn a recorder on, because I could hear what they were saying, but I didn't. It was fascinating. They started off reminiscing about playing that particular place, and then they got into telling faintly scurrilous stories about Ken Dodd and how mind-numbingly, even by comedians' standards, mean he was. How little he paid for jokes. I seem to remember Eddie going on about that. They didn't go into it in detail but the other two looked like they knew all about it.[15]

In the same year as Dodd and Braben parted company, the comedian also lost his mother at the age of seventy-one. Nearly twenty years after Sarah's death, Dodd told Professor Anthony Clare that he had been 'dreading it, but it was totally different to what one would expect'. Instead of 'fall[ing] into this tremendous trough of despair, I didn't go all to pieces. I felt some strength come from somewhere... It was very, very strong and I was able to go on and do my next show, and I remember it was a very, very good show... I knew they were with me... I think I was helped directly.'[16]

Dodd fought shy of saying it in as many words but Clare managed to pin it down to Dodd feeling that there had been some form of divine intervention. Sarah had been religious and her son said he tried 'to have conversations with my maker'. The church had been the origin of Dodd's singing, since he had been a choirboy at St John's in Knotty Ash, 'until they found out what was making the noise'. Obviously, having had the importance of being different impressed on him from an early age, Dodd didn't go for off-the-peg religion. As ever, he met God on his own terms. He said he found services 'a little bit medieval' and that he preferred to 'make my own dialogues up'. However, his faith was vitally important to him. 'We all need guidance,' he said in 2004. 'We all need help, we all need strength and courage, and God can give us courage, God can give us hope, God can give us optimism. With God, you can do anything.'[17]

One regular dialogue Dodd had was in his dressing room before a show, as he explained to Ricky Tomlinson in a 2007 radio interview. 'You never really get over stage nerves, you know. Believe it or not, all sorts of entertainers and comedians, which is what I've got on my passport, they all have their own little rituals. Some people have a little rhyme they say. Some people turn around three times. I have a little word with head office. Before every show, I have a little word with the boss and ask "Can I do a good show?", and then I probably undo it all by touching wood.'[18]

Braben was a hard act to follow. When, in 1971, it was

announced that Dodd would be taking part in the Liverpool Playhouse's diamond jubilee season, playing Malvolio in *Twelfth Night*, Dodd joked at a press conference that 'Shakespeare is the best scriptwriter I have ever had,' adding (in an aside that Braben would undoubtedly have noted with a raised eyebrow) that 'his fees are so modest'.[19] Dodd gamely fooled around in yellow tights outside the theatre for the press cameras, carrying a bust of the Bard. Dodd had mentioned his desire to appear in *Twelfth Night* in a *Liverpool Echo* article several months earlier in April, having already been offered the part. '*Twelfth Night* would have been my first choice because we did it at school,' he explained at the time. 'We all did it at school. It's a challenge to see whether I could act, it's also a bigger challenge to see whether I could accept the discipline of the straight theatre.'[20]

When Dodd received the call from director Antony Tuckey, his immediate thought was that he was wanted for the part of Feste, the fool, but Tuckey wanted a comedian to play the pompous steward. While many playing Malvolio go for the most unsympathetic of laughs, treating him as an obvious figure of ridicule, Dodd decided to paint him as a figure of pity. 'I've done six months' work because I was determined that this wouldn't be a horrible anti-climax, a horrible flop,' said Dodd, reverting to the young boy in the Picton Library. 'I read as much as I could about *Twelfth Night* and of course as much as I could about the character of Malvolio. The various theatre criticisms. And I even wrote down as many phrases as I could from these analyses that would help me to think myself into the part before going on.'

One that lodged with Dodd was that Malvolio was a tragic comedian, not a grotesque, and that the ridicule comes from upending his dignity. Another critic consulted by Dodd described the character as 'a petty tyrant', but the comedian said: 'I myself don't think he's quite as nasty as that. I think he's an orderly-minded steward, but of course you have to understand that Olivia's household is in mourning for her brother, and he is really the male head of the household because Sir Toby's not much use, he's always drunk and roistering, so it's Malvolio really who is the symbol of order in this household, and I think he takes his job quite seriously. I think he's got quite a job on, controlling these characters. I'm not playing it in the classical poetic tradition. I'm playing it in a naturalistic way. I try to be Malvolio. I have been a servant of the public ever since I left school... and this pleases me.'

The production opened on Wednesday, 10 November 1971 for two and a half weeks. Critics viewing the opening night praised Dodd's self-discipline and the way he used the tension between his natural ebullient self and the character for dramatic effect. 'Doddy sticks dutifully to the script and survives the occasional moments where the natural comedian threatens to cut loose,' said the *Liverpool Echo*'s reviewer, adding that 'the switch from scowl to smile is hilarious in the letter scene and he sustains the pathos of his final scene'.[21]

Throughout the run, Dodd had been badgering Tuckey as to why he'd cast a variety comedian like himself in the role. At the after-show drinks on the last night, Tuckey finally gave in. 'He must have had a couple of sherries... and I'd had a few...' Dodd said in 1990. 'He said, "Yes, well... his character is that of a jumped-up peasant who has delusions of grandeur far above his station."[22] Dodd took Tuckey's joke in good part and told it against himself many times over the years. However, the fact was that when Liverpool's Royal Court theatre was closed by its owners, Howard and Wyndham, in May 1970, it was a variety comedian who had the contacts and clout to get it reopened for the Christmas season. The poor old Royal Court had been reduced to running bingo sessions in the summer months, and Howard and Wyndham had spent two years trying to interest Liverpool City Council in buying it or at least offering an annual subsidy. When neither was forthcoming, the Royal Court went dark.

A 'Save the Royal Court' campaign headed by actress Margaret Lockwood made some headway but it was Dodd's having a quiet word with Bernard Delfont at EMI that brought results. EMI would take a short lease on the theatre and Dodd would put together another festive show. 'It is really thanks to Ken that the project is going ahead,' said Delfont. 'He nearly broke my arm to make me agree.'[23]

Dodd said that he 'couldn't bear to see the Royal Court standing empty' and estimated that the box office would be around £12,000 per week for a ten-week run. He had put in several thousand pounds of his own money, as he would in 1974 when the Radio City consortium bidding for the Liverpool commercial radio franchise was looking for backers. In that case, he put in £5500 and accepted a seat on the board of directors.

*

Between 1969 and 1972, Doddy's main television commitment was a Sunday teatime children's show with the Diddymen, made by the BBC in Manchester at the old converted church on Dickenson Road, Rusholme, where Frank Randle* had made his films and *Top of the Pops* had first taken to the air on New Year's Day 1964. While posterity wasn't at the forefront of priorities for most mainstream programmes, the BBC seemed to show uncommon foresight in the early days of colour television when it came to children's programmes, making many of them on film so that they could be repeated endlessly. So it was with *Ken Dodd and the Diddymen*, which began on 5 January 1969 and ran for six series until March 1972.

The shows, written by Bob Block, who had made his name on *Crackerjack* and would go on to create the long-running *Rentaghost*, were ten-minute situation comedies. In one, Little Evan became a pop star and let fame go to his head. In another, the Diddymen set up their own television station. A 'Diddy Village' set was designed by Peter Mavius to be the show's centrepiece, the tiny houses cleverly giving Roger Stevenson and his puppeteers something to stand behind, concealing the operations. In between series, Dodd borrowed the sets for his summer shows.

The shows being produced on film had a fringe benefit for Dodd, allowing him to turn up later and later. Although the intention was for the star to be present throughout the working

---

* Frank Randle (1901–57) was a Wigan-born comedian notorious for his attitude to authority. His frequent run-ins with the police in Blackpool led to him being banned from numerous venues. When a theatre manager upbraided him, trashing dressing rooms was not unknown.

day, producer Stan Parkinson soon learned to plan his shooting schedule so that all scenes involving the Diddymen without Dodd were in the can first. However, after Dodd arrived at 6 p.m. when he had been due at 11 a.m., word got back to head of North Region, Derek Burrell-Davis, who began the all-too-familiar process of threatening Dodd with breach of contract.

Doddy always had an eye for a subtle publicity stunt, having been coached well in this by his press agent, George Bartram. In 1967, he announced that 'Diddy TV' would be making a bid for the Yorkshire region ITV franchise. Despite reassuring reporters that 'this is a serious bid', no more was heard of it. Similarly, just after the first Diddymen series, Dodd told the *Guardian*'s Simon Hoggart that he intended to buy the Scottish village of Kendoon for his tiny protégés. The settlement of ten houses had been built in the 1930s for workers at the nearby power station but automation had rendered the dwellings superfluous, and now the South of Scotland Electricity Board were looking for buyers.

'I hope to buy it to go for a bit of quiet cogitation,' he said. 'They can't touch you for that yet. Yes, I'll be doing a bit of consenting cogitation.'[24] The comedian announced that he'd offered £20,000 but the electricity board told Hoggart that they were hoping for higher offers. Of course, Dodd had no intention of buying the place. He'd just noted its availability and the similarity of names, and realized that he had a perfect chance to give the papers a silly story. Even if the real-life Diddy Village never materialized, the butty miners proved to be a money-spinner for Dodd with numerous merchandising opportunities, including puppets, Letraset transfers and even Diddymen bubble bath, with the bottles in the shape of the characters.

Although Dodd maintained a steady presence on television through guest appearances – including a period when he was a semi-regular on ATV's Sunday teatime game show *The Golden Shot*, specials and children's shows – he didn't have a comedy series on TV between 1968 and 1972. One guest appearance in this period was on an English-language comedy series made by the Welsh entertainers Ryan Davies and Ronnie Williams.

After working separately for some years, primarily as comic actors and presenters, they had been persuaded to become a double act for BBC Cymru, with Williams acting as Davies' smooth straight man. Beginning in 1968, *Ryan a Ronnie* was a roaring success. Watching the handful of surviving shows, it's easy to understand why. Even if you don't speak Welsh, the humour and invention leaps off the screen. Like Dodd, Davies had a very distinctive face, almost like that of a living Mr Punch, that he used to tremendous comic effect. Also like Dodd, Davies was a chronic asthmatic, an attack of which would kill him at the tragically early age of forty in 1977.

At this time, many Welsh-language programmes made by the BBC received a repeat on English transmitters during the day, and lunchtime screenings of *Ryan a Ronnie* soon built up a small but appreciative audience. In 1971, the pair began the first of three series of English-language shows for the network, recorded in London at the BBC Television Theatre. Dodd guested on the final show of the second series, recorded on 23 May 1972 for transmission in late August, taking part in the regular 'Our House' sketch, with Davies and Williams playing the mother and silent father of the family respectively.

Sadly, no recording of the show survives but the booking of Dodd was a coup, since he was the only non-Welsh guest to appear in the three series of shows. There are close links between Liverpool and North Wales, and Llandudno was always a favourite performing spot for Dodd, so he will have been well aware of the duo's popularity. It is perhaps a measure of the respect in which he held Davies and Williams as performers that he agreed to do the show for what is described in the contract as the 'special low' fee of £50 plus his £13 return fare from Liverpool, at a time when he was getting £1000 for an appearance on *The Good Old Days*.

That spring, Dodd had been working hard at the ATV studios in Borehamwood on another bash at boxing in his peculiar magic. Going head-to-head with *Doctor Who* at Saturday teatime, *Funny You Should Say That* was a bold experiment for Dodd. 'One thing I can promise you,' he told *TV Times*, 'this television show is going to be different from anything you have ever seen', adding that he wanted to try 'more adult' humour. Unfortunately, for all of his bold proclamations, it was only a partial success.

What made it different was the inclusion of 'vox pop' interviews with members of the audience on the topic at hand. The idea had been offered to the BBC in 1970, under the title *Meet the Doddy People*, forming part of a list of proposals sent to head of variety Bill Cotton Jr by Grahame Miller and Stan Parkinson in Manchester. Although both 'Young Bill' and head of comedy Michael Mills had been keen to get Doddy talking to a grown-up audience again, none of the pitches on the list ended up happening for the BBC.

Each of the six shows was themed, albeit very loosely, with the topics over the run including Britishness, laughter, the battle of the sexes and 'the human race and aren't you glad you're running in it?' Opening each week with a burst of 'Happiness', with Doddy resplendent in the finest 1972 kipper ties and the audience all around him on comfortable chairs, the tone was established with a fusillade of gags on the set subject. 'Man is the most intelligent creature on the planet,' Dodd declared in the last show of the series. 'What other creature has the sense to go to work five days a week, vote for politicians, start world wars, blow each other up and pay income tax?'

The vox pops served as cues for sketches, with Dodd announcing, 'Funny you should say that' in response to the answers given, then cutting to the sketch. Sadly, with very few exceptions, the sketch material was weak and obvious. Not even the combined might of Talfryn Thomas (Welsh character actor, Dodd's brother in dentistry and his sidekick of many years standing) and Pat Coombs could do much to save them. The gravity of the loss of Braben had made itself very apparent, not least in the number of writers Dodd needed to replace him – typically four or five per show, both on TV and radio.

Even if the sketches weren't of the highest possible quality, they provided a vital service, keeping Dodd on screen and in the public eye without breaking into his hoard of highly valuable stage material. One stage favourite does, however, make its way into the show, namely the 'On the Road to Mandalay' routine, which had been in his act almost from the start of his professional career.

What does shine out from this fascinating but flawed series is how good Dodd was with people. He seems perfectly at ease in the vox pop segments, and among the new material, there is some treasure to be found. In one sketch, Dodd plays an interviewer attempting to make sense of the vexed issue of Women's Lib in conversation with 'German Gear', author of 'The Female Enoch'. Pin-sharp satire it is not but there is something irresistible about Pat Coombs playing a wildly broad-brush version of Germaine Greer, jumping up and down while shouting, 'Ladies, come on and wave your knickers in the air' then declaring, 'I'll tell you something, I am not a rich man's yo-yo.' The sight of Dodd corpsing as Coombs' portrayal gets broader, louder and dafter merely adds to the glee of the exercise.

As with all Dodd shows, each edition featured him in singing mode and while nothing had come close to the commercial success of 'Tears' since, his singles continued to chart respectably, with 'Broken Hearted' reaching number fifteen in December 1970 and 'When Love Comes Round Again' getting to number nineteen in July 1971. On 14 December 1971, the day that HRH Princess Margaret opened the new De Lane Lea Music Centre recording studio complex in Wembley, Dodd was in studio one with a forty-piece orchestra making another record.

However, when Dodd returned to the Liverpool Playhouse in April 1973, two years after his triumph as Malvolio, the sentimental songs were out for the duration. He was returning with a show in which he intended to harness all of his experience and study. Having spent twenty years making people laugh, he planned to explore the why and how of humour, at unsurprisingly considerable length. *Ha Ha – a Celebration of Laughter* would be, he said, 'quite suitable for children to bring adults to see', covering 'everything from Shakespeare to Diddyana, from whimsy and fantasy to satire and sarcasm'.[25]

Dodd had been expounding on his analyses in interviews for some time. A series on the philosophy and psychology of comedy had been another proposal in the abortive 1970 memo sent to Bill Cotton Jr. In a 1971 Radio 4 conversation with Michael Billington, he said: 'I'm really a catalyst. What I do is I stand on the stage and I run through a series of emotional safety valves. The audience do the work, you know, and all the people who laugh at all those sexy fertility rites are really rather very sexy fertile people themselves, releasing their inhibitions and releasing their joyous wahoos.'[26] This harks back somewhat to the days of Max Miller, who always insisted that there was nothing untoward in his material, and that it was the audience projecting themselves onto his jokes. Miller used to brandish two joke books, a white one containing clean jokes and the 'blue book' containing his fruitier material. He'd ask which they wanted and the response was always overwhelmingly in favour of the blue, giving Miller licence to proceed. Dodd tackled this conundrum in a different way, tying his filth up in absurdity and topping it off with an apparently admonitory look as if the audience had misinterpreted his purity of intention.

Dodd also knew the value of self-deprecation as a comic

device: 'I do jokes where they laugh at me. It gives them a feeling of omnipotence to see this terrible creature making himself a laughing stock. That's another kind of humour. Then we do another kind of humour, which is a fantasy, where we just turn the rules of logic upside down. This is also a kind of a release because people from childhood are taught to observe certain rules, and the mere breaking of these rules is funny, but in an act lasting, say, forty-five minutes, I try to do a kaleidoscope of comedy that runs through all the things I've learned in fifteen years.'

Dodd sometimes liked to view comedy in terms of colours of the spectrum. He described it as a rainbow, even though very few of the colours he cited feature in a standard rainbow:

> Right at the very top of the rainbow, there's white laughter, the laughter of pure joy, and you can hear this any time you want for free, pass any school playground and you can hear and see little children laughing and jumping about and celebrating the sheer joy of being alive, and that is the best kind of humour. The joy of life. The joy of feeling that this is a wonderful, wonderful experience you're going through. Further down the spectrum, you come to yellow laughter, which is the laughter of clowns, pink laughter and red laughter, the laughter of romance and love, and further down, right at the bottom of the rainbow, there's the dark colours of purple, indigo, black if you like. That's the laughter of cynicism, sarcasm and satire. My job is to make an audience happy. A relief from any stress or problems they might have. That's my job. I'm a jester.[27]

He promised that *Ha Ha – a Celebration of Laughter* would be 'an entertainment first, not a lecture', acknowledging that the audience wanted 'humour demonstrated far more than explained'. Those cited would include Dodd's beloved Shakespeare and Dickens, along with Spike Milligan, Jack Benny, Groucho Marx and Sir John Betjeman. Joke forms would be explored, as would the links between comedy and music. The show, which ran from Tuesday, 3 April to Saturday, 14 April 1973, opened with Dodd's 'wayward teeth spotlit in what looks like a conscious parody of Billie Whitelaw in Beckett'.[28] When trailing it in December, Dodd put its duration at two hours but naturally, by the time it reached the stage, it had expanded to over three, with Billington noting perceptively that it was 'as if [Dodd was] qualifying for the *Guinness Book of Records* with the longest comedy act ever'.[29]

One of the topics covered by the show was cruelty in comedy. Dodd cited the Victorians who used to visit Bedlam to laugh at the lunatics. He then told more modern jokes about simpletons to suggest that while we might think we'd made progress, we hadn't come that far. Dodd also explored surprise by telling a meandering joke about a country walk, then producing a gun, firing it into the air, causing a prop cow to fall from the lighting grid.

Billington's glowing write-up was an answer piece to the *Guardian*'s initial dismissive review by Northern arts correspondent Merete Bates, who said that 'not to underestimate the job of making a cold audience laugh… Ken Dodd does turn it into hard work'.[30] The problem was that Bates thought Dodd,

129

contrary to his earlier declarations, was overbalancing on the theory, causing him to 'lose out on the uncontrollable, belly-aching laugh'. It was 'like making love, the more talk the less action. So here: explanation, quotations and theorizing flatten take-off.' The show was, Bates admitted, 'delicately timed and fastidiously juxtaposed' and noted that Dodd had 'perfected his professionalism' but 'it is not enough... he is too calculating. Self-conscious, even self-absorbed. His technique is detached, dedicated, essentially serious... On stage, alone, for too long, his limitations grow monotonous.' Worst of all, Bates observed that at points 'Dodd begins to bully: "Now laugh!" and he counts, one, two, three and... a few willing and considerate voices conform.' The idea of Dodd as calculating with bullying tendencies chimes with the experience of several of his writers.

Writing a few days later, Billington said that *Ha Ha* was 'the funniest evening I have spent inside a theatre since I saw *Beyond the Fringe* at the Edinburgh Lyceum in 1960' and said that Dodd 'wisely perhaps... avoids too much theorizing'. One thing confirmed by the show, said Billington, was 'that comedy appeals to the head and never to the heart', placing Dodd alongside the philosopher Henri Bergson, who observed 'the absence of feeling which usually accompanies laughter', and the Victorian novelist George Meredith, who linked laughter to speed of perception. In comedy, it seems, there is no room for emotion. 'And if you listen to Dodd carefully,' Billington said, 'you realize that even at his most rude, crude and basic, he is bombarding us with images and ideas that keep us in a state of frenzied mental alertness.'[31]

Dodd followed up on Billington's suggestion in June 1974,

when he took to the stage of the Royal Court and told jokes solidly for three hours and six minutes. Nobody had thought to set a world record for joke-telling before, and the 2,000 gags he delivered were enough to satisfy Norris and Ross McWhirter and get Dodd into *The Guinness Book of Records*. The record stood for two years until an unknown called Johnny Kay managed an even greater feat of endurance.

Ha Ha sounds like a fascinating and flawed experiment. The truth of the matter probably lies somewhere between Bates's disappointment and Billington's effusive praise – at its best when Dodd was being funny rather than trying to explain funny. While Dodd was a fiercely intelligent man, he was always conscious of his autodidacticism, and throughout his life remained in awe of those he regarded as genuine intellectuals. 'I just wish I had the intelligence, the intellectual ability to do it properly,' he told Matthew Sweet in 2012, and when Sweet suggested that he did have it, Dodd demurred, admitting only 'I dabble.'[32]

However, Andy Eastwood, who would tour with Dodd for many years after graduating from Oxford University, believes the comedian was selling himself short:

Coming out of that environment and going to work with him was like going back to college, because here's another professor, literally. He only had two modes of conversation with me and with most people, I think. He was either making you laugh or he was giving you advice. Simple as that. There was no small talk. There was no 'How's your day been?' or anything like that. It had a purpose. He was either trying to make you laugh which he did very well or giving you words of wisdom.

He'd talk about agents. He didn't have a lot of time for agents at all. 'Do your own thing, shake them off, they're pickpockets with a licence' that's what he called them. He loved his own agents. He loved Dave Forrester and he loved Keith McAndrews. He thought they were great. When he was doing the gag about 'I'm going to the doctor to get a bigger bust' or whatever, it'd be Dr McAndrews. He did things like that just to tickle himself but those that knew would appreciate it.[33]

Intriguingly and frustratingly, that short run was the only outing for the show. With a firm editing hand, all accounts, even the negative ones, suggest it would have made a good basis for an edition of an arts programme like *Omnibus* or *Second House*. Like a lot of Dodd's work, it was destined to be evanescent, although he did incorporate some of the gags into subsequent television appearances and his stage act. In the autumn of 1973, he contributed a regular feature to the daytime BBC1 magazine show *Pebble Mill at One* under the heading 'Ken Dodd's Anthology of Humour'. Meanwhile, a 1977 *Guardian* write-up of his Christmas show at the Palace, Manchester, expressed delight that 'Dodd hardly pauses in his patter [when] a full-sized stuffed cow drops from the flies to bounce alarmingly behind him', noting that 'some of the young telly comics would "milk" that cow for laughs'.[34]

As traditional a comic as Dodd was, he was always keeping an eye on fads and trends to incorporate into his shows.

On New Year's Eve 1972, the day before Britain joined the EEC, there was a one-off show for Radio 2 called *Ken Dodd's Comical Market*. The jokes are broad-brush rather than hard-hitting political satire ('What if Michael Foot has to go metric? It's alright for Mr Heath. He lives at Number 10. He's off to a good start. It's just as bad for the Europeans. They'll all be having to buy English phrase books with such useful English colloquialisms as "What's your inside leg measurement?" and "Eeeeee, I'm fair clemmed, Gladys."'[35]) but full marks to Dodd for spotting the tenuous opportunity.

A brief vogue for oompah bands and bierkellers resulted in a diversion from the sketch and stand-up shows he'd been doing for the BBC in London, back to the Playhouse in Manchester, where he did German-tinged variety bills under the heading *Doddy's Oompah Show*. For this series, he was reunited with producer Peter Pilbeam, nicknamed 'the Illuminated Aspirin'* by Dodd, who drew upon his previous experience with the comedian to work around his relaxed attitude to time:

Whenever you booked Ken, you always booked him for at least an hour before you needed him because you knew he wouldn't be there at the time you'd booked him. You got to know the tricks of the trade with him, as it were. Trouble was, he realized after a while that people were doing that, and played up accordingly. I got a reputation for being the first producer who'd managed to get a script before recording day, and also to get him there on time.

*   Pill-beam.

I don't know why that was. Ken and I hit it off quite well as producer and performer, and I had an arrangement with him that I used to drive out up the East Lancs Road, and meet his driver halfway to Liverpool to pick up the script on the day before we were doing the actual show, so that I could get it back in time for my PA to type it up and get it duplicated for the studio the next day.'[36]

The direct approach was always the best way in that pre-email, even pre-fax era. Dave Dutton remembers Doddy visiting his home to collect new material before a show. 'A crowd would gather round outside, kids. Because they'd seen the Diddymen and all that.' On one occasion, Dutton's Uncle Ned was in attendance when Doddy turned up. Slightly the worse for wear, he overstepped several boundaries: 'He was a pit man, my Uncle Ned. He was just very down to earth. And he poked him in the teeth with his finger and said "Are them real, Mr Dodd, or are them ones you have specially made for television?" So I went, "Oh, Jesus Christ." Doddy didn't bother, you know. When he had gone, my uncle, I said, "I'm really sorry about that." He said, "Don't worry, lad. We all have an Uncle Ned."'[37]

The *Oompah Shows* are not among the delights from the Dodd archive that get regular airings on BBC Radio 4 Extra but Pilbeam remembers one gag with great fondness: 'One lovely line that came out of one of the *Oompah Shows*. There was a sketch where he was Robin Hood, and he and his merry men were crawling along the side of a road in Nottingham somewhere, and they came upon this lump of stone. Little

John says, "There's a strange thing", so Ken as Robin said, "What's that?" "There's somebody buried here. It says it's a Vi Miles from Nottingham." That's always stuck in my mind for some silly reason.'[38]

Writing about the production of Dodd's radio shows in his 1977 book *How Tickled I Am*, Michael Billington gives a flavour of what Pilbeam and Dodd's London producer, Bobby Jaye, were up against. The normal length of script for a half-hour radio show would be around thirty pages. On the occasion chronicled by Billington, Dodd turned up with seventy-six pages. Sketches overstay their welcome. Of one, where a worker talks like management and vice versa, Jaye says, 'It's a funny idea but it's jolly floggers* for about half a page.'[39]. Jaye kept an eye on dubious gags and cut quite a few, but even after this, the script was far too long.

After over four hours rehearsal, the recordings routinely produced ninety minutes of material, which then had to be cut down to a half hour. The reason why the long-suffering Jaye had put up with it was simple: 'I just stand on one side and watch this man. He's a bloody genius. He just comes out onto that stage and radiates total likability. When he gets out on that stage, people just love him. I've watched this man and I can't analyse it and I don't think even he quite knows what it is.'[40]

After his brief sojourn with ATV, Dodd returned to BBC television for a new series with Michael Hurll producing once again. On the face of it, an experienced variety ringmaster-type

* Hard going.

producer like Hurll was ideal for Dodd, but he tended towards excess. 'The only problem he had was that he would do things in wonderful taste, and in very bad taste, and he never knew the difference,' said a senior colleague who also had close family connections to Hurll. 'He was like the Americans. If it's successful, he doesn't care.'[41] A self-indulgent comic like Dodd needed a firmer hand, and the result is that *Ken Dodd's World of Laughter* is frequently messy across its three series. It is also, regrettably, a product of its time, veering all too frequently into racial stereotypes and jokes about limp-wristedness in a manner that the younger and elder Dodd would not have countenanced. Again, it's the sketches that let the side down most. Firing gags at the camera, Dodd is as good as ever.

Dodd also did a lot of jokes about the work-shy and workers on the fiddle but those had always been a theme in his act. 'Every night, you know, I have the supper, I have meat pie on toast, and I go down and stand on the banks of the Mersey, listening. [Impersonates ship's hooter very convincingly] I always do that after meat pies. It's funny, I wonder what it is? I stand on the banks of the Costa Mersey and listen to the dockers knocking off from working. Knocking off tins of paint, rolls of lino, cases of salmon...'[42]

On the face of it, this ties up with Dodd's Conservatism, as the jokes give him a chance to do a bit of union-bashing. But at the same time, he's almost admiring of the layabouts. This was a man who was almost certainly incapable of work or of being an employee in any conventional sense. He couldn't have held down a job to save his life. He worked for himself for most of his life and he was paid handsomely for his hobby. He was lucky enough to be able to buck the system many times over. He admitted as much after his trial: 'It is all I can do. I cannot hang wallpaper or decorate anything, but comedy is something I love. As an art form it is as enthralling to me as music is to other people. I just love communicating with an audience. It is a love affair really. Some love affairs do not go on very long, but we have been together since 1954.'[43]

Even when several entertainers were trying their hands at authordom – Les Dawson wrote a series of novels, Eric Morecambe came out with *Mr Lonely* and even Max Bygraves had a go with *The Milkman's On His Way* – Dodd kept his writing strictly for the stage. The closest he came to producing a work of literature was putting his name to *Ken Dodd's Butty Book*, published in 1977. The writing had been done by Dave Dutton and a former colleague from his days as a journalist. Alongside the obvious jam, the butties on offer include savoury options like 'First Night Fare' ('Chop hard-boiled eggs and blend with minced, cooked liver in mayonnaise'[44]), 'Nomad's Nosh' ('Rye bread and butter with a tasty filling of devilled kidney spread... the kids'll "lapp" this up.'[45]) and the self-explanatory 'Anchovies Aweigh'.

The book marked the end of Dutton's association with Dodd, in circumstances not unlike the parting with Braben. Dodd was receiving a £350 script fee for each *World of Laughter* on top of his £1500 appearance fee. By the 1970s, Dodd preferred to take the full fee then pay the writers himself. As a result, Dave Dutton spent much of the time he worked for Doddy on £15 a week. In comparison, Eddie Braben had been paid directly by the BBC, receiving a pretty respectable 100 guineas per programme for Dodd's radio show in 1963.

Dodd pulled a similar stunt with backing musicians on the road. After a week working with Doddy at the Spa in Bridlington, drummer Tony MacDonnell was offered the forthcoming 1979 summer season at the Opera House in Scarborough:

I did that week and a couple of corporates with him and he was lovely. He was a delight to be with. As far as my personal taste in comedy, I used to sit in the pit and piss myself laughing every night. I loved him.

The MD said, 'Ken would like a word with you before you go.' I thought, 'This is nice,' so I go round to the dressing room. 'Would you like to work with us? Because we're looking for a drummer for the full season. Phone Stan in the morning.' So I phoned Stan [Clarke, Dodd's musical director], and said, 'I could be up for that.' Stan said, 'Did he talk to you about the money?' I said, 'No.' I can't remember what it was, but it was about 120 quid a week and the Union rate was £165. I said, 'That's less than I got last year, Mr Clarke,' and he said, 'Well, that's all Ken'll pay.' And that was it. I didn't do it. I politely declined.[46]

Dodd's unwillingness to pay the going rate or overtime led to a story that became a legend among theatre musicians working in Yorkshire. As MacDonnell recounts:

The band that did do it all came from Hull in the end, which is a fifty-mile drive. There was a big thing about the second house. He would go on and on and on and on, and they didn't get any overtime for it, and they wanted it. So, they sent the saxophone player, who was the band's steward, to say, 'Mr Dodd, we can't carry on like this, we've all got to get home, if you insist on us staying, we should be getting overtime.' Ken said, 'I'll see you right. Come and see me at the end of the week.' I think it was a ten- or twelve-piece band, and the story goes that he gave them a fiver for a drink. What happened after that was that they said, 'We're going' and they left the MD to close the show himself. I think that's what happened for the rest of the season.

That Scarborough season wasn't the happiest of times for the comedian, as his father had become increasingly unwell. As late as the shows finished, Dodd was dashing back to Thomas Lane every night to see how Arthur was doing, but when he died on Thursday, 19 July 1979, Dodd returned to Scarborough and did the show.

Arthur's passing came just two years after the death of Dodd's fiancée, Anita Boutin. This was a period of heavy industry for Dodd and the workload helped distract him from his private sorrows. With both Arthur and Anita, he gave no indication to the outside world that anything was amiss but, inside, Dodd was in turmoil. Stricken by a brain tumour, Anita had spent months in hospital. When she died, Dodd made a rare public comment about her importance to him. 'She was a lovely and wonderful person,' he told the *Liverpool Echo*, but most importantly, it seemed, she was 'very much my partner in show business, and the architect of my success, helping me and sharing my decisions. While she was with me, she inspired me to be a successful entertainer, and I hope that her memory will continue to inspire me.'[47]

Dodd allayed fears that grief would force him into early retirement. 'It'll certainly be a time before I'm back. At the moment, I certainly don't feel like being an entertainer.'

5

Back to the boards

'Freud said that a laugh is a sudden explosion of psychic energy. Of course the trouble with Freud was that he never played second house Friday night at Glasgow Empire.'

After Anita's death, business as usual had resumed in 1978. *Ken Dodd's World of Laughter* had come to an end in 1977 and now Dodd felt free to accept overtures from the commercial companies again. A one-off Christmas special for Thames in 1978 was the prelude to a six-part series beginning in January 1979, *The Ken Dodd Laughter Show*.

Dodd made reference to the change of channel in the first of the run, informing the audience that 'you can't overrun on ITV, otherwise you're likely to find yourself swimming across a lagoon with a Bounty bar between your teeth, or slipping down a plughole with 99 per cent of household germs. When I told the BBC I was coming across to this channel, no less a person than Billy Cotton went down on his knees before me. And bit my leg.'[1]

At the time, Thames Television used the New London Theatre on Drury Lane as an adjunct to its Teddington studios, and producer Dennis Kirkland wisely chose to locate the Dodd series here rather than in a studio. Being a modern theatre in regular television use, it was dogged by none of the problems of lighting, sound and sightlines that afflicted Dodd's 1960s BBC shows from Ardwick, Bolton and Blackpool, but had all of the atmosphere Dodd needed.

One advantage of being on ITV was that each half-hour show was just twenty-five minutes long (to allow for the commercial breaks), meaning that Dodd's stand-up comedy didn't have to be eked out quite as much as in the BBC shows. However, there were issues with the material. The quality was fine but the origin was under dispute. The scripts were credited to Dodd, Frank Hughes and Norman Beedle, but watching the shows, Dodd's former writer Dave Dutton thought some of the items seemed oddly familiar.

Dutton wrote to Thames, indicating that the shows included some material he had written, without payment or permission. He received a brush-off from head of light entertainment Philip Jones, who said that the material in question had all been written by Dodd, who had been paid for its provision. Via his agent at the time, the firm Curtis Brown, Dutton was able to supply copies of the sketches and documentation from the BBC to prove that the disputed material was his work. Thames paid up immediately and Jones intimated that the situation was a black mark against Dodd's name at Teddington.

The series did enable Dodd to make up for past misdemeanours, though, with Rita Webb appearing in three of the shows and being given a lot to do, including one sketch where she claims to be Miss World, complete with sash and tiara:

Dodd: You're Miss World?

Webb: Course I'm Miss World, cock.

Dodd: Miss World Cock. Charming. Miss World? What happened?

Webb: Well, I let meself go a bit. It's opening all them supermarkets what done it. 'ere where are all the others?

Dodd: All the others? What others?

Webb: The contestants for Miss Universe.

Dodd: What contestants?

Webb: I was told to report here with a clean pair of drawers on. And I've turned me corsets too. 'ere, you ain't that Eric Morbid, are you?[2]

The following year saw Dodd returning to the Palladium for a third season, taking to the stage in a Mini Metro ('It does eighty-three miles per gallon, more if you both pedal.').[3] During the season, he talked of branching out overseas. He'd been to Mexico once for a corporate gig, booked as the entertainment for six hundred British plumbers. He said that making it abroad, particularly America, was 'a matter of timing', just as his first Palladium season had been. Whatever he did, he wanted to be in control: 'I came to the Palladium on my terms in 1965. I could have been here earlier, but not as top of the bill.'[4]

During this time, Dodd was picking up the pieces of his life emotionally with Anne Jones, who was to become his second

143

long-term partner. They first met when Cheshire-born Jones was one of the Bluebell Girls in Doddy's Christmas show at the Opera House, Manchester, in 1961. For the number 'Love Is Like a Violin', a giant violin prop was hung from the flies with dancers perched precariously on top of it. Jones made herself known one night when she fell off the violin.

The pair had stayed in touch through the years, even after Anne left show business to become an air hostess and later a personnel manager. After Anita's death, they grew closer, and for Dodd, Jones was the perfect partner. Just as Anita had spurred him on and taken care of the tedious details, Anne knew the business and had experience outside it, enabling her to give the disorganized Dodd the support he needed.

Recovering from his double bereavement, Dodd had to process another sad loss when Dickie Mint was stolen from his car in early January 1982. Mint had always been Doddy's favourite and in interviews he, with obvious sincerity, said he regarded him as a real person. Dodd had parked by Liverpool Cathedral while he attended a dentist's appointment. 'This is the most untattiferlarious thing that's ever happened to me,' he told reporters, while the Chief Constable of Merseyside took the PR initiative by announcing that Mint would be placed on the missing persons list.[5] It might be assumed that the Cathedral was a relatively safe place to park, but Liverpool-based writer Tim Worthington explains that it wasn't so:

> The city centre had fallen into quite a state of neglect by then and if you didn't fancy the multi-storey fees, you could park in places like the Cathedral but it was considered

very much at your own risk. It's hard to explain but even a couple of footsteps outside the main shopping area felt a bit like a sort of empty no man's land and you didn't see many people walking about there. My father was never especially concerned by this, although he was paranoid about leaving anything on display in the car, and one day when we were returning to the Cathedral car park, we saw a distressed-looking Ken Dodd chatting to a policeman who looked a little bemused. We kind of guessed what had happened, but we were still a bit startled when we found out what had actually been stolen. I remember wondering what kind of market there could possibly be for it.[6]

The loss must have been an unwelcome distraction as the comedian prepared for his new BBC series. After Dodd's successful appearance as the sole guest on an edition of *Parkinson* in 1980, producer John Fisher had turned his mind to the matter of how to get the best out of Dodd on television. Fisher had first met Dodd in the mid-1960s, when he was a student at Magdalen College, Oxford. 'When Dodd used to take his Blackpool shows on the road, and he always stopped for three weeks in Oxford at the New Theatre,' Fisher recalled in 2006. 'One year I was there, wrote him a note saying how much I admired him and asking if I could pop round to see him. No performer has more time for his public than Ken Dodd. He was absolutely wonderful. I sat with him and chatted about the old-time comics, magic and spesh [speciality] acts. It was fabulous, but it was no more than a passing acquaintance.'[7]

Or so Fisher thought at the time. After graduating, Fisher went to work at BBC Television in Manchester, making trailers and assisting Stan Parkinson, producer of the *Diddymen* series. 'He remembered me as somebody who'd been in his dressing room at Oxford. There's no reason why he should have done.' When Fisher was himself in a position to offer Dodd a series, everything went back to that first dressing room conversation nearly twenty years earlier. A loose format came together where Dodd would do a little stand-up, talk about his career, sing songs and introduce some of the best speciality acts from around the world.

The result, which went out in March and April 1982, was *Ken Dodd's Showbiz*, a lavish production with dancing girls, a big orchestra under the direction of Ken Jones and the full use of TC1, the largest studio at BBC Television Centre. At the start of each show, Dodd would be lowered from the lighting grid in a cylindrical lift. This was a hell of a way to make an entrance. When it worked. On one occasion, the gear used for raising and lowering the lift got stuck, leaving the star suspended in mid-air until it was fixed.

Those who worked on the show also recall one of the dancers' headdresses catching fire and a big production number where Dodd sang 'I Talk to the Animals' (from *Doctor Dolittle*) to a menagerie assembled in the studio, including a baby leopard, a beagle and a lion. Production assistant Lesley Taylor remembers the last of these with especial clarity:

> I nearly lost my right arm to a lion. I was taking a break down on the floor and his handler was in with him. It

wasn't fully grown, but it was large. It wasn't a cub. I said, 'Is he alright to pet?' and this guy said, 'Yes, fine.' So, I put my hand through the bars, was petting him and got a bit nonchalant during the time I was there. All of a sudden, the lion just put his paws around my right arm, which is my writing arm, but the claws were ever so slightly out, so I couldn't move my arm for fear of the claws ripping it. So, I had to go to the keeper, 'Excuse me, do you think you could help?' And I think there was talk of John being goosed by an elephant, but I didn't witness that.

Taylor recalls other tensions at play on the studio floor, largely down to the star's attitude to rehearsal, which remained unmodified from his earliest days in television: 'He didn't like coming down to London. I have a feeling he only came down for the actual record day. Certainly, we'd do a show and then congregate in his dressing room for the run-through for the next week's show with Ken Jones, the musical director, and anyone present. It was late night after a busy show and a long day and you weren't getting out of the dressing room until gone midnight/one o'clock. And then he was driven back to Liverpool straight away.'[8]

The series got a sniffy response from Peter Fiddick in the *Guardian*, who dismissed it as '*Café Continental* with a Knotty Ash accent',* in a review bemoaning several shows that weekend that gave 'a sense that the medium fell asleep

---

* *Café Continental* was a BBC TV variety show that ran from 1947 to 1955, showcasing numerous European acts.

147

some time in the 1950s... Doddy... did his saucy jokes, sang a song, introduced some Continental magic and puppets, and it all happened in a vacuum... Just once there was a sight of the audience, but never any feeling that the solitary star and the rest had any contact. That made all the pre-teen giggle-jokes sillier and the years of hard work a bit sad.'[9]

Reading Fiddick's criticism, it seems likely that Dodd would have defended the suggestions of anachronism robustly. If the show looked old-fashioned, that was because it was meant to be. Nonetheless, Fiddick had a point about Dodd's isolation from the audience and his fellow performers. The highlight of the series is when Dodd sits down in a set designed to look like a theatre bar and interviews Arthur Askey over a pint of beer.

In public, Dodd was always positive about his fellow professionals. Over the years, few performers were as feted by Dodd as Askey. 'Arthur Askey was like a firework display going off, so dynamic,' he told Ned Sherrin on Radio 4's *Loose Ends* in 2004. Discussing wartime comedians, he added that 'Arthur Askey was my hero'. In private, though, he wasn't always as complimentary about the *Bandwaggon* star and bee enthusiast, sometimes grumbling that Askey was 'just a concert party turn'. This duality of attitude seems to be evidence of the description Dodd gave Dave Dutton of himself as a 'sincere hypocrite'.

What lay behind this attitude? It could well have been that he felt stung by Askey's claim that he'd invented some of the comic concepts that Doddy made famous, but had been told to cut them out of his act because audiences wouldn't get it.

'I talked about diddymen, jam buttie factories and treacle mines,' the elder comedian told the *Guardian* in 1975, talking about his early days, 'but at that time, they said "You can't use that sort of thing, no one will understand you."' He was also told to lose his Liverpool accent: 'I was a bit tonsils and adenoids then, you know.'[10]

Given that Askey was talking about his concert party days in the 1920s, it seems very unlikely if not impossible that Dodd would have seen the act that Askey was talking about. A strange bitterness seems to pervade most of the interviews Askey gave in later life, giving the impression that he wasn't quite the big-hearted beacon of fun he made out on stage. And while Dodd was a lifelong Conservative, in interviews Askey sounded like he'd gone so far to the right that he'd fallen off some years earlier.

After *Ken Dodd's Showbiz* had finished its run, the rest of the year was a quiet one in television terms for Dodd. He turned up in an edition of *In at the Deep End*, a series where former *That's Life* reporters Chris Serle and Paul Heiney tried their hands at various jobs. Dodd advised Heiney on how to be a stand-up comedian. Then in September he made his debut on the cheerfully cheap game show *Blankety Blank*, with his old radio chum Judith Chalmers turning up as a fellow panellist. There was no Doddy Christmas special, and a call from his stout protector Barney Colehan to top the bill on a special live New Year's Eve edition of *The Good Old Days* came to nothing at the last minute when technical issues meant the show was replaced with a repeat.

The nation did not go without tickle tonic over the festive

season, though. Mr R. Bramhill of Knotty Ash had sent a letter to *Jim'll Fix It*, explaining that he'd promised his grand-daughters Kate and Ruth a visit to the famous jam butty mines, and that they were now trying to hold him to his pledge, putting him in 'a big bit of a fix'.[11] Doddy obliged, presenting the girls with a tickling stick each, 'made from the feathers of the Knotty Ash giggle goose... the only bird in the world that lays a fluffy egg'. Thus equipped, Dodd gave them a demonstration of 'open crust mining', seeing Diddy people hacking away at loaves with pickaxes. The mine, he claimed, was on the site of a former 'porridge volcano' and had been 'discovered in 1627 by the famous Liverpool explorer Sir Dingle Jetty [who] fell head first into a vat of raspberry jam and uttered the immortal words "Heaven preserve us".'

Doddy was absent from the presentation of the 'fix it' badges in the studio but the whole exercise gave producer Roger Ordish an experience of the comedian's rather less restrained off-stage humour when he went up to Liverpool to plan the location shoot:

He met me at the station and drove me to Knotty Ash in his van. The conversation went something like this:

'Good morning, Roger. and how are you today?'

'To tell the truth, Ken, I have had better days. My wife has just left me and run off with another man.'

'I'm sorry to hear that, but we have a saying here in Liverpool: "An empty home is better than an unwanted tenant."'

'Yes, I suppose that's true.'

After a perfectly timed pause Ken added, 'Mind you, we usually say that after someone has farted.'[12]

A similar insight into Dodd's earthier side, saved for private audiences, came after he appeared on London Weekend Television's *6 O'Clock Show* on 10 February 1984 with Michael Aspel, Paula Yates and Danny Baker, to talk about ventriloquism. When the credits had rolled, Dodd joined Aspel and company in the hospitality suite on the seventeenth floor of Kent House, LWT's headquarters on the South Bank of the River Thames. Claiming that he had another appointment elsewhere in forty-five minutes, Dodd said he'd stay for a drink. Danny Baker and researcher Paul Ross – brother of Jonathan – took up position with Dodd at the bar. Baker remembers:

Well, his first pint in hand – I remember being surprised he drank pints of lager – I, knowing how to gain an 'in', asked him about Frank Randle. BANG. We were off. He seemed startled that Paul Ross and I knew anything pre-Jimmy Tarbuck and the LONG night began. His poor PA kept bobbing up saying, 'Ken, if we leave now we can get the 7.40...' that became the 8.10, then the 8.35, then the 9.05. He would say, 'I might have to give that thing a miss, I'm talking comedy with some fellow AFICIONADOS!' He actually used that word and, as you can imagine, I've never forgotten it. Man, but he could drink beer. Pissed as you like, we walked to the lifts in LWT his arm around my neck.

It is one of the warmest memories I have of all the guests we had in that six-year run. A colour 8 x 10 arrived the following week signed 'To the GREAT Danny, In the spirit of Frank R'. A tickling stick was in the package. I think Paul got one too.

Baker suspects that the prior engagement was an escape clause should Dodd have found himself being buttonholed by bores, but given Dodd's attitude to timekeeping, it's equally possible that somewhere, people were waiting for him to arrive. Like David Hamilton many years earlier and Roger Ordish, Baker found that while Dodd was as clean as a whistle when working, he was not a whit averse to a bit of filth among fellow professionals.

The conversation moved onto much-married comedians like Stan Laurel, and Dodd ventured a gag that wouldn't have found room in his stage act, about the male attitude before and after the act of sex. It concerned a couple on their wedding night. Pre-coitus, the bride broke wind, to which the groom cooed about 'botty burps'. When she repeated the release after the consummation, he was less understanding, berating his love for 'stinking the place up again'. As well as illustrating Dodd's off-duty love of mucky jokes, it also indicates a deep understanding of the battle of the sexes, in favour of the female.

*

Just as comedians go in and out of favour, so do long-running drama series. In 1987, twenty-four years after its first episode, the children's science fiction series *Doctor Who* was very much out of favour with BBC bosses. In particular, it displeased Michael Grade, who had been appointed controller of BBC1 in 1984.

The son of the agent Leslie Grade and nephew of Lew Grade and Bernard Delfont, Michael Grade had made his name as director of programmes at London Weekend Television, after a period as an undistinguished head of light entertainment. After a few years out working in the US, Grade arrived at the BBC seemingly intent on achieving what the Daleks had failed to do: killing off the time-traveller in the blue police box. The show was, he declared, too violent. Many years later, he expanded on this in an interview with Graham Barnard of BBC Radio Norfolk. 'I thought it was horrible, awful,' he said. 'I thought it was so out-dated. It was just a little show for a few pointy-head *Doctor Who* fans. It was also very violent and it had lost its magic and I killed it.'[13]

At the end of the twenty-second series in March 1985, an eighteen-month 'rest' was ordered. When the twenty-fourth series began on 7 September 1987, with Sylvester McCoy replacing Colin Baker as the Doctor, Grade told the press that 'the jury is still out on this show'.[14] The decision to move *Doctor Who* from its traditional Saturday teatime slot to Monday evenings directly opposite *Coronation Street* was seen as a measure of Grade's lack of faith in the project, if not a straightforward case of constructive dismissal.

Long-serving producer John Nathan-Turner had taken the criticism about violence to heart and responded by seeming to make the show lighter and more fun. He accompanied the announcement that Dodd was to make an appearance in the show, alongside Hugh Lloyd and Stubby Kaye, by saying the show had 'become [like] *Morecambe and Wise* – everybody wants to be on'.[15]

In fact, Dodd was the second choice for the role of the Tollkeeper in 'Delta and the Bannermen', the second story in the new series, Bob Monkhouse having proven unavailable. Director Chris Clough recalls that Dodd preferred to deal direct rather than go through the Forrester George office, and was quite hard to track down. 'He was quite reclusive,' the director remembers. 'I think we had to go round the houses.' In the end, Clough went to see Dodd at the Hackney Empire to sound him out about taking the part. 'We had a meeting backstage, after the show, which was obviously very late at night,' says Clough. 'This was the late *Ken Dodd Show*. There he was, tickling stick, all his bloody bits he was trying to flog. He was complaining that Ken Campbell was sitting in the front row every night, trying to steal his gags. I thought that was very funny. He found that quite off-putting, old Ken with his swivel eyes looking up at him.'[16]

The plot of the three-parter finds the Doctor and his assistant Mel, played by Bonnie Langford, arriving at space tollport G715, approaching the gate with trepidation. Instead of the feared onslaught of hostility, they are greeted by Dodd as the Tollkeeper, resplendent in spangled lilac jacket and peaked cap. They are, he declares, the 10,000,000,000th customer and they have won the grand prize of a week in Disneyland in 1959. They are to make the trip on a space cruiser disguised as a coach with the Navarino 1950s Club, 'squat wrinkly purple creatures' who have been transformed to look human. Unknown to everyone, the coach also contains Delta, the queen of the Chirons, trying to escape the deadly Bannermen, who are intent on killing her and the egg that is the future of the Chiron race. The coach hits a satellite and is blown off course, landing not at Disneyland but in a South Wales holiday camp. The Tollkeeper is killed by the Bannermen after he is forced to reveal Delta's destination.

Speaking in a behind-the-scenes report for the children's programme *But First This*, Dodd described the character as 'a sort of a galactic car park attendant' and observed that 'although it's a zany character and rather a jolly person, he's very much a jobsworth'.[17] Dodd's scenes serve almost no purpose other than putting Ken Dodd in an episode of *Doctor Who*, and it would be stretching a point to call Dodd's contribution acting. But the objective of successfully casting Dodd in an amusing role in a long-running TV show was achieved. 'As a director, you've got to know that you're not going to get Ken Dodd and turn him into King Lear overnight,' Clough observes. 'He'd make a bloody good King Lear, but anyway, you're not going to turn him into a classical actor. So, you've got to harness what you've got and actually that's what the role wanted.'

Most of the serial was shot at the former Butlin's holiday camp in Barry Island and nearby. Dodd's scenes were done in a single evening, something that fitted with his natural working pattern. However, the lack of immediate audience response put him off his stride a little. Between takes, he was able to get the crew laughing but not when the cameras were rolling.

'Nobody was laughing on the set, so he was completely out of his comfort zone,' Clough observes. 'On stage, he's getting the bounce back from the audience, but on that occasion, it was just like chucking it out into a void. Nothing came back. I think he found that really quite hard. Also, it's kind of strange, we were outside an aircraft hangar in the middle of the night and people were going through this sort of metal detector thing, which he had to imagine was happening, because it was all done with visual effects. He was quite shy about how the process worked because obviously it was alien to him completely.'

While Dodd's live shows were feats of memory, they relied strongly on his long-term store of comic material. Short-term retention was another matter, and his television shows tended to involve heavy use of cue cards and teleprompters, a necessity disguised skilfully by Dodd. 'He found it quite difficult to remember the lines,' says Clough. 'After each take, he'd huddle off with his wife and just go over it.' Clough encouraged Dodd to take liberties with the script as he saw fit. 'You don't want to constrain him. You want him to feel at his most confident and that's when he's at his most confident, when he's running free, really. He was just fantastic. He threw himself into it and just turned it on.'[18] The gusto of his performance left many hardcore Whovians unimpressed, making it clear that they felt it was a sign of the ongoing trivialization of a children's show about a 900-year-old man who travels through time and space in an item of early twentieth-century street furniture. 'It was a shame, I thought,' says Clough. 'He was a great man.'

All through this busy period, Dodd gave the distinct impression of being a man on top of his game and in control of his destiny. Only those closest to him had even an inkling of the worries that had been on his mind for a few years. In June 1988, though, the whole world was to find out.

6
The trial of Kenneth Arthur Dodd

'Self-assessment. I invented that.'

When Ken Dodd took to the stage of the Arcadia Theatre in Llandudno on Tuesday, 7 June 1988, the 1,100-strong audience were even more pleased than usual to see him. There had been questions as to whether the show would go on that night. Dodd's timekeeping was notorious but it was exceedingly rare for him not to turn up eventually.

The doubts were prompted by the headlines in that morning's papers. The *Daily Mirror* led on the front page with 'Ken Dodd on tax fraud charge: Diddymen comic accused'. It reported that the following morning, the Inland Revenue were to put eighteen charges of tax evasion before Liverpool magistrates' court. The charges – relating to Dodd's companies Ken Dodd Enterprises, Diddy Scripts and Happiness Music – dated back to 1973, and it was reported that the 'amount involved in the probe was more than £900,000'.[1] Journalists seized on the description of Dodd as a 'common law cheat'.

In Llandudno that night, Dodd broke from his usual barrage of gags to open up in front of the loyal punters. One audience member was sitting with his hands clasped and Dodd thanked him for his prayers. 'Hand on my heart, I haven't done anything wrong,' he was reported as saying. 'I haven't hurt anybody. I haven't burgled anybody. I haven't stolen anything... Time will tell and the full story will come out. Thank you very much for supporting me here this evening. Believe me, it has meant a great deal. To see you all in here when I first came in, I thought, "Well, they're with me"... I have always given good value. Thank you for being so supportive – you are like a family. Please God, I will be here every Tuesday till September.'[2]

Just a few weeks before the story broke, Dodd had appeared on the Saturday evening TV show featuring the popular puppet Roland Rat and ventured a joke that seemed innocuous enough at the time, but rather more pointed with the benefit of hindsight: 'Stand-up comic? That's a very, very dangerous profession, you know. So many of them around these days. There's MPs, double-glazing salesmen, driving examiners. Then there are the alternatives. Vicars and VAT inspectors. Terrible. They'll do anything for a laugh.'[3]

On 8 June at court, Dodd was absent for the brief hearing but this was entirely expected. He had an engagement he couldn't miss, having travelled down from North Wales to Hove for the funeral of his agent, mentor and friend Dave Forrester. Journalists approached him for a comment at the ceremony but he, not unreasonably, refused. The case was adjourned until August and when it resumed, the Inland Revenue had added a further nine charges to the sheet. David Hartnett, the inspector in charge of the investigation, told the court that the case was 'much more serious' than thought originally.[4] Dodd was ordered to surrender his passport, with Hartnett saying that the magnitude of the charges 'gives us cause to believe he would not attend the trial'.[5] In a somewhat curious utterance, Hartnett added that he had 'confidential information that Mr Dodd might not be at any trial which may take place' while admitting that he 'had no opportunity to check out that information'. Dodd's barrister Susan Klonin responded that Dodd had been advised to take a break in warmer climes for the sake of his bronchitis and emphysema, but had 'no intention of fleeing the country and being a fugitive on the run', adding that he had been 'fully co-operative' throughout.

Indeed, he had. It's hard to believe that Dodd, a man who holidayed rarely and went abroad even less often, had any intention of skipping bail, casting a question over the source, or indeed the existence, of Hartnett's 'confidential information'. Moreover, two days before the hearing, Dodd had paid £475,000 to the Inland Revenue in cash and bought £350,000 worth of tax reserve certificates, as a means of settling his debts. This made it clear that Dodd had no quibble with the Inland Revenue's calculations. The issue was whether he genuinely didn't realize that he owed the money or whether he'd been trying to pull a fast one over many years. Having settled the debt, the trial would hinge on whether his claim of honest mistakes and bad advice would be believed over the Inland Revenue's claim that he had been guilty of long-term systematic fraud.

It seems clear that the Inland Revenue thought they had

this one in the bag. They were riding high after the successful prosecution of retired jockey-turned-trainer Lester Piggott the previous year. Confirmation that Dodd was to appear in court on tax evasion charges came on Monday, 6 June 1988, the same day it was announced that the Queen had stripped Piggott of his OBE. The following day, many papers chose to link the stories for greater effect. This is likely to have been skilful news management by the Inland Revenue rather than coincidence. Piggott was a favourite in the racing-mad Royal household, and his defenestration sent the message that nobody was safe from the taxman. Deliberate or not, the timing of the announcements sent a message. They were coming for Doddy.

Meanwhile, as an illustration of what Dodd could expect from the press in terms of accuracy and fairness, the *Mirror* claimed that Piggott 'cried like a child who had had his favourite toy taken away from him in his moment of need',[6] while the *Express* reported a prison officer as saying: 'He was told but it didn't seem to register. Lester never lets on how he feels. He just shrugged.'[7]

Piggott had been arrested in December 1986 and elements of the handling of his case correspond with how tax officials tackled Dodd in the early stages. He had to sign over his house and his stables, worth £950,000, as bail, and he was ordered to surrender his passport. The fact that the bail was almost immediately halved and his passport returned suggests that this was a standard tactic – an exercise in humiliation rather than because of any real concern the accused would jump bail.

One of the main charges concerned false statements about Piggott's bank accounts. He claimed he had only three, all held at the National Westminster Bank in Newmarket. Investigators found that he had seventeen accounts, spread across different banks in various names. When he came to trial in March 1987, he faced twelve charges over undisclosed income of £3.75 million. Found guilty, in October, he was sentenced to three years in prison. Passing sentence, Mr Justice Farquharson said he might have been able to spare Piggott from a custodial sentence if he had disclosed the details of his various accounts at the outset of the investigation.

Whether prompted by the details of the Piggott case or because he believed he had nothing to hide, Dodd's apparent co-operation indicated that he wasn't going to make the same mistake. He knew that he was on his own. Just as Piggott had been a favourite of the Queen, Dodd had his own friends in high places who could do nothing to help or protect him. A loyal Conservative, Dodd had built an especially good relationship with Margaret Thatcher. Dodd offered his help at the 1979 Conservative Party conference, the first after Thatcher became prime minister. Her political secretary, Richard Ryder, noted that there didn't 'seem to be any way of directly involving him' but asked 'would you like him to be asked to attend any particular occasion?' Thatcher's handwritten response to Ryder's note said she 'should so much like to see him'.[8]

When Dodd was at the Palladium in October 1980, Thatcher asked if she and Denis could attend a performance. Despite correspondence in which Denis declared Dodd to be 'a very, very nice man but not my favourite comedian',[9] the Thatchers

163

attended the show on Thursday, 23 October and visited the comedian backstage before returning to Number 10. A week later, the PM wrote a warm note thanking Dodd 'for receiving us afterwards when you must have felt exhausted' and telling him, 'You were <u>wonderful</u>.'[10]

Then, when the Conservative Party conference was held in Blackpool in October 1981, Thatcher spent the evening before it began watching Dodd at the Opera House, joining him for drinks afterwards. Following riots in the Liverpool district of Toxteth that July, the city's problems – not least unemployment and deprivation – were making news. It seems that Dodd had theories about what needed doing. Writing the following week to thank him for his hospitality, Thatcher said, 'I was most interested to hear what you and Lady Pilkington* had to say about Liverpool and the solution to its problems. I do so agree with you that the people of Liverpool need to have their sights uplifted. However, as you know only too well, that is easier said than done.'[11]

That early closeness dissipated in time and by 1988, Dodd's name was absent from a draft guest list for a party to thank all the sports and show business personalities who helped with Thatcher's victory in the general election the year before. It seems that by the time of his trial, Dodd was out of favour in Downing Street.

He coped with the interregnum between the initial hearings

---

* Mavis, Lady Pilkington, was the widow of Lord Pilkington, the St Helens glass tycoon, and very much a member of the Merseyside great and good.

and the trial proper, set to begin in June 1989, by keeping as busy as he could. Given that his lawyers had told the court that 'he very much needs a break', he didn't want to overdo it but a pantomime commitment to play Idle Jack, with the ever loyal Anne as Puss, in *Puss in Boots* at the Civic in Halifax saw him through the festive season. Reviewing the production for *The Stage*, Geoff Mellor referred to Dodd as 'the Knut from Knotty Ash' – a pun on the silent K rather than a reference to the waterlogged Danish king or anything ruder – and stated that the booking was 'a wise investment… as tinkling tills and block bookings are the order of the day at the box office'.[12] Mellor's comment is interesting, with its suggestion that Calderdale Council were cashing in on Dodd's current notoriety, but public support for the comedian seems to have been overwhelming throughout. The BBC were less supportive and in March 1989 it was announced that *A Question of Entertainment*, on which Dodd had served as a regular panellist, was being repackaged for its second series without Dodd or host Tom O'Connor, who had experienced some difficulties of his own after a brush with the tabloids. Controller of BBC1, Jonathan Powell, denied that the controversies surrounding the comedians had anything to do with their ousting. 'We were just not happy with the show as it was,' he said.[13]

Cannily, having learned well from George Bartram, Dodd knew that giving the press a bit of a story every so often would keep his name in the public eye for positive reasons. So it was that in February 1989, the always-sympathetic *Liverpool Echo* reported his investment in a Preston-based racehorse-owning syndicate, being one of 250 people who had put in £250 each. Although he was happy to pose for photographers clowning around with jockey Geraldine Rees and Dalsky, one of the syndicate's seven horses, he had to admit that his asthma made him allergic to the animals. He also said he wouldn't be betting on his investments, with an aside about his father's weakness. 'My dad was a regular punter, so I have always had an interest... [but] I only ever bet on the Grand National,' he said.[14] In any case, once the story appeared, positive and glowing, he'd already had his money's worth out of the venture.

The following month, he appeared on Granada Television's *This Morning* with Jean Alexander, who played Hilda Ogden in *Coronation Street*, to help choose a new cat for the re-shot opening titles of the soap opera.

Doddy also knew the value of charity work and worthy causes. When he heard that his friend Johnnie Hamp was putting on a big gala benefit at the Liverpool Empire in aid of Barnardo's, he was most put out not to be asked. It wasn't to be taken personally. Hamp had merely thought that he'd have trouble getting Dodd off once he was on:

> Right in the middle of the lead up to the concert, I'd fixed the whole cast, and Doddy rings me here, at home. He said, 'This show you're putting on, this charity thing for Barnardo's. I want to be in it.' I said, 'Why? Frankie Vaughan is topping, big orchestra, Les Reed with the Liverpool Philharmonic.' He said, 'Yeah, but I want to be in it. I need the publicity during this trial, doing a charity show.' I said, 'Ken, I'm full.

I'll tell you what, I can offer you a fifteen-minute spot.' He said, 'I'll do it.'

I said, 'Ken, if you over-run, the crew have all got to be paid at the Empire. It's a charity show, all the lighting people, front of house. You've got to stay to your time.' Come the day, I put him on almost at the end but we had a big finale with the walk-up. I had two fellas in white uniforms with a straitjacket. I said, 'Now, Ken, if you go over fifteen minutes, these two are going to come on. It'll get a big laugh because people will know the reason for doing it.' I gave him a bit of leeway. He did seventeen minutes, and it would have got a good laugh. People would have known that. Must have been the shortest set he ever did.[15]

In May, he posed with schoolchildren at St Michael's RC Primary in Kirkby to kick off the Keep Knowsley Tidy campaign. Waving a pair of tickling sticks for the photographers and perching one of the campaign's promotional paper hats precariously on top of his head, he told reporters: 'When I see rubbish, it makes my hair stand on end.'[16] That same month, he did a benefit show at the Grafton Rooms on West Derby Road for the charity Victims of Violence.

Doddy, like many Liverpool entertainers, helped raise money for the families affected by the Hillsborough tragedy of 15 April 1989, when ninety-six football fans were killed and 766 were injured by incompetence and negligence at an FA Cup semi-final match between Liverpool and Nottingham Forest. Dodd arranged a solo gig at the Kingsland Cabaret Restaurant in Birkenhead and agreed to appear at the Empire on 4 June with Cilla Black, Jimmy Tarbuck, Freddie Starr and the Searchers, among others.

Dodd's trial was due to start the following morning, Monday, 5 June, but Dodd was a no-show for the big show. He had consulted a GP, Dr Rhys Williams, who had diagnosed a cardiac arrhythmia. The court was told that 'his life would be in danger if he was to become too excited', a statement seemingly belied by Dodd's frenetic on-stage manner over the previous thirty-five years. Dodd's QC, George Carman, requested an adjournment to allow for further checks on the comedian's health, and it was agreed that, all being well, the trial would resume a fortnight later.

When proceedings began again on Monday, 19 June, Dodd arrived in good form, joking with reporters about being unable to get a seat. His appearance was somewhat different to the 'haggard… worried and sombre-faced' look he had presented at the adjournment hearing. Tests had confirmed the arrhythmia but found no damage to his heart or arteries. Once the court had settled, prosecution counsel Brian Leveson QC began laying out the case against the comedian, consisting of eleven charges: seven of being a common-law cheat and four of false accounting. Aptly enough, given Dodd's own aversion to brevity, he began by warning the jury of five men and seven women 'that his opening statement would take a considerable time', given the intricacies of tax law and the investigation, all of which would have to be explained in full.

The investigation into Dodd's arrangements had begun in June 1984, after the Inland Revenue started investigating his former accountant Reginald Hunter, who would eventually be found guilty of twelve counts of dishonesty with other clients. Leveson noted that there had been no evidence that Hunter had acted fraudulently on Dodd's behalf, but said that the inspector in charge 'did... think it appropriate to start an inquiry into Mr Dodd's tax affairs'.[17] The prompt for the decision became apparent two days into the trial when tax inspector Joseph Atkinson began giving evidence for the prosecution. He cited two letters sent by Hunter to his client, making jokey reference to the comedian's assets. 'You will notice again,' Hunter wrote to Dodd on 2 June 1976, 'that the Ken Dodd balance sheet omits its greatest asset, i.e., the great drum, better known in Stock Exchange circles as the Aladdin's Cave of Knotty Ash. Long may that priceless possession remain in the Merseyside mangrove swamps to be seen but rarely and by the very few.'[18]

Leveson said that Dodd had furnished investigators with a list of his bank accounts, including one at Barclays in Water Street and another at the National Westminster in Old Swan. The barrister explained that the investigators had been speaking to Dodd under a protocol known as the Hansard Extract. 'The Extract,' he explained, 'can be taken as a very broad hint that full disclosure and telling the truth will lead to informal resolution rather than prosecution. It is an opportunity for the taxpayer to come clean... The carrot is the prospect of no prosecution. The stick is that if... it can be proved he has lied it is likely he will be prosecuted.'[19]

Dodd had appointed the accountancy firm Thornton Baker (now known as Grant Thornton) to audit his finances after the initial approach from the Inland Revenue. During the course of the investigation, he declared a forgotten Trustee Savings Bank account, opened in 1963, containing £1200, but Leveson said that investigators had found an account in Jersey and six accounts in the Isle of Man, into which Dodd had deposited £406,000, a sum that had grown to £777,453 with interest. It was suggested that Dodd had taken the cash personally, travelling by air. In a chilling echo of the Piggott case, it was stated that Dodd had failed to mention these extra accounts to both his accountants and the Inland Revenue.

As if that weren't damning enough, Leveson went on to indicate that Dodd had been routinely falsifying his income for years. The barrister said that there were numerous examples of Dodd being paid two fees. One would be settled by cheque and put through the books. The other would be in cash and not declared. Leveson went on to allege that Dodd had continued this sharp practice throughout the period when he was being investigated.

Dodd had been asked early on about the possibility of cash payments being involved. He had told them that '95 per cent of his income' was paid by cheque and that the 5 per cent in cash would have been declared too. He admitted that it was possible that he had 'failed to remember' some cash transactions, but that these would not come to 'more than a few hundred pounds'. He added that it was not unknown for clubs to operate their own fiddles by inflating the fee they said they were paying a turn, and creaming off the difference. He stated that he would be challenging any figures presented by the Inland Revenue on this basis.

One of the problems, Leveson suggested, was that Dodd

tended to treat the money held by his companies – Ken Dodd Enterprises, Happiness Music and Diddy Scripts – as his own, dipping in and out as he saw fit. Whether this was the case or not, Dodd's finances were in an unholy mess and the auditors' attempts to make sense of them were akin to plaiting sawdust. According to the Inland Revenue, Dodd's gross income between 1949 and 1982 had been £1,154,456, leaving £575,783 after tax. They wondered how he had managed to spare £406,000 in deposits to the Jersey and Isle of Man accounts. According to their calculations, just £93,000 of the money could be classified as savings.

A further audit undertaken by Arthur Young and Co (now Ernst & Young) suggested that Hunter had been writing down as expenses amounts of money that were in reality going to Dodd in cash. Dodd had asserted that if this had happened, it was without his knowledge. One possible explanation for how Dodd was able to save so much was how little he seemed to spend. It was worked out that over the thirty-three years covered by the audit, the comedian had spent just £23,100 in cash. The Thornton Baker audit worked out his annual living expenses at a modest £12,600 a year, while the Young survey found them to be a mere £3500 per annum.

If this frugality sounds implausible, and Dodd had admitted to inspectors that he routinely carried up to £5000 in cash when away from home, it rings all too true to many of those who had worked with him. David Nobbs recalled one night after a radio show recording at the former Paris cinema on Lower Regent Street, when Dodd turned up at the Captain's Cabin pub behind the studio just as last orders were being called and announced that he was getting a round in. He returned from the bar with a pale ale for himself, and nothing else. He told the thirsty hordes that the barman was closing up and had let him have one because he'd arrived after everyone else.

Nobbs' friend and writing partner David McKellar says, though, that 'different rules applied in certain places'. He explains:

> If he was just with me it was alright, but not if there was a crowd around. He came in the pub after one of the recordings, the radio recordings, which was surprising. We used to all go for a drink then I used to rush to Victoria to get the last train back to Brighton. He came in and he bought everyone a drink. He put the money down on the counter and the bloke behind the counter didn't know who he was. Foreign bloke. He'd obviously underpaid by hell of a lot. The barman said, 'Excuse me, sir, when was the last time you bought a drink?' and he said, 'April the 3rd 1943.'

This tightness extended to Dodd's clothes shopping. When Dave Dutton was writing for Dodd, the Lancashire cotton industry was still extant, and Dutton's mother worked in a mill. 'Because she worked there, she could get the shirts with no labels cheap,' says Dutton. 'I think they were about five shillings or something like that. They were perfectly good shirts. So, she used to get me the shirts, and then Doddy saw one on me and he said, "That's a nice shirt. Where did you get it from?" I told him I got it for five shillings from the mill. So he had a word with her and gave her thirty bob or whatever. Next time he came, she gave him half a dozen shirts with the labels out. And this is a multi-millionaire who could have the finest bloody tailored shirts anywhere.'[20]

Dodd, knowing how much was at stake, had decided not to make false economies when it came to choosing his defence barrister. Only the best would do, and in 1989, George Carman QC vied with Peter Carter-Ruck for the top spot. Primarily known for his specialism in libel cases, Carman was a grand inquisitor with a knack for a memorable and funny line. When Conservative politician David Mellor took an inappropriate holiday in Marbella, and his benefactor sued *The People*, Carman joked: 'Marbella has sand, sea and sunshine and, if a politician goes there and – in the honest view of some – behaves like an ostrich and puts his head in the sand and thereby exposes his thinking parts, it may be a newspaper is entitled to say so.'[21]

More importantly, he had a reputation for coming up trumps when the odds seemed stacked against him and his client. In 1973, he had defended James Hogan, the manager of a rollercoaster in Battersea Park that had derailed and killed five children. Sir David Napley was representing the surveyor involved in the case and noted Carman's skill. 'It didn't seem to me that the chap had much of a defence, but George got him off. I said to my partner that if he could get that chap off, he was worth watching,' Napley recalled in 1992, and it was Carman who came to mind in 1979 when Napley was representing former Liberal leader Jeremy Thorpe, who faced charges of conspiracy to murder his ex-lover Norman Scott. The case put Carman firmly in the top tier.

Apart from his professional skills, Carman would have appealed to Dodd because he was a fellow northerner. Born in Blackpool in 1929, the son of a furniture salesman and a women's clothier, the lawyer had lost his Lancashire accent very deliberately when he was studying at Balliol College, Oxford, but could lapse back at will, something he found very useful in his early years on the Manchester circuit. The foundations of Carman's success were 'meticulous hard work, a thorough preparation of his case aided by a prodigious memory that enables him to conduct a cross examination over many hours with only the sketchiest of notes'.[22] He would script his opening and closing remarks, but extemporize from notes in between, a method not unknown in comedy. In particular, Carman had an impatience with jargon, and would repeatedly press witnesses to explain complex matters in simple, clear terms.

He was far from perfect, though. All three of his marriages failed and, in the words of Alan Rusbridger, who as *Guardian* editor brought in Carman to defend the paper against a libel suit from Conservative politician Jonathan Aitken, 'he seemed to lead an empty and lonely life away from the law'.[23] He was, Rusbridger noted, 'bad at holding his drink. He could be difficult and ill-tempered. His insecurity and vanity were always near the surface.'[24]

None of that seemed to matter in the courtroom and from the moment he got to his feet for Dodd, Carman delivered fully on his reputation. It soon became clear that a significant part of Carman's strategy was to cast doubt on the abilities

LET'S HAVE FUN!

1. "LET'S HAVE FUN."

    Dancers   ORCHID ROOM LOVELIES
    Singers   JOY HARRIS and JOSEPH WARD

2. JIMMY JAMES and JIMMY CLITHEROE

3. ROY CASTLE.

4. JIMMY JAMES, JIMMY CLITHEROE and CORINNE.

5. DENNIS SPICER with JAMES GREEN.

6. "ON THE MISSISSIPPI."

7. JIMMY JAMES, with his B.B.C. Discovery.
    The Discovery, ELI   BRETTON WOODS

INTERVAL

PLEASE NOTE SPECIAL

PETER WEBSTER SUNDAY SHOW

at 6.10 and 8.15 p.m.

with

STAR GUEST ARTISTES ONE PRICE ONLY

2/6

All Seats Bookable

8. ORCHID ROOM LOVELIES.

9. JIMMY CLITHEROE interrupts ROY CASTLE

10. "YELLOW ROSE OF TEXAS."

    Dancers   ORCHID ROOM LOVELIES
    Singer   JOY HARRIS

11. JIMMY CLITHEROE and CORINNE.

12. JIMMY JAMES. "The Spare Room."
    Reveller   JIMMY JAMES
    Long-suffering Wife GLORIA BANNISTER

13. TRIO VEDETTE.

14. KEN DODD. The Unpredictable One.

15. FINALE.

RULES AND REGULATIONS

1. Dodd the apprentice: In his early days on the variety circuit, Dodd took full advantage of his access to elder comic legends, watching them like a hawk from the wings. Not least of these was Jimmy James, with whom he worked at the Central Pier, Blackpool, in 1956.

2. Dodd preparing props at home in Knotty Ash, aided by the funniest man he ever knew, his father Arthur Dodd.

3, 4. Although Dodd did summer seasons in all of the top English resorts, his heart was always in Blackpool.

5. A lifelong fan of Shakespeare, Dodd fools around in 1964 with Yorick, a part he would later play.

6. Looks familiar: BBC TV's new star sees himself on the small screen.

Programme One Shilling

Leslie A. Macdonnell &
Bernard Delfont present

"doddy's here!"

Staged by Robert Nesbitt

at the famous **London** PALLADIUM

7, 8, 9, 10.
The London
Palladium is the
pinnacle of any
performer's career,
even if it's just a
one-nighter. Dodd
was resident there
for eight months
in 1965, visited
along the way by
the entire Cup
Final-winning
Liverpool FC
team...

...and the Prime Minister, Harold Wilson. At the end of the year, he appeared there in his first Royal Variety show, in the presence of Queen Elizabeth. Spike Milligan and Dudley Moore look on, while Max Bygraves pretends to be blasé.

11. David Hamilton attempts to keep Dodd and Graham Stark under control in a sketch from *Doddy's Music Box*.

12. The lady's not for tickling: Even Margaret Thatcher, not noted for her sense of humour, found Dodd's comedy irresistible.

13. A defiant Dodd arrives at court during his tax trial, 1989.

14. A tattifilarious day at the Palace for Doddy and Anne, as he receives his knighthood, 2017.

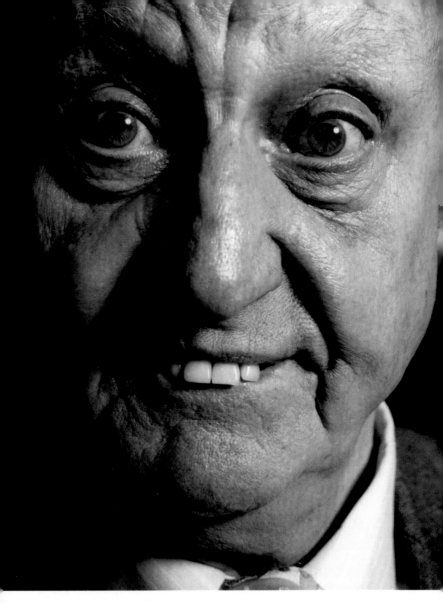

15. The face of comedy: Andy Hollingworth's 2003 portrait
of Dodd, a masterpiece capturing the essence
of the man and his work.

and professionalism of Reginald Hunter. This was in contrast to the Inland Revenue, who seemed determined to play down the accountant's contribution to Dodd's woes. In this, the QC was aided by Hunter's record with other clients, which had led to prosecution on twelve counts of dishonesty. Carman stopped short of suggesting that Hunter was a criminal, preferring to depict him as merely incompetent.

Carman began his offensive in earnest on the fifth day of the trial, when he accused Hunter of 'Alice in Wonderland behaviour'. The accountant had routinely put off dealing with Dodd's PAYE returns for as long as four years after they were due, which Carman called an 'unusual... unacceptable' state of affairs.

Then there was the matter of the expense sheets collated by Hunter, of which Carman said 'it looks as if Mr Hunter quite arbitrarily plucked some figure out of the air in respect to some expenses incurred by Mr Dodd'.[25] He indicated that one set of expenses had been inflated by £37,000, including £20,000 being added to travel expenses of £5401 and £5000 being added to a wardrobe and props total of £7600.

He used these figures in his cross-examination of John Collier, one of the accountants at Grant Thornton who had taken Dodd on in 1984. Collier was guarded and cautious, refusing to accept that Hunter had inflated the figures personally, while admitting that someone at Hunter's office must have done it. Either way, he seemed to be saying that Dodd was not to blame. Pressed by Carman to agree that Hunter was incompetent, Collier replied diplomatically that 'there was evidence to suggest that Mr Hunter was careless'.[26]

Having demolished Hunter and persuaded Collier to agree cautiously with the assessment, Carman would later express bafflement as to why the Inland Revenue had not interviewed Hunter for their Dodd investigation. It was, he asserted, 'to put on *Hamlet* without the Prince'. David Hartnett replied that he did not think Hunter could be of any assistance to the inquiry, and that even if he could have been, nobody knew his whereabouts. Carman argued that it was impossible to establish whether Dodd's discrepancies were the result of negligence or dishonesty without interviewing the accountant who had prepared the figures. The suggestion was that the Inland Revenue had deliberately avoided looking for Hunter in their keenness to pin the blame wholly on Dodd.

Carman had earlier seized on Collier's hedging and began to question whether the Grant Thornton team had not been compromised in their loyalty to their client by 'a degree of persistence and no doubt pressure' from the Inland Revenue, forcing them to surrender evidence that could be used against the comedian. 'It is always possible in some cases... that the Inland Revenue, if it is ever appropriate, can point an accusing or critical finger at the chartered accountants advising,' Carman told the court. In response, Collier said that any evidence he had supplied had been intended to 'assist rather than prejudice' Dodd.[27]

However, later in the trial, Dodd himself indicated that there had been a significant breakdown in relations between him and Grant Thornton. 'They were not friendly,' he told the court. 'They certainly were not very patient. They were quite brusque. I think they thought they were rather superior.'

Gordon Hope, the head of the team, was 'very aloof', Anthony Brown was 'very haw, haw, haw' and Dodd 'lost complete confidence in him... because he kept making facetious remarks', while the comedian asked not to deal with John Collier due to 'a personality clash'. Dodd said that Brown had told him he'd need to find everything, even old bus tickets, for a full audit. 'He said it was like a Chinese launderette: No tickee, no laundry,' claimed Dodd.[28]

It also emerged that Dodd had reacted badly to the inspectors early on in the investigation. Following a long interview, tax inspector Joseph Atkinson told Dodd he wanted to go immediately to Thomas Lane. Dodd had replied that this would not be convenient, as he had his cousin's funeral the next day and family commitments to fulfil before then. Dodd suggested a visit at 4.30 the next afternoon, and said that the demand to go there immediately had been a 'Gestapo' tactic. This had been left out of the typewritten report of the meeting but was present in handwritten notes.

Dodd's reaction to the inspectors and the accountants is, perhaps, an indication of his need for control of any given situation. For the first time in his life, someone had a problem with him and he couldn't disarm them with a joke or charm them with a flattering nickname. In his hour of greatest need, his superpower had been neutralized and he didn't like it at all. This episode possibly underlines why he persisted with the Widnes-based Hunter for so long, despite it being obvious that the accountant was, at best, out of his depth. To a corporate entity like Grant Thornton, Dodd was just another client, and a difficult one at that. To Hunter, Dodd was a trophy, a status symbol. Hunter was grateful for the patronage and easier to push around.

Also, Dodd seemed to like to keep his money within the local economy where possible. 'Ken was very frightened to spend money outside Liverpool,' says David McKellar. 'He was very generous but he didn't trust anyone outside Liverpool with money. So I don't know whether he'd been done a few times and whatever.'[29] Grant Thornton had a Liverpool office but was a London-based firm. Liverpool-based writer Tim Worthington always noted with approval Dodd's support for local businesses. 'Near to where I grew up, on Booker Avenue in Liverpool, there was a row of shops that included a photographer's that Doddy used for a lot of his publicity shots. There were always framed photos of him with balloons and Diddymen and so on – I think the one from the cover of [Michael Billington's] *How Tickled I Am* might have been in fact – and I remember feeling impressed that he was a big star but still used local tradespeople he trusted.'[30]

Carman was intent on establishing the idea that Dodd had been failed not only by Hunter, but by Grant Thornton. Answering questions from Brian Leveson, prosecuting, Paul Marshall, one of the firm's tax managers, said that there had been 'no hint at all' of the Jersey or Isle of Man accounts. Carman countered by asking Marshall if he had given Dodd 'a specific warning about the danger of criminal prosecution' in the case of 'any omission or false statements' in the certificates where assets were declared. Marshall replied that he could not remember doing so. Carman pressed further, asking Marshall if he'd 'accept that it was your duty to give him such advice'. Marshall said he'd 'warned Dodd how vital it was' but couldn't 'remember using the words criminal prosecution'. The QC went on to ask Marshall whether he now accepted that such specific advice 'is a prudent thing to do when you have a client who is a layman'. Marshall said yes.

Masterful work, but how could Dodd have not realized that he was withholding vital information about these extra holdings? Carman produced some leaflets and magazine articles outlining the benefits of banking in the Isle of Man. One stated that while the island was within the British Isles, it was not in the UK and as such not subject to UK tax legislation, resulting in interest being 'paid gross to non-residents with no tax deducted'.[31]

In the early 1970s, the Isle of Man Bank, owned by the UK-based National Westminster Bank, took advertisements in UK newspapers inviting people to get in contact if they were 'interested in 1) being furnished with information regarding residence in this delightful Island with its substantial tax advantages, or 2) having an account in Sterling with a bank in the Scheduled Territories but outside the United Kingdom of Great Britain and Northern Ireland'.[32] Carman asked Gordon Hope, a senior partner at Grant Thornton, if this coverage were not 'potentially seriously misleading', to which Hope could only agree. The advertisements and articles contained 'an ambiguity... we are not told if customers are non-residents in the Isle of Man or non-residents in mainland Britain'. At no point was it clarified that UK residents would be liable for UK tax at the usual rate, and it was on this basis that Dodd maintained that the Isle of Man accounts contained money on which he had already paid income tax, and that he was unaware that he was liable for further taxation on the interest.

The prosecution had gone to great lengths to establish that Dodd had deposited the money secretly, even furtively. Carman argued that this was an impossibility, given how well-known and easily recognized a personality Dodd was. He asked his client if he expected to be recognized. Dodd replied that he had 'rather enjoyed' his trips to the bank and that the visits had 'quite a carnival atmosphere' as he handed out tickling sticks to staff. 'There was a lot of whispering going on, a lot of twittering and fluttering,' he said, 'and they would say "Oh, it's Ken Dodd" and I would be introduced to Gladys who they would tell me was celebrating her birthday.'

He admitted that he had stuffed the money away into wardrobes and cupboards because he knew that interest in the UK would be charged at a high rate. 'I was misled,' he told the court, and added that 'as soon as I found out, I told the Inland Revenue about every one of the bank accounts.'[33] Carman was making a lot of the running, casting doubt on the Inland Revenue's methodology and findings, but it was far from a walkover. In particular, the evidence given by Jack Oatley, an agent who had booked Dodd for fifteen years until February 1987, looked damning. He said that the comedian had instructed him directly to seek cash payments for tax avoidance purposes.

Ending their association in a somewhat florid letter, Oatley told Dodd that he could 'no longer tolerate the deceit and double dealing which has crept in over the past few months' and would not 'join in with the rat race of sycophants and hungry fighters who seem to have taken over'. He concluded by castigating Dodd for a 'ruthless disregard for the ethics of the business' and telling the comedian that 'things have a strange habit of levelling out and knowing you are a superstitious man I think you will ultimately find out that Friday February 13 was not a lucky day'.[34]

Oatley told the court of a booking at the Stirk House Hotel in Clitheroe in August 1984, where Dodd received £230 by cheque and £600 in cash. Carman asked Oatley if his resignation missive was not 'a most unpleasant letter to write to anyone you have been associated with for years'. Oatley replied that it was merely the truth. Carman seems not to have made explicit the problems with the evidence, with Oatley claiming the deceit had 'crept in' during the latter part of 1986, while admitting to being complicit in the deceit over two years earlier.

It's entirely possible to read Oatley's letter as the work of a frightened man trying to save his own skin after direct threats from the tax inspectors, an impression supported by evidence given by Ronald Craven, the proprietor of the Chestnuts restaurant in Lincoln, where Dodd had appeared three times in 1987 and 1988. Dodd's payments for the engagements had come to £3100, of which £2525 had been handed over in cash. Carman pointed out that the cash sum included money for transport, crew and musicians. Craven 'told the court how Inland Revenue investigators had told him to tell them what they wanted to hear or "they would go through my books with a fine tooth comb".' Certainly, Craven had no problem with Dodd apart from the length of his act sometimes depressing bar sales, and the comedian not leaving the venue until 3 a.m.

As the trial progressed, details emerged, many of them volunteered by Dodd himself, about his strange relationship with money. The tax inspectors told the court that Dodd had admitted to keeping over £330,000 in cash, withdrawn from the overseas accounts, in the attic at his Thomas Lane home, in the house next door, which he also owned, and at another property, 66 Bankfield Road, Broadgreen, where Anita Boutin's brother, Billy, lived. The reason given for this hoarding was that Dodd thought 'the whole economy was going wrong' and 'I thought we were going to have civil war in this country'.

Later in the trial, when he was being questioned, he said that apart from fearing the collapse of the banking system, keeping large amounts of cash close at hand made him feel like a star, with a 'feeling of security and accomplishment'. Dodd's friend David Hamilton suspects this was a sincere summary of the comedian's attitude: 'I think there was a thing among those old pros, that they all had the same thing, that terrible insecurity, they'd seen it happen to other people before them. They could go out of fashion. And particularly with the comedians, they might wake up one day and just not be funny anymore. I think what Ken did, he stuffed all the money under the bed and that was his security.'[35]

This revelation stands in marked contrast to what Dodd told Professor Anthony Clare when he was the subject of *In the Psychiatrist's Chair* on BBC Radio 4. Dodd admitted cheerfully to being 'a hoarder of anything, magazines, newspapers', but when Clare asked if he was also a 'hoarder of money', Dodd replied in the negative. 'Oh no, no, well, I like money, why have you got some?'[36] Dodd went on to describe himself as 'a businessman' and noted that 'a lot of entertainers, particularly light entertainment people, are absolutely abysmal when it comes to handling money. They're absolutely dreadful and that's why they're always in trouble. You know they're always, you know, bankrupt or they let other people look after their money and I won't do this.'[37]

The interview with Clare was transmitted in August 1987, nearly three years into the Inland Revenue's investigation into Dodd's finances, and months after Dodd had been forced to reveal the existence of his overseas accounts. Presenting himself publicly as shrewd and in control of his money was at odds with the image of vulnerability on which his defence now depended. Dodd talked, albeit hesitantly, about the feeling that he had benefited from divine guidance in a way that, in retrospect, sounds like he was asking for some assistance in dealing with the taxman. 'I believe that I am helped quite a lot,' he told Clare. 'If I have a guardian angel, if God is looking after me, I don't want to be bothering them all the time… but there are occasions when you do need, you feel perhaps a little extra, a little extra confidence would come in handy.'[38] Dodd admitted that he lived in fear of money. Fear of having it, fear of not having it.

Throughout his career, Dodd had done his best to give away as little information about his private life as possible. However, in his eagerness to prove his innocence, he felt it necessary to reveal some very personal details. Carman having forced the Grant Thornton accountants to admit that they should have tried harder to impress on Dodd the importance of the documents they wanted him to sign, Dodd claimed that he had signed them at a time of great fatigue and anguish, related to his and Anne's attempts to have a child.

The day before Dodd was due to sign the declarations, on 3 October 1986, he was in Hunstanton in Norfolk with Anne, where he was performing two shows at the Princess Theatre. At the time, Anne was receiving a fertility treatment that required sexual intercourse to occur within thirty hours. Without going into details, he admitted that there were problems in achieving this, and said that he had driven Anne back overnight to Liverpool. Normally, the driving would have been shared but this was impossible 'on medical advice' and so he arrived home 'shattered' and went to sign the documents in this fragile state.

When Anne herself was called to give evidence, she corroborated Dodd's stories of their attempts to conceive a child. Jones's evidence painted a picture of a man who lived in a state of chaos. On moving in with Dodd at Thomas Lane, she found that the wiring was so old and dilapidated that lights routinely went off with a bang as soon as they were switched on, while most of the rooms in the house were stuffed with old props brought home by the 'vanload' and offloaded at the end of a season. As soon as a room was full, it would be shut and locked.

Anne explained that she had noticed how confused Dodd got with accounting and that she had begun to help him keep track of everything, despite admitting that she had failed O-level maths. As well as appearing in all of Dodd's shows, it was Anne who arranged the support acts, backing musicians and technical assistance.

On the same day as Anne gave her evidence, several of Dodd's show business associates were called as character witnesses, including comedians Roy Hudd and Eric Sykes, TV producer John Fisher and general secretary of the Entertainment Artistes' Benevolent Fund, Reg Swinson. Hudd, who had been approached by Dodd during the fortnight's adjournment at the start of the trial, was at the time appearing in a revival of a seventeenth-century play, *The Birth of Merlin*, at the Theatre Clwyd in Mold. When Doddy turned up one night during the run, it was initially assumed he was there in his capacity as a comedy historian. Hudd told Dodd that he had no idea whether he was innocent or guilty, but would be happy to show up and speak for his friend.

Hudd had always felt a special affection for Dodd, as he'd been booked by James Casey for his first *Workers' Playtime* on Dodd's recommendation. Similarly, Sykes, who spoke of the 'great debt' the nation owed to someone who brought so much pleasure. He said that he'd seen audience members leaving to catch last buses backing up the aisles gingerly so they missed as little of the show as possible. Meanwhile, Fisher talked about Dodd's extreme disorganization and frequent lateness, but said that people soon forgave him because of his spirit.

During preparations for the trial, Hudd had mentioned to George Carman that Dodd had, during one summer season, been the only big name to agree to turn out for a special prisoners' show at Dartmoor. Audaciously, Dodd chose to open with a song, 'The Key', which he recorded for Decca in 1962, and which begins with the line: 'There is a key that will open all doors for me.' Thankfully, the inmates saw the joke and from then on, Dodd could do no wrong. After the show, when Hudd asked why Dodd had agreed to appear, he replied: 'There, but for the grace of God go I.'[39]

Carman loved the story and begged Hudd to tell it in court, before getting cold feet. Between their initial meeting and the trial, Carman kept ringing Hudd saying the story was either in or out. In the end, sensing the way the wind was going, Carman decided it was safe to tell, and Hudd got a good laugh with it. Hudd told the court that Dodd's primary focus was his work. 'Everything comes second in his life,' said Hudd, but he also stressed Dodd's commitment to smaller 'Cinderella charities'. Hudd said: 'A lot of people hitch their wagon to high-profile charities that will attract the maximum amount of publicity for themselves. Ken Dodd would never do that... he has never refused a cry for help.' He also noted the accused's support for younger performers and theatres under threat of closure. This Dodd did by practical action. He supported newcomers by putting them in his shows and teaching them the craft, and he helped save theatres by underwriting long runs of his own shows.

All of these tributes were doubtless lovely to hear, but Leveson went in hard and told judge and jury that they were irrelevant to the matter in hand. Mr Justice Waterhouse disagreed, saying that the picture it painted of a single-minded individual dedicated to his work was worth bearing in mind. In his summing up, before releasing the jury to deliberate on its verdict, Waterhouse said that 'all the witnesses agreed that the defendant is a very hard-working man and a dedicated performer' and instructed the jury to 'give appropriate weight, according to your assessment' to Carman's comment on the prosecution's failure to call Reginald Hunter to give evidence.[40]

The jury retired at 11.30 a.m. on Thursday, 20 July. A tense twenty-four hours later, the jury began delivering its verdicts on the eight charges. On the four charges of false accounting and one of the charges of cheating the Inland Revenue, the answers were unanimously not guilty. On the remaining three charges, majority verdicts of not guilty came forth. Dodd had been cleared. Rarely lost for words, he could only whisper 'Thank you', while Anne fainted, being rescued by Dodd's musical director, Stan Clarke.

It's hard not to detect a note of disappointment in some of the coverage of Dodd's acquittal. The uber-Tory *Daily Express* used the verdict to argue that Mrs Thatcher should cut taxes even further than she had, but sounded a sour note in suggesting that 'anyone paying PAYE... surely ought to be affronted by tax avoidance on a Dodd scale' and that 'taxmen... are probably a little puzzled by what happened yesterday'.

The puzzle was why 'Millions of us who do not keep our affairs in pristine order feel we have more in common with a man who stashes thousands of pounds all over the City of Liverpool than we do for anyone who works for the Inland Revenue... the verdict clearly shows... the public's true feelings about having to pay tax... they believe that a man's money is his own business and he can do what he likes with it, even if what he likes to do is cram it into tin boxes and never spend it.'[41]

The *Daily Mirror* went a lot further than the *Express*, carrying a 'Mirror Comment' piece that teetered on the brink of libel, hinting heavily that Dodd was guilty as hell and had been very lucky to get off:

> Lester Piggott was a dishonest man who honestly pleaded guilty to defrauding the taxman. Ken Dodd is an honest man who didn't think he had to pay tax on all his income. Piggott must regret that he didn't plead not guilty, didn't have George Carman to defend him and isn't known for his sense of humour. Without casting doubt on the correctness of the jury's decisions yesterday, Mr Dodd is a fortunate man… His experience may now prompt other equally innocent performers to examine their accounts, if not their consciences, before they, too, end up unjustly in court. Mr Carman can't be everywhere and no two juries are alike.[42]

The short piece reeks with very heavy irony. 'Honest', 'innocent' and 'unjustly' are all intended to convey the exact opposite meaning and when the *Mirror*'s anonymous leader writer, possibly editor Richard Stott, said 'Without casting doubt', he was intending to cast every possible doubt on the correctness of the verdict.

It is undoubtedly true that Dodd had been very lucky indeed. The verdict depended on the jury believing his defence, and had they not, he would have been looking at the same fate as Piggott, possibly even a longer sentence for not accepting his guilt. However, the jury did believe Dodd's claims of innocence and chaos. The sour grapes in the leader columns read like the papers were ready to go to town on Dodd as they had with the jockey, and were bitterly peeved at having to run positive coverage. A flavour of this can be obtained from the *Mirror*'s two-page spread inside the paper headlined 'The mad, sad, mean and lonely world of a Diddyman'.[43] As unpleasant as this was, if he'd been found guilty, the tone would have been even worse.

A kinder eye was cast on Dodd by the *Observer*'s John Sweeney:

> Dodd had suffered his private finances, childlessness and grief all held up to the public gaze… Television audiences who may never have seen Dodd live could perhaps write him off as a tiresome and unfunny clown… [but] that would be to miss the soul of this complex and intriguing man. Farcically disorganized and punctiliously unpunctual he may be, but the fool with the tickling stick is no idiot.
>
> Time and again during Dodd's trial as evidence about his pinched lifestyle came out – no Rolls-Royce ('How can you collect fish and chips in a Rolls-Royce?'), dry rot in his house, the opposite of luxury – the picture of a classic miser would begin to crystallize before Carman would tease out some marathon charity fund-raising feat performed by the comic. A cash-miser maybe, but with his time one of the most generous comics in Britain… [and] not an emotional miser… when John Fisher… told the court about a ten-page letter Dodd had written him when his wife was ill with cancer, it was hard not to feel warmth for the creased figure who had written it… Dodd left Liverpool Crown Court – to the wild applause of several hundred – an honest fool and not a knave.[44]

One element that undoubtedly worked in Dodd's favour was being tried on his home turf. 'Money was Ken's Achilles heel, in terms of all the trouble he had later on with the court case,' says David Hamilton. 'Obviously, he was very lucky where that was concerned. I think what happened with the court case was a) a very good QC in George Carman, and his famous saying that a lot of accountants are comedians but no comedians are accountants, and I think the other thing was a Liverpudlian jury. Liverpudlians adored Ken Dodd and were probably not too fond of the Inland Revenue.'

In a 2012 Radio 3 interview with Matthew Sweet, Dodd said of Merseyside audiences, 'They love jokes about the come-uppance of people in control, when it happens to them,' 'The downfall of dignity, the downfall of authority. It would be a very brave man who walked down Church Street with a top hat on. He'd be taking a chance.'[45]

7

The last of the variety comics

*'What a beautiful day for creeping into Eamonn Andrews'
bedroom, tapping him on the shoulder and saying "There
you are now. How do you like it?"'*

The trial had generated a lot of interest in Ken Dodd. The
week after the verdict had been delivered, his agent Keith
McAndrews told *The Stage* that 'the phone hasn't stopped
ringing. Interest in Ken has always been very keen. His spring
tour this year was a sell-out. But the extra interest the court
case has started is phenomenal... [he's] the hottest property
in Britain.'[1]

This was good news to a comedian who had been unable
to work for several months. Although cleared resoundingly,
Dodd would have to pay costs on top of the money he owed,
and also faced a potential civil court action from the Inland
Revenue. George Carman had not come cheap, his total fees
for the trial being estimated at £250,000. The knowledge of a
full diary, beginning on Sunday, 27 August with a show at the

Arcadia in Llandudno where the public hell had begun, was some comfort, at £1 500 for a one-night stand, but this had to be balanced against concerns for the comedian's health.

Dodd's professional renaissance, however, came at a great price. Although Dodd began joking about the whole situation immediately, it had been a very hard time for him and Anne. He said that they had 'not had one happy day' since the investigation began five years earlier. Indeed, it rankled to the very end. 'It still hurt him forever,' says entertainer and *Happiness Show* colleague Andy Eastwood. 'He joked about it, but it wasn't a joke at all.'[2]

Although television bookings were always welcome, it was after the trial that the idea of Dodd travelling constantly, playing every theatre in the British Isles in a comedy equivalent of Bob Dylan's 'Never Ending Tour', began to take hold. Few of the venues he played at this stage were grand variety halls holding 2000 people. Many of the theatres now booking Dodd were municipal venues like the 600-capacity Beck Theatre in Hayes, Middlesex. However, the impression that he was operating in reduced circumstances is belied by the fact that these venues were now the backbone of British theatreland, the home of the touring stand-up circuit and that he sold out wherever he went. Younger stand-ups often had the aggressive backing of agencies like Avalon and Addison Cresswell's Off the Kerb, but for Knotty Ash's finest, it was all done by him and Anne.

'When I watched him, he had quite a kind of punk attitude, I thought, towards the business,' says Ashtar Al Khirsan, who made a documentary about Dodd for the BBC. He remembers:

When people, presumably, were telling him or there was a perception that he was too old or had his time, he just refused to bow to any of that, and he and Anne, on the road, together, with a few friends who were helpers, and the dog. It was him and Anne, really doing it. They did everything. They got the show on the road. They were the machine behind the whole thing. From the time they were together through the whole of his career.

I'd just actually come off making a film about Pete Doherty, and I used to say to him, 'You and Anne, you're like Pete and Kate [Moss]. You're like a couple of punks just keeping the show on the road.' I remember standing in the wings, watching Anne do all the whistles and things for Ken's act, and she was hidden behind the curtain doing all these things. She was surrounded by his things, his drum, his props and everything. And there was Ken on stage doing his thing, and I just thought, 'Actually, you know what? You don't need much, just to really do something. You just need the drive and you need the talent.' Quite a lot of people have talent, but you need the drive, and just those two together, they really fitted in terms of keeping the show on the road.[3]

Word of mouth was a major element in Dodd's later success, as was the idea that in seeing the show, you were witnessing the last living example of a rare breed. Cleverly, Dodd amplified the stories of his worst excesses, making them a unique selling point, as Andy Eastwood explains:

He'd be off-stage at half-twelve, but the people would still be there, leaving at two o'clock, and then the rumour would go around, 'Oh, he was still on stage at half past two', and the word of mouth would add another five hours. That was the whole beauty of that, because there's no better publicity than word of mouth, and that was the one way he ensured he had it, by being late. Every single person, if you got to a brilliant show, you go home, people say 'What was the show like?' and you say 'Yeah, it was great' and that's the end of the story, but with him, it was all 'We missed the bus, we couldn't get up for work the next morning, we missed work, we were late, everybody thought we'd gone missing.' They've got a story to tell.[4]

The length of the shows had crept up over the years. In 1965 at the Palladium, Dodd was doing forty-five minutes of a two-hour show. When he returned there in 1980, the show was over three hours. By 1994, four hours was nothing unusual. Dodd was always keen to stress that he wasn't on stage himself for the whole time. It was a variety show and, among other acts, Anne, billed as Sybie Jones, was a part of it, singing country songs and playing the flute.

Many said that the shows were too long but Dodd was adamant that he was only concerned with giving the punters a good night out. 'They've come along there, they've put hard-earned money down and I feel very, very aware of this,' he said in 2012. 'Going to the theatre these days, it's not cheap by any means. I think that's possibly why I probably do a bit of overtime. I just really want to earn my money.'[5] In reality, Dodd was as concerned with enjoying himself as he was with the audience's satisfaction. He liked a pint of lager but was never a heavy drinker, and his only drugs came in an inhaler. The show was Dodd's intoxication of choice.

However, while Dodd craved the love of his audiences, not all of it was welcome or appropriate. In November 2003, a Bristol woman, Ruth Tagg, was detained indefinitely under the Mental Health Act, having stalked Dodd and Anne Jones for over a year. Suffering from a psychopathic disorder, Tagg had attended one of Dodd's shows and become convinced that he had been speaking directly to her. After this, she began attending as many shows as she could, sitting as close to the front as possible.

In January 2001, she sent Dodd a framed tapestry she had made but was upset when it was returned. She then sent a letter asking how she could become part of Dodd's 'extended family'. These were unsettling enough but the situation escalated when she sent Dodd and Jones three T-shirts with offensive messages printed on them and a dead rat drenched in perfume. To Dodd she sent communications calling herself 'your secret love' and on one occasion included a pornographic photograph of herself wearing a mask. In October 2001, she caused £11,000 of damage to a house owned by Dodd by pushing lit rags through the letterbox. When she turned up at one of Dodd's shows in New Brighton in May 2002, the police were waiting for her and arrested her on suspicion of harassment. When the case came to court, a charge of arson with intent to endanger life was dropped in favour of a lesser charge of arson being reckless as to whether life was endangered. Tagg pleaded guilty to that and the charge of harassment. As sentence was passed,

Tagg told the judge, 'Thank you very much My Lord, I am very grateful.'[6]

It was always common for show business personalities to shave a few years off their real age – Jack Benny made a joke of it by claiming to be thirty-nine for most of his life – and Dodd was no exception. 'Say I am this year forty-eight and next year I shall be forty-five,' he joked in 1980. 'Let it be known that I am on the sunny side of fifty.'[7] When he played Southport Theatre on his birthday in 1991, he billed it as his sixtieth when it was actually his sixty-fourth. However, as the show was a fund-raiser for Broadgreen Hospital's cancer unit, it's unlikely that anybody would have quailed at the subterfuge.

Moreover, he could still fill the Palladium many times over, as he did for six weeks in late 1990, with a show once again directed by Dickie Hurran. Before then, Dodd was to receive the accolade of being not only the subject of *This Is Your Life*, but the subject of the 500th show made by Thames Television since it had been revived in 1969. Due to be transmitted in early May, the double-length show was recorded at London's Royalty Theatre on 19 February, with Frank Carson, Jimmy Jewel, *Twelfth Night* director Antony Tuckey and Doddy's mentor Hilda Fallon turning up to pay tribute. However, the programme didn't get underway without a little light tabloid controversy.

The *Liverpool Echo* reported that 'a newspaper' had spoiled the surprise on the morning of the show, but that the recording had proceeded 'in the hope that neither Doddy nor any of his friends would have seen the article'. A Thames spokesman was quoted as saying that the reveal had been 'purely malicious' but added that 'this newspaper is read by so few people he's unlikely to have read it'. Not naming the newspaper in question is revealing in itself. The article refers, of course, to the *Sun*, regarded with justifiable contempt across Merseyside for its horrific coverage of the Hillsborough tragedy, in which the fans were accused of all manner of atrocities. Writer and former *Echo* sub-editor Gary Bainbridge confirms that 'The *Echo* continues to have a house style of never referring to the *Sun* by name. The closest it ever gets is The S*n.'[8]

Back on the road, Dodd and Anne were clocking up between 75,000 and 100,000 miles a year in a series of unflashy, practical cars. Dodd had never been one for the status symbol motor. 'Ken didn't have expensive tastes,' says David Hamilton, recalling that when they met in the late 1960s, Dodd 'had a Karmann Ghia. Nice car, but it wasn't a Rolls-Royce. It wasn't a star's car.'[9] After the sporty Volkswagen, Dodd favoured big cars like Ford Granadas and Mercedes, with ample room for props.

The mileage built up because, wherever possible, Dodd and Anne preferred to return to Thomas Lane after a show. There was always a third presence in the car, wherever Dodd went: the dog. 'He loved the dog,' says Andy Eastwood, who worked extensively with Dodd on stage from 2002 onwards. 'They had a boxer when he was much younger, then he had a few poodles. There was Boodle, Doodle, Pippin, George and Rufus. He still mentioned the boxer in the act. He used to say, "My grandad was having a bath in front of the fire in an old tin bath, and the boxer dog came in and said 'Oooh, they're putting my meat in a bigger bowl'." He still got a mention in for the dog. I think he wanted to have his memory of the dog.'

In September 1984, Dodd had been persuaded by Dennis McCarthy, a BBC presenter in the Midlands and a friend since that first Nottingham engagement in 1954, to appear in the first show of a new series, *The Dog Show*, to talk about his canine companions. The interview took place at the Birmingham Hippodrome and featured Boodle waiting patiently in his master's dressing room. 'It's a sensible name, isn't it? Boodle, because he's a blooming big poodle,' Dodd replied when asked how he'd chosen the dog's name.

Boodle, Dodd explained, was the third in the line. He'd bought a dog in Torquay many years before, and he'd named him Touché, who had fathered another Dodd family pet, Marco, who went on to father a litter himself. 'When you're the owner of the sire,' Dodd explained, 'you're allowed to choose the pick of the litter, so I chose the strongest. Enter Boodle. He's about twice as big as he should be, but that doesn't matter because even if he never wins any dog shows, he's still my best pal... All dogs are beautiful, because they give all the affection that human beings could learn a lesson from.'[10]

Dodd had kept three dogs at one time but that was when Arthur was still alive. 'He looked after them when I was away,' Dodd said, 'but you can't travel with three dogs. We travel with one. Smuggle him in all the hotels under my coat.' The boxer of blessed memory, Dodd joked, had 'won the Lonsdale belt'. The breed had been a rich source of gags for Dodd. During the 1979 Thames series, a sketch had required Talfryn Thomas to bring on a basket of boxer puppies, and Doddy picked one up with obvious delight. However, under the glare of the lights, the nervous creature began to piddle on the comedian, causing him to name 'this one Henry Cooper because he's been splashing it all over'.

When giving evidence in the trial, Roy Hudd had touched upon an interesting aspect of Dodd's ethical outlook. The causes he supported were never glamorous and all seemed to be rooted in his personal values. If something he thought was a good thing hit trouble, he'd be there straight away. Theatres were the most obvious example. After the Royal Court experience in 1970, he'd repeated the gesture there again in 1976, then again in 1978 when both the Manchester Palace and the Frank Matcham-designed Grand in Blackpool were in trouble. The Grand would become a favourite regular stop for Dodd in later years.

Similarly, he shied away from making a killing in television advertisements and came to loathe corporate bookings. In May 1970, he was enlisted by British Rail's Eastern Region to drum up trade for the threatened line between Hull and Scarborough. There was no slick promotional campaign. Instead, 100 children from Hull went for a day trip to Scarborough, and 200 children from Scarborough went to Hull. With tickling sticks to the fore, Dodd entertained the East Riding passengers as far as Driffield, renamed 'Diddytown' for the day, then picked up the service from the north back to Hull, for a second house. It was an endearingly old-fashioned exercise rooted in Dodd's love of live performance.

The summer seasons that had formed the backbone of a comedian's year when Dodd started, with big names taking up residence at a resort for several months, were a thing of the past by the early 1990s. However, Dodd adapted and built the resorts into his 'continuous tickle tour'. In the summer of 1990, he did ten weeks of Thursdays at the Embassy in Skegness and Sundays in Scarborough. The following year, he did Thursdays in Clacton and Sundays in Llandudno.

Somewhat perversely, once Dodd had begun to focus on relentless touring, he gave the television performance that had eluded him throughout his career. It only took until 1994, a full forty years into his career as a professional comedian. Beginning with Dame Edna Everage in 1980, London Weekend Television had been producing *An Audience with...*, a series of occasional spectaculars in which a celebrity took questions from a star-studded audience. Dodd got the call for the fourteenth show, following Dudley Moore, Mel Brooks, Billy Connolly and Victoria Wood, among others. It was the first time the comedian had topped the bill for LWT since a one-off Christmas show in 1969.

There were no sketches, no variety acts to break up the flow and no sentimental songs. It was just Dodd doing jokes, and some of his best ones at that. Previously, he'd been careful to preserve his A-grade material but, having four decades' worth of gags banked and no great desire to have a regular show again, Dodd clearly felt he could spare the ravenous monster of television a few of the biggest successes from the giggle ledger. This was clearly what the medium needed. Platinum-grade Dodd.

Making his entrance with a brace of tickling sticks, Dodd addressed 'ladies and gentlemen... gracious Lord Mayor' then put one stick under his leg in a suggestive manner and exclaimed with mock surprise, 'Good gracious, Lady Mayoress'. He instructs a member of the front row to put away her binoculars. 'You're looking down the wrong end, anyway.' He declares 'How tickled I am, how completely discomknickerated, knockerated, how full of plumptiousness' it is to be asked to such an occasion. LWT, he says, stands for 'a long wait for a titter'.

The celebrity audience ('The last time I saw so many stars, I'd banged my head on a mangle') was an eclectic gathering. Dame Hilda Bracket sat next to Samantha Fox, while Clive Swift – Richard in *Keeping Up Appearances* – sat next to his brother David – Henry in *Drop the Dead Donkey*. The show was such a roaring success that in 2001, Dodd was one of the few accorded the honour of *Another Audience with...* One of the highlights of the show is Dora Bryan asking Dodd to sing a song without pulling silly faces, and being rewarded with a version of Ray Noble's 'The Very Thought of You', interrupted at every turn by an invasive trumpeter. It's a superb old gag, reminiscent of Stan Freberg's version of 'The Great Pretender'.* Bryan doesn't get her wish, as Dodd grimaces at every interjection, before edging forward to strangle the trumpeter, but it all ends sweetly as the trumpeter is revealed to be Joan Hinde, an old friend from the variety circuit and a very fine musician. There's no meanness in the gag, no going

* Even Frank Sinatra did a variation of it on *Sinatra at the Sands*, becoming engaged in a running battle with tenor saxophonist Eddie 'Lockjaw' Davis on 'I've Got a Crush on You'.

for the easy laugh with bum notes. It only works if the inter-ruptions are musically excellent.

In the multi-channel era, of which Dodd was a keen follower, watching obscure satellite channels late into the night, there was precious little need for Dodd to do any more big television shows. He'd distilled it all into these two shows, which could now be repeated endlessly.

Between the two shows, in 1996, Dodd returned to his beloved Shakespeare, this time on film, playing Yorick in Kenneth Branagh's adaptation of *Hamlet*. Dodd, who tended to refer to Branagh as 'Kenneth Allbran', was quick to note that Yorick didn't have much to do. 'I said "He's a skull"', Dodd said in a 2006 radio interview, 'and he said, "Ah yes, but we're going to show him in a flashback in the film, when he was fully fleshed."'[11]

As the Yorick scene was a modern invention, Dodd had some concerns about the dialogue. 'He couldn't actually put words into my mouth,' he noted reverently. 'You can't invent words for Willie. He said, "Would you tell some jokes?" I'd sussed that I'd have to do this, so I swotted up on some actor and actress jokes. Of course, around the table, they were hooting and laughing. If anybody's trying to lip-read, I'll be in trouble.'

The question of why Dodd hadn't returned to Shakespeare after *Twelfth Night* in 1971 is answered by the discipline required. Having proven to himself that he could do it, he felt no need to continue with it. Antony Tuckey had told Dodd to let Shakespeare get the laughs, and the uncommon restraint of Dodd's performance was highly effective, but the comedian admitted many years later that it was hard 'subduing my natural enthusiasm to play a part, to not ad lib, to not try to improve on it, to not try to embroider it'.[12] And the question of why Dodd didn't do more movies is perhaps answered in an observation from the *Hamlet* experience. 'You'd got to be in the make-up chair at about half-past six,' he said. 'An unearthly hour. Shepherd's hours.'

On the road, Dodd always tried to test out between six and ten new jokes every night. He was also keen to showcase new talent. When he'd started, there was a variety circuit. Now he *was* the variety circuit. Andy Eastwood joined the company of Dodd's *Happiness Show* in January 2002, when he was fresh out of Oxford University:

> He was very generous in that even the first time he booked me, he gave me four dates as a try-out, not just one. I think it was two nights in Sheffield, two nights in Leamington Spa, which for a twenty-two-year-old green kid, it's nice. He could have said just one, and if I'd made a mess of it, tough, but he gave me a try-out of four. He gave you a chance. Everyone can have a bad night.
>
> Anne did the bookings. That was via an agent in Liverpool called Tony West, who he'd had a few acts from, but I dealt with them directly and then used to pay Tony his commission afterwards, because it was easier to deal with Anne directly. She was in charge of all that. She'd always run it past Ken, but she made those decisions. They must

have liked me because they booked me for another fifty dates right away, for the rest of the year.[13]

Eastwood had been obsessed with variety from an early age, thanks to his grandfather's George Formby records. He first saw Dodd performing live when he was fourteen.

I went to see him at Bournemouth Pavilion, which he did every Easter. My father and I went round the back to see him. You know how you are at that age. My dad said, 'Tell him you want to go into the business' and all that, you know, like you do. So I said 'I want to be a musician. I want to be an entertainer' because I was already doing it as a kid. Like you do at that age. As he'd done and so many do. He was quite almost dismissive, he said, 'Oh, you've got to really, really want it.' He spoke with such conviction that it really hit you, the forcefulness of his tone would hit. It felt like I was being told off. Then I thought 'But I do want it' and he said 'No, you've got to really, really want it', and I thought, 'Well, I do want it'. He was so forceful, anyone with half a doubt in their mind would be put off by it on the spot.

As David Hamilton had done thirty years earlier, Eastwood knew that he would be wise to just watch Dodd and learn. What became immediately apparent was the elder man's generosity with material, and the lack of jealousy present. The show was the thing and the star didn't mind who got the laughs, as long as they kept coming. This was an echo of

Dodd's early experience in variety, where far from trying to undermine the rising talent, older turns would provide endless encouragement. When Dodd had spent six weeks in the *Birthday Show* at the Coventry Hippodrome in late 1956 as the newcomer on the same bill as Tommy Cooper and ventriloquist Arthur Worsley with Jewel and Warriss topping it, Jimmy Jewel kept calling Dodd into his dressing room and giving him new gags he could use. 'He'd give me all the jokes to go on and try and do my best to steal the show,' Dodd said when Jewel turned up on his *This Is Your Life* in 1990.[14] Years later, he was the veteran providing the helping hand. Eastwood recalls:

If you listened to him, he would go on and on giving you help. If people ignored it, then they were out of the door, but I took it on because I thought where else can you get that kind of expertise. For a variety act, that was invaluable. I remember coming off, I think at City Varieties, Leeds, probably the first year I worked with him, and he'd written a whole page, an A4 page of notes. He didn't have to do all that, but he would do it, and if you listened, he'd keep on and on doing it. I soaked it up like a sponge.

He was always giving me gags. I'm not a comedian, I'm a musician, you know, but he used to say, 'Try this one, try that one.' He'd give me them all the time. It's a highway to hell to go on in the Ken Dodd show, when they'd just seen him for a couple of hours, and do gags. He'd tell me, 'You cocked that one up, you got that one.' He made me do them. I did sixteen years with him, about 350 gigs I think it adds up to, and really when you think about it, half of my act by the end of it was stuff that he'd suggested.

He always used to say, 'We want everybody to pull the place down.' He wanted to follow a good act. I used to open the second half, by which time they'd already been in the theatre for three hours, and of course, they needed a wake-up, they needed a bit of reviving, so he wanted me to really get it going after the interval. He used to say, 'The best thing for me in the world is following a good strong act.' He wanted it to be electric. He told me a story. He said, 'The best act I ever followed was Max and Harry Nesbitt, one of them played a uke, they used to sing "How You Gonna Keep 'Em Down On the Farm?" and absolutely rip the balls off the place.' He remembered standing in the wings, it had to be in the fifties, he remembered standing in the wings, thinking, 'Oh God, how can I follow these? They're absolutely blowing the roof off' and then of course, he walked out and the atmosphere was already there. You've just got to keep them up there. You don't have to work. And that was his principle. He wanted the whole thing to work like that. There can't be any low points. So, yeah, he loved everybody to do well.

Anne used to do a spot, and going back right to when I started with them, she used to say, 'Well there'll never be any jealousy. I'd like it if you pull the place down and go better than me. We're very happy if you do.' And that's very encouraging because at that age, a bit green, you might think, 'I hope she doesn't mind if I do a good one.' There was none of that ever. It was all encouragement, all the time. It was the most positive environment to be in, you know. There was pressure as well, of course, in a packed place, obviously, when you're on the bill with somebody like that, you think 'Oh God, I'd better get it right' but absolutely encouraging all the time.[15]

Perhaps surprisingly for a man noted for the length of his shows, Eastwood says that 'the best principle he taught me was editing your material'. Dodd's aim wasn't brevity, it was maximizing the amount of material that could be crammed into a show. If the jokes were shorter, you could tell more of them. 'He used to say, "If you can say something in six words or you can say it in ten, do it in six." If I was ever doing a song, and it had three verses, he'd say "Do the best two", or "Do the best one." That was his principle all the time. He did it with gags, he'd cut a word out. He'd cut half the routine out when he found which half was getting the result and going best. He would trim everything all the time, put more in and then trim that, and that's why, although the show was notoriously long, there was not a wasted second when you look at the words on the page.'[16]

After the shows, Dodd would reflect on the past, which was a never-ending source of delight and fascination to the young Eastwood:

He used to reminisce. It wasn't so much ever a conversation as a soliloquy. 'Come in,' while he was unwinding after the show. Whoever was there, whoever was with him, he'd just wind down by talking, oddly enough. He'd reminisce about the people that he'd worked with. Jewel and Warriss, Max and Harry Nesbitt, talking about people like Morecambe and Wise and Tommy Cooper. He was in awe of those old comics, those top of the bill comics, like Ted Ray, who would go on and do fourteen minutes, top of the bill Moss Empires or whatever, and he used to say they could do it in fourteen minutes. 'They didn't have to batter the audience into submission like I do, they could do it. They could score in fourteen minutes and get off.' He admired that, but he outlived and outgrew that whole era.

8

Dodd not go gentle...

'I wheeze. When I walk down the street, people think I'm following them with an accordion.'

Throughout his career, Dodd had given almost the same interview, no matter what questions he was asked. On chat shows, he had an act, every bit as venerable as some of the jokes he told on stage. The story of seeing the advertisement in *The Wizard*, the tale of riding his bike with his eyes shut, a namecheck for the influence of Arthur Askey. Dodd's eyeline in interviews was telling. Early on, instead of looking at the interviewer, he would hunt around for the red light and address his answers to the camera. It was a performance.

In 2012, on Radio 3's *Night Waves*, Matthew Sweet brought up some points about Dodd's manner. Was his hold over audiences a form of Stockholm Syndrome, the phenomenon where hostages begin to like their captors? Was it a control thing? Dodd bridled. 'Not controlling. Entertaining. People don't come to the theatre to be controlled,' he said, not entirely convincingly, given his private admissions that he did indeed love to be in control.

With regard to Stockholm Syndrome, Dodd said: 'You went too deep now. You're going very, very deep. You're using other psychological terms.' It's a little rich to hear Dodd, who analysed his effect on audiences so minutely, and read psychological texts avidly, accusing Sweet of going 'too deep'. Listening with a little knowledge of Dodd's interests makes it sound like he feels Sweet hasn't gone too deep, but instead has got too close to the truth, something to be avoided not because there was anything to hide, but because Dodd felt it was letting light in upon magic. All through his career, he practised the art of concealing the art, and he was not alone among comedians in deflecting. Anyone asking a question that looked likely to get Dodd off script would be disarmed with a joke.

Director Ashtar Al Khirsan was one of the very few to get Dodd away from his script when she made a documentary about the comedian for the BBC's arts strand, *Arena*, in 2007. Speaking to him in dressing rooms before and after shows, being with him as he browsed in bookshops, following him through the streets of Liverpool as people stopped him for autographs and pictures, the impression that comes across is that Dodd had become comfortable with Al Khirsan and her crew. If it is a performance, it is good, subtle and understated, and an accurate picture of what Dodd was like 'off', or as 'off' as he ever managed.

'I made a film about Eric Sykes and we actually had twelve chat show versions of him explaining why there was no glass in the glasses,' says Anthony Wall, series editor of *Arena* since 1985. 'We actually cut them all together into just one straight-forward story that didn't deviate from any of the individual pieces. That is, I think, another self-protective thing. People are expecting you to be funny so you go out pat. I think Ashtar did break through that. She really, really liked him and he trusted her.'[1]

Al Khirsan had worked with Dodd in 2003 when she directed a two-part special for BBC1 with Bob Monkhouse called *Behind the Laughter*. When she began working on *Arena* two years later, she suggested a film about Dodd. Recalling their first encounter, Al Khirsan says:

> I thought 'Oooh, he's smart' and very articulate. He was a complete surprise to me when I met him. When I was younger, I thought, 'Oh they're all misogynists, these people, these kind of comics' and a lot of them are, but I honestly don't think Ken was like that at all. He was not what I was expecting. He spoke about comedy in a way that had a lyrical quality to it, which I thought was really interesting and really revealing and it just resonated with me really, because although he was a gag man, he understood the craft and the art. I knew that he was interesting, and that there was a film to be made that was somehow a bit more intimate, a bit closer to him.[2]

'They're not necessarily the things we're best known for, but Eric Sykes, Charlie Drake, Max Bygraves, all that stuff is so important to me, crossing over into Sellers,' says the

Cambridge graduate Wall of *Arena*'s occasional forays into comedy history. 'I grew up in a sort of working class-y sort of environment, we'd watch *Sunday Night at the London Palladium* every week. It's not like it's something I've had to come to later in life.'

As for Dodd, Wall admits that he had 'always had somewhat of an ambivalent attitude to him... the fact that he did go on for ages [and] to someone of my generation, [I was] not overly amused by keeping The Beatles off the number one spot.' However, any such resistance was overridden by 'what I've always felt about those people is that they are the ones who have the true social history of Britain at their disposal, because they saw it, they lived it, they lived amongst it. I thought, "Anyone who's been around that long and done what he's done is going to be really, really interesting."'

A meeting was arranged at the Charlotte Street Hotel in London. 'He obviously just wanted to check us out,' Wall says. 'We seemed to get on pretty well. He'd obviously got a lot to say, he was interesting and he was very funny. What I didn't realize was the extent to which he was quite an intellectual. The commitment to the study of the whole thing. I remember thinking that he could actually have been an academic.'

Sensing that Dodd 'liked the idea' of 'someone from a posh arts programme' taking him seriously, Wall notes that the off-stage Dodd was 'more thoughtful' but that 'there wasn't that much difference', with gags rising to the surface at every turn. Wall sensed that, like many comedy greats, Dodd was always thinking in terms of jokes, and recalls an encounter with Bob Monkhouse. 'A fire engine went past the window and he rushed to the window, turned and said, "I've got to tell you. I just can't not. I've got to tell you. I've now got twenty-five jokes about fire engines in my head. I can't stop it. You know we phone each other up, you know? You know we phone each other up, because I'm not the only one who's got this problem."'

There is a sequence in the film that illuminates the difference between the gagsmith and the thinker. 'Sometimes you'd like to think very seriously about something, and jokes keep popping into your head, so you have to learn how to control it,' he tells Al Khirsan, before going on to explain his internal monologue. '"That's all for now, thank you. That's quite enough. Kenny, go to your room." He goes there. "Kenneth, you can come out now" and you start thinking about something serious then. There's two or three people in here, I think. Two or three personalities. Two or three characters. Two or three strong personalities who would like to be heard. I think there's the show business Ken Dodd, I think there's a thinking Ken Dodd and hopefully there's an amusing Ken Dodd. I hope so, anyway. One who can see the funny side.'[3]

Wall knew how private Dodd was and that the level of access Al Khirsan had achieved was unprecedented. 'I think this is the trust factor, isn't it?' he says. 'I feel very pleased about that in that sense. I'm pretty sure he was pleased with the film.' The filming took place over 'three months, something like that', explains Al Khirsan. 'I went to various gigs around the country, and towards the end of the shoot he was in a residency in Blackpool, at the Grand, every Sunday, so I would go up every Sunday for a good month or so.' Al Khirsan found that the best material emerged the longer she spent with Dodd and Anne:

> I did a sit-down interview with him and I don't think I used any of it in the end, because I'd heard a lot of it before and I didn't want to use anything that I'd heard before, but you do need the luxury of time to be able to get that, to build the relationship with somebody, to get that on camera. He would get annoyed with me, because I was always there. It was in a jokey, but it wasn't really jokey, way. It is irritating having somebody around, and I am irritating, because I am always there in the background. That's part of what you do when you make those kinds of documentaries. He gave me the stock answers to begin with in the first sit-down interview, but you know after that, when you're around people just sort of forget you're there.
>
> I remember him saying to me, 'Why are you always trying to get inside my brain? Why are you always trying to do that?' It was just me and him, and I was standing at his dressing table, just putting on his make-up or something, and I said, 'Ken, I really want to know what's going on inside there.' He said to me, 'Look, Ashtar, there's only two things that you need to know about me. I'm afraid of women and I'm obsessed with money.' I said, 'Will you say that on camera?' and he said, 'No, absolutely not,' and that was it. And I loved him even more after that, really. I don't think he was afraid of women. If he'd been afraid of women, he wouldn't have gone for such strong women in his life.

The building of the 'trust factor' was noted by comedy historian and photographer Andy Hollingworth, who photographed Dodd on four occasions between 1996 and 2003, the final session resulting in a picture that seems to capture both Dodd himself in all his facets and at the same time the whole history of variety:

I looked at the photographs from the first time I photographed him, which was at the Civic Theatre in Barnsley, and he's totally in control. Absolutely in control. He's doing all sorts. He's lifting his leg, he's in front of the curtain and he's waving his Doddy stick, but it took me another seven years for me take that picture which I am pleased with, and say something, rather than Ken just rolling through his poses, and being in control. I do remember him saying 'Oooh, that's jolly close' and I was working on a Rollei with a close-up lens, so I'm probably two feet away from him. He knows. I did hear that other people had sent him the picture and he liked it. He would never have said that to me, I don't think.[4]

From the *Arena* documentary, Wall is particularly proud of the sequence where Dodd returns to the Picton reading room where he spent so many hours as a boy, studying laughter. Wall says: 'If you didn't know he was a comedian at that time, and hadn't been talking about something else, it might have looked more like a film that had been made about Ewan McColl, you know. It was very important to have that kind of film made about him as a testament, which will stand there.'[5]

There was no mention in the *Arena* film of the low points in Dodd's life, like the death of Anita or the tax trial, but Wall explains that this would not have been the *Arena* way. 'Unless the personal life is inextricably wound up with what's been written about, painted or performed or whatever, we're not doing it,' he says. 'That's pretty much axiomatic with us.' There was also no mention of Anne, only a couple of shots where she was visible at Dodd's side. 'My vague memory is that was what she wanted,' says Wall. 'It was about him and not his personal life.' Similarly, in 1965, when *The People* ran a feature about Dodd and Anita, it was noted that 'She prefers to remain in the background', with Dodd declaring, 'I speak for her.'[6]

One of the recurring themes in Dodd's life was the lack of time available for certain things, despite the abundance of time he allotted to his great obsession, comedy. He claimed there was never time to get his hair cut ('Short back and sides, and a little off the shoulders') or to marry Anita or Anne. He also delayed his initiation into the Grand Order of Water Rats* for over forty years. 'It was a very special afternoon as he was nominated in the late Sixties and we had to wait till November 2011 for him to officially come in,' comedian Jeff Stevenson recalls. 'He was shown round the packed room and intro-duced to his brother rats. They came to me and mentioned my name and Ken said "Young Jeff". I was 50. We all fell about laughing.'[7]

Stevenson had met Dodd on several previous occasions,

---

* The Grand Order of Water Rats is a charitable organization estab-lished by music hall performers in 1889.

including a dinner where Stevenson was performing. 'I had a gag he liked. It was, "I've got a strange ambition. I would like to be a coroner for ten minutes. I'd like them to bring in a traffic warden who's still breathing. I would survey the body and if the traffic warden says, 'I'm still breathing', I'll say, 'I'm sorry, I've already started the paper work.'" Doddy did it on TV, and I took it as the biggest compliment that he'd 'borrowed' it from me, but weeks later someone accused me of stealing it from Ken.'

In January 2016, Ken Dodd made an appearance as a panellist on BBC Radio 4's *Museum of Curiosity*, then in its eighth series. Although Dodd's archive shows were doing good business for BBC Radio 4 Extra, this was his first involvement in an all-new radio comedy production since the *Ken Dodd's Comedy Club* series had finished on Radio 2 in July 1994.

The Museum of Curiosity follows a loose format that allows scientists, authors, comedians and other experts to talk about their enthusiasms, each panellist being required to bring along an object or, quite often, a concept, for inclusion in the museum's collection. Host John Lloyd, a comedy producer of distinction and a long-time admirer of Dodd, observes that the comics like to show off a little in intellectual company, while the academics like to come across as funny.

'I think the comics are usually keen to show off that they aren't just jokesmiths,' he says. 'Obviously, no comic is. If you're bright enough to be a stand-up, you're very bright indeed. Stand-up comics who are any good are among the cleverest people in the country. There's no question about it. Arthur Koestler wrote a whole book about this and how creative comedy and creative science are very similar. It's looking at the world in a surprising way and making up new constructions.'

For Dodd's visit to *The Museum*, he was paired with historian Greg Jenner and mathematician Dr Hannah Fry, who contributed the US prohibition law and the mathematical formula for a perfect marriage respectively. Dodd's contribution was an old favourite subject of his, the 'chuckle muscle', specifically the one owned by William Shakespeare, whom Dodd referred to once again as 'a wonderful scriptwriter'.[8] Not the greatest playwright in history, but a scriptwriter, although given Dodd's relationship with Eddie Braben, this can be read as high praise indeed. 'He had a wonderful, almost unbelievable insight into human beings, into their minds,' Dodd explained. Of course, Shakespeare and Dodd both enjoyed good honest vulgarity and mentioning the 'chuckle muscle' always gave Dodd a chance to indulge: 'If you exercise your chuckle muscle every day, you will always stay young and healthy. If you don't use it, it dries up and drops off.'

The booking was a chance for Dodd to dust off some of his greatest hits in the guise of exercise. Lloyd had direct experience of how the old boy could appeal to younger audiences. 'When my son Harry was a teenager, he came into my office in the school holidays and said, "Dad, have you heard of a stand-up called Ken?"' says Lloyd. 'I said "Ken is a very old-fashioned name", and he said, "He's absolutely brilliant." It was *An Audience with Ken Dodd*, and Harry was absolutely in stitches.'

Dodd was given a minute in which he had to score 'seven titters', with Museum 'curator' Sarah Millican adjudicating.

Opening with his trusty standby about cucumbers and Martians, Dodd hits the target with ease. Along the way he covers seaside B&Bs – 'Mrs Digger's dignified digs, no dogs, 30 shillings a week all in, use of cruet... She says "You'll have to make your own bed, here's a hammer and nails"... I looked under the bed and there was a mousetrap with a fish in it. I told the landlady, and she said "I forgot to tell you, the room's damp"... For tea, you've got a special pork pie with an egg through the middle. Some hens are clever, aren't they?'

Dodd goes down well, despite his routine being resolutely stuck in 1954, the year he turned professional. There is no acknowledgement that holidays have changed. No mention of going overseas. No attempts to update the gags with references to Airbnbs. In a 2012 radio interview, Matthew Sweet suggested that 'much of the act alludes to things that are rooted in a world that has slightly passed... jokes about milkmen, rent collectors, coalmen.' Dodd replied: 'You have to talk about things that people know about. You have to talk about well-worn concepts.' When Sweet said that these concepts weren't so well known to younger audiences, Dodd laughed and admitted that it was because of his age. Sweet was right but in a way, it didn't matter. At 6.30 p.m. on Radio 4 in 2016, Dodd – always more a Light Programme Sunday lunchtime turn – is an anachronism but he still goes down a storm. Maybe he goes down so well precisely because he is a man out of time. Possibly a man out of space – a gleeful alien sent to Earth in the 1950s to take it over with jokes. The gags still work, because they're rooted in bathos, steeped in absurdity and delivered with brio. They work for all ages because Dodd supplies the context. Indeed, by 2016, Dodd was the context.

As old as the jokes are, Millican laughs generously but some who were at the recording speak of a distinct off-mic *froideur* between her and Dodd, recalling her taking exception to some comments that came across as patronizing and sexist. Listening to the recording, the only hint of an edge comes when Millican and Dodd discuss the perfect condition for audiences, with reference to alcohol and Jenner's donation to the museum:

Millican: Comedy seems to work better if the audience are well-oiled. Do you agree with that?

Dodd: No. I think it slows your mind down. That's why you shouldn't drink and drive. That's why you shouldn't drink and propose marriage.

Millican: Doesn't it help people lose their inhibitions?

Dodd: You can lower your inhibitions with a good strong cup of tea, I think. [...] A drunken audience is awful. I like an audience to know what they're thinking.

Millican: And full of tea.

Dodd: Not full of, because...

Millican: Then they'll be going to the loo all the time. I've not thought this through, have I?

Dodd: You can't fight nature.

Millican: So, full of tea, but on commodes. The ideal audience.

The commode line gets a woof of approval from the audience and in the hubbub, Dodd says something indistinct that also gets a laugh, suggesting that it was accompanied by a visual element. There is a faint sense that Dodd doesn't like being 'topped' by anyone, and it may be that he is doubly put out by a woman doing it.

Perhaps, though, this is unfair. 'He embodied some kind of notion of very old-fashioned values and traditions, but Ken went for really strong women,' says film-maker Ashtar Al Khirsan. 'He really liked strong women. Anne is a highly intelligent, very, very cultured, well-read woman, who gave as good as she got. She's a fantastic person, really. The fact that he'd gone for somebody like her and clearly Anita, from the way that Ken described her, was another very strong woman, it really, really endeared me to him. This is somebody who is interested in his equals.'[9]

In reflecting on this episode, Lloyd notes the nature of the comedy business and the massive age gap between Dodd and Millican. 'Professional comedians are about the most competitive people I know, really. What we like to do is mix up, you know, senior people who are often in their seventies and eighties. People who are National Treasures. Cricket commentators and explorers and so on, and they haven't really caught up, you know, the way you don't speak to young feminist comics, like "My dear" or "Girls do this". So, there's a little bit of that, you know. I'm always in the middle on these things. Be a bit forgiving. It's not impertinent. It's just the way that people spoke to each other, the language they used is different. On the other hand, I don't know. I'm probably on the dinosaur edge of things.'[10]

Although he was of a different era, Doddy kept a keen eye

on the comedy scene to the very end and was quick to praise younger comedians who appealed to him. He was always proud of his part in the rise to fame of Joe Pasquale, who won a 1987 edition of *New Faces*, on which Dodd was a judge. In a 1992 television interview with Michael Billington, Dodd came out very strongly as an admirer of Vic Reeves and Bob Mortimer as practitioners of what he described as 'whimsy'. 'He has a table full of odd objects,' Dodd explained. 'He has a man coming on with a paper bag over his head and a stick. There are no jokes, but it's just lovely, beautiful whimsy.'

Dodd also had a great appreciation for good situation comedy from both sides of the Atlantic. Ashtar Al Khirsan recalls a pleasing discovery she made on visiting Thomas Lane during the making of her *Arena* film. 'His favourite television programme was *Frasier*. He used to love the wit. I remember sitting in his house at Knotty Ash and it was on in the morning. He loved it. He thought it was brilliant. Which is a mark of, I think, his smartness.'[11]

In Dodd's later years, there were some changes in his manner. At some point, his real wayward teeth were replaced with a far less unruly false set, but it is a tribute to the skill of his dentists and to the enduring memory of the originals that the absence of his trademark gnashers is barely noticeable until it is pointed out. Even after their removal, the teeth were implicit. The difference between on-stage and off-stage became more marked. When not performing, he seemed increasingly frail. Nothing more than could be expected from a man of his years, but some way from the vim and vigour of his younger self. In front of an audience, though, Dr Theatre provided a rejuvenating tonic and the years fell away. The shows got a little shorter but not by much.

Danny Baker remembers the figure cut by Dodd when they met again in January 2017 at the National Television Awards at the O2 Arena ('By Jove, what a magnificent shed'), where Dodd was presenting the award for best comedy programme to the situation comedy *Mrs Brown's Boys*. Baker recounts:

> He was in the corridor backstage, not exactly holding court, but being rightly feted. I remember how absent he looked even though he was responding as best he could to the amount of people wanting selfies. He was not so much confused as exhausted. I said hello but he didn't either recognize or remember me. I got to tell him how much I enjoy his records, something largely forgotten now. I think I'd even played 'Eight by Ten' and 'They Didn't Believe Me' that very day, unaware he was going to be at the function. He thanked me distractedly a few times and then said, 'I still do songs in the act' and took from his pocket a flyer for, I think, the Wimbledon Theatre, where he was playing later that month. 'That's the number there for the tickets.' Then he was pulled away to have his picture taken with some of the *Strictly* people.

In presenting the award, Dodd got the envelope containing the winner's name upside down, a detail seized upon by the tabloids. Dodd's genuine laugh when he turns the paper over indicates that it was indeed a mistake and not a deliberate bit of business.

The NTA appearance came shortly after it had been announced that Dodd was to become Sir Ken in the Queen's New Year's Honours list. While high-achieving sportspeople routinely become knights and dames in their thirties,* and rock stars get their high-level gongs in their fifties and sixties,† variety entertainers and comedians have to wait until their eighties, if ever. Few were more aware of the strange relativity of standards than Bruce Forsyth, who was eighty-three before he got his knighthood in 2011, having spent several years musing to friends on why Tom Jones had got his at a mere sixty-six.

In Dodd's case, the tax trial, even though he was acquitted, did not help matters and it is possible that his closeness to Margaret Thatcher worked against him rather than in his favour. However, on the ninth nomination, he was judged worthy of a K. The previous nominations had mostly come from those who had worked with Dodd on charitable causes, and included strong support from former prime minister Gordon Brown, who had been lobbied by Norma Hornby of the Canal Boat Adventure Project, a charity for deprived children.

When it came to Dodd's investiture in March, at which Prince William, Duke of Cambridge, officiated, salvers of dainty circular jam butties were added to the ceremonial buffet. Dodd promised to repay the favour if the Duke ever paid a visit to Knotty Ash.

---

* Dame Kelly Holmes was thirty-four and Sir Steve Redgrave was thirty-eight.

† Sir Mick Jagger was fifty-eight and Sir Elton John was fifty.

For the rest of the year it was business as usual. In June, Dodd took the *Happiness Show* back to the Hay Festival as part of its thirtieth anniversary programme. Another notable date in the work diary was Dodd's traditional annual home-town Christmas show at the Philharmonic Hall. At the start of December, though, the venue announced that the show had been cancelled due to unforeseen circumstances. Given that Dodd hardly ever cancelled shows – his sudden hernia operation in 2007 having resulted in only one cancellation and a couple of postponements, with the others occurring after the deaths of Anita and his parents – some fans worried for his health. Doddy was quick to allay their fears. The show would take place on the scheduled date in the 1350-seat theatre auditorium in the Echo Arena complex.

The show was a roaring success. 'The stamina involved in doing shows like this throughout the year would exhaust a performer a third of his age... A Ken Dodd show is an event everyone should have at least once in their life,' wrote the *Liverpool Echo*'s Jamie McLoughlin, noting that Dodd received a standing ovation, and saying 'never underestimate how difficult that is to summon from a crowd you've held captive for the best part of five hours'.[12]

The Philharmonic cancellation had genuinely been due to an issue with the venue, but barely a fortnight after the show came the worrying news that Dodd had been hospitalized with a severe chest infection. Dodd had already been feeling unwell before the gig but insisted that the show had to go on. 'I thought I was Mr Happiness,' he said later, 'but then, all of a sudden, just before Christmas, bang.' After the show, his condition worsened and when he began to have trouble breathing, he was rushed to hospital. Doctors managed to rule out flu but whatever the cause, chest infections are a serious matter for a nonagenarian. A spokesman, probably his long-serving publicist Robert Holmes, told the press that Dodd was being treated with antibiotics and was expected to make a recovery.

The message on social media was different and hoax stories of Dodd's demise began to spread. When the *Liverpool Echo*'s Paddy Shennan visited Dodd in Broadgreen Hospital, he was able to relay a message to the hoaxers: 'They are horrible monsters. I don't think they are human beings. I think they are evil, but I think they will get theirs. I can tell you now, there is a God, and He will punish them.'[13] Finally, six weeks after he was admitted to hospital, came the news that everyone had been waiting for. Doddy was well enough to go home. Flanked by children in Diddymen costumes, he gave a performance from his wheelchair for the waiting press in the foyer of the hospital, praising the NHS and in particular the miracle qualities of the hospital porridge. He vowed to be back on the stage as soon as he could. 'I'll teach my legs to work again, because they've forgotten, you know. Once I've recovered myself, I'll get back to doing the job, which is the only job I've ever had...While I was in here I wrote some new jokes, so it should be alright.'[14]

Doddy never returned to work. On Saturday, 10 March 2018, it was announced that all Dodd's forthcoming shows up to June had been cancelled. The official line was that he was 'doing OK' but needed time to convalesce before making his comeback, but in private, the end was drawing near. The day before, Friday, the registrar visited Thomas Lane and Sir Ken and Anne were married in the presence of close friends Peter and Colette Rogan and Reverend Julia Jesson, the vicar of St John's, who blessed the rings after the civil ceremony. On Sunday, 11 March, Doddy died peacefully in the home he'd lived in since childhood.

The lights were dimmed at the London Palladium as a mark of respect. Among the first to pay tribute was Doddy's friend, *Royle Family* star Ricky Tomlinson, nicknamed 'Rickety' by the comedian. Tomlinson said that they had been 'great mates' and that 'everyone loved and adored' Dodd. This might sound like a standard show business tribute but it speaks volumes. Dodd was a true-blue Conservative all his life and Tomlinson is the exact opposite, and yet the pair held each other in immense personal regard. Liverpool is not, by inclination, a Tory heartland but very few on Merseyside seemed to mind Dodd's leanings. John Martin, a Liverpool-based comic and a regular scriptwriter for Doddy, said the news was a shock, as they had been talking on the telephone about material for the comedian's big comeback show.

In addition to the tributes from friends in the business, there were memories from Dodd's audiences, including Veronica Yorke of Horwich near Bolton, described by her local newspaper as a 'Ken Dodd super-fan'. Arthur Dodd had delivered coal to Yorke's mother's family in West Derby, and Veronica had first met Dodd when she was fifteen. After that, she attended as many shows as she could and served as a 'plant' for gags. 'There was one routine where Ken would come on in a wig and ask who he looked like. I'd have to count a few seconds in my head and shout out 'Shergar!'... [he was] one of the warmest, kindest gentlemen you could wish to meet.'[15]

Dodd's funeral took place at Liverpool's Anglican cathedral on Wednesday, 28 March, with 2700 inside and hundreds more outside in the rain watching the ceremony on large screens. Friends from the business, including Tomlinson, Roy Hudd and Jimmy Tarbuck, sat alongside the Liverpudlians who greeted Dodd every day when he went out and about in the city.

The cortège had left Thomas Lane with Doddy's coffin in a carriage pulled by plumed horses, and processed through the city to be greeted at the cathedral by a brass band playing 'Tears' and 'Happiness'. It was a sad occasion but also a celebration of a man who'd lived a long, contented life largely on his own terms, and in the process brought joy to millions. This wasn't just the death of a man. It was the end of an era in light entertainment.

9
Epilogue

'A man retires when he stops doing what he doesn't want to do and starts doing what he does want to do. And I'm doing what I do want to do.'

Although Doddy emerged from the hospital adamant that he'd be returning to the stage, and indeed Anne had equipped the house for convalescence, including the installation of a stair lift, there is an impression that he had an inkling he might not make it. Dodd wanted to set his affairs in order, not least by marrying Anne.

There were other loose ends to be tied up. During their long association, he'd encouraged Andy Eastwood to add jokes into his act and given him the material. He'd also been brutal in the notes he gave Eastwood after the performance: 'It was just a nightmare to have to do it, really. He wanted to coax me into doing gags, and in fact he always told me I couldn't tell gags. He said I was useless at telling gags.'[1] Then, when Dodd was in hospital, comedian Don Reid, a mutual friend, went to visit and came back with a message from the patient. 'Ken asked Don to tell me to keep on telling the gags and that I'd do them well. Isn't it funny? For someone who'd tell me I couldn't do it, he sent me this message. "Keep telling my gags, you'll do them really well." And that's the last I ever heard from him.'[2]

It seems likely that Dodd had been using elements of reverse psychology to goad Eastwood into doing better and trying harder, but couldn't bear dying with his young protégé thinking he'd meant it. Certainly, there are no signs of rancour in Eastwood's obvious affection for his mentor, and affection on a city-wide scale was evident on the day of Dodd's funeral. 'Ken stayed,' David Hamilton rationalizes. 'I think Cilla became a sort of arch-Liverpudlian, and towards the end, that accent I don't think anybody believed. She was playing up to it. The great thing about Ken was that he was almost the only one who never left. The Beatles went, Cilla went, everybody went, Ken remained. They just absolutely adored him. The crowds at the funeral. One of the interesting things, you know the old saying "A prophet is without honour in his own country", not Ken. Ken was adored in his own back yard. Who's going to turn up at a bingo hall or a supermarket to see somebody they can see out shopping in their own time? But they still did.'[3]

Even people who had professional grievances with Dodd, like former writer Dave Dutton, still admired him as a comedian.

He was a hero when I was a kid. And he was still a hero on stage to me, because he was irreplaceable. The guy was magic. When you can make people laugh by coming out with *Beano* jokes, and have grown men with tears in their eyes, there's some magic going on and skill involved there that not a lot of people, well, I don't know anybody else who could do it. Tommy Cooper, he had the same facility with childish jokes, but Doddy, it was the way he built them up until people were pounding in their seats begging him to stop. The amount of material he put in a performance. No other act in the country or in the history of show business I think had his range. [4]

In February 2019, it was announced that Dodd had left an estate worth £27.7 million. The will he had written years before had been superseded by his marriage to Anne two days before his death, with the result that she inherited everything. Almost immediately after Dodd's death, the accountancy trade press had noted that marrying Anne had avoided 40 per cent inheritance tax, giving Dodd a 'last laugh' at the taxman. The mainstream press caught up with this angle in the coverage of the legacy.

However, Lady Dodd was quick to state that she would be honouring the original will in full, carrying out Sir Ken's wishes, which include restoring the clock at their local church, St John's, where Dodd was a regular worshipper, and providing funds for numerous charities that he had supported. One of these is Shakespeare North, a Prescot-based trust aiming to promote Shakespeare's work and the Tudor heritage of Merseyside.

Apart from the tax trial and the losses of his parents, siblings and Anita, Dodd's life was full of happiness. Early on in his life, he knew what he wanted to do and who he wanted to be. He wanted to be a comedian. Having decided that, he achieved it with a notable lack of struggle. He achieved and maintained contentment.

'He was just a very positive bloke,' says Anthony Wall. 'I think the fact that he never left Knotty Ash... suggested a remarkable degree of stability for a comedian, who one thinks of as being not necessarily that way. I always imagined Knotty Ash was some kind of working-class hellhole, but of course it turns out to be a rather nice suburban area. There was an air of contentment. He was a content man who wasn't paralyzed by his talent. As far as I know, he never tried to play Las Vegas. I think he felt, "My home is with these people and these places that I play."'

Everything took second place to comedy. It always had. Many have wondered if that wasn't hurtful to both Anita and Anne, the fiancées that Dodd was always 'too busy' to marry. However, this is perhaps to misunderstand the nature of the relationships. Both loved and were loved by Dodd. The sentimentality of his songs betrays a romantic soul. Just as important, though, both Anita and Anne loved the business as much as Doddy did. These were double acts. 'Both his fiancées were incredibly devoted to him, he had that incredible devotion from them,' says David Hamilton.

In his early days, Anita spurred him on, telling him which bits of his act to develop and which bits to sideline. As for marriage, Anita's brother, Bill Boutin, explained the situation as he saw it in 1965: 'At first, they put it off because Ken felt he ought to establish himself. He said he had nothing to offer a wife. But he's very ambitious and is never satisfied. As soon as he has fulfilled one success, he's looking for the next step to climb.'[5]

Later on, it was Anne who put the bills together for Dodd's shows, booked the musicians, and made sure the props and sound systems were up to spec. The fact that Anne had begun as a dancer, but later worked in administration, meant that she had both business experience and show business experience. Both women were in the background but their quiet strength was vital to all of Dodd's achievements. For all of his talk of Gestalt psychology and his love of control, Anne was the boss, making it so that all Doddy had to worry about was his act. 'Anne was absolutely integral,' says Ashtar Al Khirsan. 'She was part of Ken Dodd. She's a very smart, well-read woman. A strong character. A strong woman. Didn't take any nonsense from him.'

Did he get away with the crime of the century? There is a strong possibility that without the services of George Carman QC and the help of a hometown jury, this story could have had a very different ending, with Dodd's career over in 1989, living out his final years in disgrace. And yet his obsession with comedy was so complete and total that it is easy to imagine he regarded the organization of his finances as an unimportant detail right up to the moment when it suddenly mattered a great deal.

The way in which Doddy valued his privacy provoked interest in what he was like 'off'. 'He kept saying to me, "Why are you always trying to lift the curtain?" says Al Khirsan. 'He said, "Don't you understand people really like the curtain?

They don't want to see behind the curtain." I suppose I was always trying to burrow around, and to get inside his brain.'[6]

The truth was that behind the curtain, there was a man who enjoyed being with family and close friends. Show business parties weren't for him. 'He adored his family,' says Al Khirsan. 'I met his brother. When I spoke to him on the phone after I'd made the film and I kept in touch with him, the first thing he would say to me was, "How's your mother? How are your family?" Always. That was very, very important to him. He adored his parents, absolutely adored his parents. I think he'd had quite a lot of stability in his life. I don't think, like many comedians, he'd come from a family that was loveless or dysfunctional. I don't think there's much personal darkness there.'[7]

Andy Eastwood has a similar story to tell. 'He used to advise me, "There's a lot more to life than doing shows. Look after your mum, look after your family," all that kind of thing. He was always hammering that message home. There's more to life than doing shows. He used to mention his grandad, his dad, all in the act. There was a lot of warmth about him that was, I think, quite hidden to some people.'[8]

If a gig was within a hundred miles of Liverpool, he, Anne and the poodle would head home after the show and pull up the drawbridge. He was a man of complexity who maintained a simple life. There was no dark side. He didn't pretend to be full of fun and then, the moment he was off-stage, become a snarling misanthrope, unlike some beloved performers. Off-stage, Dodd was still funny, but more of a gently spoken wit than a manic gag machine.

Maybe the boy ventriloquist remained that throughout his career. Perhaps the on-stage Ken Dodd was a ventriloquial figure, to be put back in his box at the end of the night. Bob Monkhouse observed that some performers 'send a character on stage. A persona they've invented, that they can project on stage, they will hide behind that. Or they will wear a disguise, a funny costume.' Monkhouse believed that Doddy's 'entire presentation has been a disguise':

> So Doddy sends out a madman on the stage, a wonderful organized clever spinning dervish of a madman that he has invested with life, and he animates him, and he keeps him alive as long as it gives him pleasure and the audience is laughing, and he'll make them laugh longer than they ever expected. When he comes off, I think he dies a little death and becomes once again the ordinary bloke that Kenneth Dodd is in real life. He's not an exciting person like the chap on stage. He's a quieter man. He's just as sweetly natured, but he's waiting to go back on. I think he's waiting to go back on. I think everything off stage is an interval.

Dodd's big ambition was to play every theatre in the British Isles, a touring comedy version of the old actor-managers. If he hadn't achieved it by the end of his long career, that was only because new venues had popped up. Had he been immortal, he, Anne and the poodle would have driven there eventually. Now, though, the interval is permanent. In some ways, however, Doddy is immortal. People still talk with reverence of Dan Leno and Sir George Robey, and they left almost no legacy other than fading memories and a handful of crackly recordings.

Now that we're past the days of television companies reusing old video tapes, the *Audience with Ken Dodd* shows will last forever, and chances are the humour within them will too. 'Happiness' and 'Tears' will keep turning up on the radio. Radio 4 Extra will keep repeating the surviving shows from the 1960s. He'll be commemorated every time the bells ring at St John the Evangelist in Knotty Ash.

Moreover, the considerable indentation he made in the British way of life will be impossible to erase. There will be references to 'Ken Dodd' hair and teeth for years, decades, possibly centuries to come. He never wrote the great textbook on comedy that he always promised, but he could only have provided insight and guidance, not a sure-fire manual on how to be a great comic. Even he couldn't be sure which gags would work best. He couldn't teach anyone to be Ken Dodd. There was, and will ever be, only one of those.

Doddology

The following is an extensive, but not exhaustive, listing of Sir Ken Dodd's broadcast appearances from 1954 to 1990, and of his live work in variety between 1952 and 1960. A full listing of his live work would be a whole other highly useful book, but the aim here is to give a flavour of the world in which Dodd cut his prominent teeth.

Radio appearances

LP = BBC Light Programme
HS = BBC Home Service
HS(N) = BBC North of England Home Service
R1/2 = BBC Radio 1 & 2 combined
R2 = BBC Radio 2
R3 = BBC Radio 3
R4 = BBC Radio 4
R4(N) = BBC Radio 4 (northern transmitters only)

Starring vehicles

Northern Variety Parade presents Ken Dodd in 'What a Life'

HS, Tuesday, 16 April 1957, 1900–1930

Recorded: Playhouse Theatre, Manchester, Sunday, 31 March 1957.

KD, Eddie Leslie, Irene Handl, Herbert Smith, Fred Fairclough, the
    BBC Northern Dance Orchestra conducted by Alyn Ainsworth.

Writers: James Casey and Frank Roscoe.

Producer: James Casey.

Fee: 25 guineas.

It's Great to Be Young

Series 1:

HS(N), 2 October–6 November 1958

Thursdays, 1830 – 6 x 30m

Recorded: Playhouse Theatre, Manchester, Sundays 14 September–19 October 1958.

KD, Peter Goodwright ('as everyone else except...'), The Barry
    Sisters, Judith Chalmers, the BBC Northern Dance Orchestra
    conducted by Alyn Ainsworth, Jimmy Leach at the electronic
    organ.

Writers: James Casey and Frank Roscoe.

Producer: James Casey.

Five editions of this run were repeated nationally – LP, Mondays,
    2100, 9 March–6 April 1959 as a prelude to six new shows
    made especially for the network.

LP, 13 April–18 May 1959

Mondays, 2030 – 6 x 30m – repeated HS(N), Tuesdays, 1900

Recorded: Playhouse Theatre, Manchester, Sundays 15 and 29 March, 12 April–3 May.

KD, Peter Goodwright ('as everyone else except...'), Leonard Williams, The Barry Sisters, Judith Chalmers, the BBC Northern Dance Orchestra conducted by Alyn Ainsworth, Jimmy Leach at the electronic organ.

Writers: James Casey and Frank Roscoe.

Producer: James Casey.

Series 2:

LP, 14 November 1960–2 January 1961

Mondays, 2000 – 8 x 30m

Recorded: Playhouse Theatre, Manchester, Sundays.

KD, Peter Goodwright, Leonard Williams, Judith Chalmers, Karal Gardner, Jimmy Goldie, The Littlewood Songsters, the BBC Northern Dance Orchestra conducted by Bernard Herrmann (Tommy Watt on shows 3, 7 and 8).

Writers: James Casey, Frank Roscoe and Eddie Braben.

Producer: James Casey.

Star Parade

LP, Thursday, 18 June 1963, 2000–2030

KD, John Laurie, Judith Chalmers, Harold Berens, Cardew Robinson, The Springfields, the BBC Revue Orchestra conducted by Malcolm Lockyer.

Writers: Eddie Braben and Ken Dodd.

Producer: Eric Miller.

The Ken Dodd Show

Series 1:

LP, 29 September–3 November 1963

Sundays, 1400 – 6 x 30m – repeated Wednesdays, 2000

KD, John Laurie, Judith Chalmers, Wallas Eaton, Percy Edwards, Peter Hudson (Ray Fell in show 1), the BBC Revue Orchestra conducted by Malcolm Lockyer (shows 1–4), the BBC Variety Orchestra conducted by Paul Fenoulhet (shows 5 and 6).

Guests: Gerry and the Pacemakers (show 1 – 'How to make yourself invisible'), The Four Ramblers (show 2 – 'How to make yourself more invisible'), Edmundo Ros (show 3 – 'How to make yourself even more invisible'), The Barry Sisters (show 4 – 'How to make yourself most invisible'), Wilfrid Brambell (show 5 – 'How to wash an invisible shirt'), The Beatles (show 6 – 'A last frantic attempt to make yourself visible').

Writers: Eddie Braben and KD.

Producer: Bill Worsley.

Series 2:

LP, 24 May 1964–19 July 1964

Sundays, 1400 – 9 x 30m – repeated Wednesdays, 1931

KD, Duncan Macrae (shows 1–4), John Slater (shows 5–8), John Laurie (show 9), Wallas Eaton, Percy Edwards, Patricia Hayes, the BBC Revue Orchestra conducted by Malcolm Lockyer.

Guests: Val Doonican (show 1), The Barry Sisters (shows 2 and 8), The Bachelors (show 3), Edmundo Ros (show 4), Rosemary Squires (show 5), The Caravelles (show 6), Brian Poole and the Tremeloes (show 7), The Migil Five (show 9).

Writers: Eddie Braben and Ken Dodd.

Producer: Bill Worsley.

Series 3:

LP, 11 April–4 July 1965
Sundays, 1400 – 13 x 30m – repeated Wednesdays, 1931
KD, John Laurie, Patricia Hayes, Wallas Eaton (shows 1–4 and 13), Alan Curtis (shows 5–6, 9 and 11–12), Mike Yarwood (show 7), Graham Stark (show 8), Percy Edwards (shows 1–3, 6, 8, 10, 12 and 13), Judith Chalmers, Doddy's Diddy Orchestra conducted by Malcolm Lockyer.
Guests: The Swinging Blue Jeans (show 1), The Countrymen (show 2), The Migil Five (show 3), Brian Poole and the Tremeloes (show 4), The Searchers (show 5), The Barron Knights (show 6), The Honeys (show 7), Dave Berry and the Cruisers (show 8), Unit 4 Plus 2 (show 9), The Barry Sisters (show 10), The Yardbirds (show 11), Vince Hill (show 12), The New Faces (show 13).
Writers: Eddie Braben and Ken Dodd.
Producer: Bill Worsley.

Series 4:

LP, 12 June–17 July 1966
Sundays, 1330 – 6 x 30m – repeated Wednesdays, 2000
KD, John Laurie, Patricia Hayes, Graham Stark, Judith Chalmers, Percy Edwards (shows 2 and 6), Doddy's Diddy Orchestra conducted by Malcolm Lockyer (shows 1, 2, 4 and 6) or Paul Fenoulhet (shows 3 and 5).
Guests: Dave Berry and the Cruisers (show 1), The Honeys (show 2), The New Faces (show 3), The Barron Knights (show 4), Unit 4 Plus 2 (show 5), The Spencer Davis Group (show 6).
Writers: Eddie Braben and KD.
Producer: Bill Worsley.

Series 5:

LP, 4 December 1966–5 February 1967
Sundays, 1330 – 10 x 30m – repeated Wednesdays, 2000
KD, John Laurie, Patricia Hayes, Cardew Robinson (shows 1 and 2),
  Graham Stark (shows 3–10), Peter Goodwright (show 4), Judith
  Chalmers, the Augmented BBC Northern Dance Orchestra
  conducted by Bernard Herrmann (shows 1–3), Doddy's Diddy
  Orchestra conducted by Malcolm Lockyer (shows 7–10).
Writers: Eddie Braben and KD.
Producer: Bill Worsley.

Series 6:

R2, 19 November 1967–7 January 1968
Sundays, 1400 – 9 x 30m – repeated Wednesdays, 2000
KD, John Laurie, Patricia Hayes, Graham Stark, Judith Chalmers,
  Doddy's Diddy Orchestra directed by Geoff Alderson.
Writers: Eddie Braben and KD.
Producer: Bill Worsley.

Comedy Parade: Nobody But Doddy

LP, Thursday, 22 October 1964, 2000–2030
KD, the BBC Revue Orchestra conducted by Malcolm Lockyer.
Writers: Eddie Braben and KD.
Producer: Bill Worsley.

The Ken Dodd Experience

R2, 16 November–21 December 1969
Sundays, 1400 – 6 x 30m – repeated Monday 2045
KD, Peter Goodwright (shows 1–3, 5 and 6), Talfryn Thomas,

Colin Edwynn (shows 1 and 4), Barbara Mullaney, Mike Newman (shows 2, 3 and 5), Daphne Oxenford (shows 3–5), Jan Edwards (shows 2 and 6), John Laurie (show 6), Doddy's Diddy Orchestra directed by Geoff Alderson.

Writers: KD, Gordon Pleasant, Eddie Foxall, George Moffat, and (shows 2–6) David Nobbs.

Producer: Bobby Jaye.

Doddy's Scarborough Fair

R2, Saturday, 29 August 1970, 1201–1302

KD, Pearl Carr and Teddy Johnson, Barbara Law, Syd Francis, the BBC Northern Dance Orchestra conducted by Bernard Herrmann.

Producer: Peter Pilbeam.

Doddy's Daft Half-Hour

Series 1:

R2, 27 December 1970–14 March 1971

Sundays, 1401 – 12 x 30m – repeated Mondays, R4, 1815

KD, Peter Goodwright (shows 1–2, 5–7, 9–12), Mike Newman (shows 1 and 4), Pat Coombs, Teddy Johnson, Talfryn Thomas, Jo Manning Wilson, John Graham (shows 2–4 and 8–12), Doddy's Diddy Orchestra directed by Geoff Alderson.

Writers: KD, David McKellar, Norman Beedle, Malcolm Cameron (shows 1–3, 5–10 and 12), George Moffat (shows 1–6), Eddie Foxall (shows 4 and 5), Ron Freedman (shows 5, 8 and 11), David Macauley (show 10).

Producer: Bobby Jaye.

Series 2:

R2, 25 June–27 August 1972
Sundays, 1402 – 10 x 30m – repeated Mondays, 2002
KD, Peter Goodwright (show 1), Pat Coombs, Hugh Paddick
(shows 4–6, 8–9), Teddy Johnson (shows 1–3), Talfryn Thomas,
Jo Manning Wilson, John Graham, Wallas Eaton (show 7),
Miriam Margolyes (show 9), Roger Delgado (show 10).
Writers: KD, Malcolm Cameron, Stewart Campbell (shows 1–2
and 4–10), David McKellar (shows 1 and 2), Norman Beedle
(shows 1–3, 8–10), Peter Tonkinson (shows 3–5, 7 and 9),
Maurice Bird (shows 1, 2 and 5), Charles Sheills (shows 4 and 6),
Cyril Walker (shows 3 and 7), Dave Dutton (shows 8 and 9),
John Pye (show 9).
Producer: Bobby Jaye.

Doddy's Blackpool Bonanza

R2, Monday, 30 August 1971, 1102–1202
KD, Kenneth McKellar, Freddie and the Dreamers, Lyn Kennington,
the BBC Northern Dance Orchestra conducted by Bernard
Herrmann.
Producer: Peter Pilbeam.

Doddy's Comical Market

R2, Sunday, 31 December 1972, 1402–1430
KD, Peter Goodwright, Jo Manning Wilson, Miriam Margolyes,
Talfryn Thomas, Teddy Johnson and John Graham.
Writers: KD, Norman Beedle, Dave Dutton, Malcolm Cameron,
Maurice Bird.
Producer: Bobby Jaye.

Doddy's Oompah Show

R2, 21 July–25 August 1973
Sundays, 1202 – 6 x 60m
KD, Barbara Mullaney, Peter Wheeler, the Massed Oompahs of the
   BBC Northern Dance Orchestra directed by Alan Moorhouse.
Guests: George Chisholm, Robert Young, Candy Devine (show 1);
   Pat Mooney, David and Marianne Dalmour, Lynn Kennington
   (show 2); Adge Cutler and The Wurzels, Jacqui and Bridie, Louisa
   Jane White (show 3); The Grumbleweeds, Alan Randall, Keeley
   Ford (show 4); Rosemary Squires, Candlewick Green, Maxton
   G. Beesley (show 5); Chester Harriott, Lynn Kennington, The
   Fivepenny Piece, Maxton G. Beesley.
Producer: Peter Pilbeam.

Doddy's Comic Cuts

R2, 30 December 1973–3 February 1974
Sundays, 1402 – 6 x 30m
KD, Talfryn Thomas, Jo Manning Wilson, Michael McClain, John
   Baddeley, Gretchen Franklin (show 1), Miriam Margolyes
   (shows 2–6).
Writers: KD, Dave Dutton, Ross Edwards (shows 1 and 2), Dennis
   Berson (shows 2–6), Maurice Bird (shows 2–5), Malcolm
   Cameron (show 3), Terry Ravenscroft (shows 4 and 6), Mike
   James (show 6).
Producer: Bobby Jaye.

They Can't Touch You For It

R2, 3 August–21 September 1975
Sundays, 1402 – 8 x 30m

KD, Talfryn Thomas, Jo Manning Wilson, Miriam Margolyes (shows 1–4), Gretchen Franklin (shows 5–8), Michael McClain, John Graham (shows 1 and 3), Chris Emmett (shows 2–8).
Producer: Bobby Jaye.

Doddy's Different Show

R2, 4 October–8 November 1981
Sundays, 1330 – 6 x 30m
KD, Peter Wheeler, Talfryn Thomas, Marlene Sidaway (shows 1–3, 5 and 6), Paula Tilbrook (show 4), Peter Goodwright (show 6), Brian Fitzgerald (musical director).
Producer: James Casey.

Ken Dodd's Palace of Laughter

Series 1:

R2, 23 January–6 March 1986
Thursdays, 2200 – 8 x 30m
KD, Peter Goodwright (shows 1, 2, 4 and 8), Paula Tilbrook (shows 1, 4 and 8), Marlene Sidaway (shows 2, 3, 5–7), Sybie Jones, Simmons Brothers, Gary Anderson (shows 3 and 5), Colin Edwynn (show 6), Paul Melba (show 7), the Ken Adams Palace Band.
Venues: Wigan Little Theatre (show 1), Southport Little Theatre (show 2), Todmorden Hippodrome (show 3), Tyldesley Little Theatre (show 4), Ince Blundell Village Hall (show 5), Altrincham Garrick (show 6), Bolton Little Theatre (show 7), Blackpool Grand (show 8).
Writers: KD, John Pye, John Walker, Barry Roberts, Roy Dixon.
Producer: Ron McDonnell.

Series 2:

R2, 3 September–22 October 1987

Thursdays, 2200 – 8 x 30m

KD, Peter Goodwright (shows 1, 2 and 4–6), Paula Tilbrook (shows 1 and 3), Colin Edwynn, Sybie Jones, Michael McClain (shows 2 and 5–8), Jennifer Stanton (shows 2 and 4–8), Adam Daye (shows 2, 7 and 8), Johnny More (show 3), the Brian Fitzgerald Palace Band.

Writers: KD, John Pye, Barry Reeves, Ken Rock, Norman Beedle, Colin Brown.

Venues: Crewe Lyceum (show 1), Cheadle Hulme Chad's Theatre (show 2), Hanley Theatre Royal (show 3), Stockport Garrick (show 4), Altrincham Club Theatre (show 5), Wilmslow Guild Theatre (show 6), Northwich Harlequin (show 7), Tyldesley Little Theatre (show 8).

Ken Dodd's Easter Fayre

R2, Monday, 31 March 1986, 1300–1400

KD, Peter Goodwright, Rosemary Squires, The Wurzels, Syd Francis, The Minting Sisters, Frankie Howerd, the Brian Fitzgerald Band.

Producer: Ron McDonnell.

Ken Dodd's Christmas Cracker

R2, Thursday, 25 December 1986, 1230–1300

KD, Peter Goodwright, Sybie Jones, Moira Anderson, the Brian Fitzgerald Band.

Producer: Ron McDonnell.

Thursday, 24 December 1987, 2200–2230, R2

KD, Colin Edwynn, Sybie Jones, Michael McClain, Jennifer Stanton, the Brian Fitzgerald trio.

Writers: John Pye, Colin Brown, Ken Rock, Barry Reeves, Roy Dixon.

Producer: Mike Craig.

Monday, 25 December 1989, 1230–1400, R2

KD, Colin Edwynn, Sybie Jones, Michael McClain, Paula Tilbrook, David Ross, Brian Fitzgerald Trio.

Writers: Eddie Braben, John Pye, Norman Beedle, John Brown, Richard Jones, Jeremy Browne.

Producer: Mike Craig.

Pull the Other One

Series 1:

R2, Thursdays, 2200

22 January–12 March 1987 – 8 x 30m

David Frost (host), KD, Frank Carson, Leslie Crowther (shows 1 and 5), Mike Burton (shows 2 and 6), Bernie Clifton (shows 3 and 8), Bernard Bresslaw (shows 4 and 7).

Devised and researched by Nell Brennan and Andrew Palmer.

Producer: Edward Taylor.

Series 2:

R2, Thursdays, 2200–2230

19 May–21 July 1988 – 10 x 30m

David Frost (host), KD, Frank Carson, Bernie Clifton (shows 1, 2, 5 and 6), Alfred Marks (shows 3 and 4), Dame Hilda Bracket (shows 7 and 8), Peter Goodwright (shows 9 and 10).

Christmas special – Pull the Other Cracker

R2, Sunday, 25 December 1988, 1300–1330
David Frost (host), KD, Frank Carson, Bernie Clifton.

Series 3:

R2, Thursdays, 2200
14 December 1989–15 March 1990 – 14 x 30m
David Frost (host), KD, Frank Carson, Max Boyce (show 1), Bernie
   Clifton (shows 2–4, 11–12), Dame Hilda Bracket (shows 5–6,
   13–14), Ray Alan and Lord Charles (shows 7 and 8), Mike
   Burton (shows 9 and 10).

Series 4:

R2, Thursdays, 1900
29 November 1990–2 February 1991 – 13 x 30m
David Frost (host), KD, Frank Carson, Leslie Crowther (shows 1,
   3 and 13), Bernie Clifton (shows 2, 11 and 12), John Martin
   (shows 4, 7 and 9), Adrian Walsh (shows 5 and 6, 8 10).

Ken Dodd's Easter Parade

R2, Monday, 20 April 1987, 1300–1400
KD, Peter Goodwright Paula Tilbrook, Sybie Jones, Michael
   McClain, the Brian Fitzgerald Band.
Writers: Norman Beedle, John Pye, Barry Reeves, Ken Rock,
   Colin Brown.
Producer: Ron McDonnell.

Ken Dodd's Easter Special

R2, Monday, 4 April 1988, 1300–1400

KD, Johnny More, Paula Tilbrook, Sybie Jones, Colin Edwynn, Michael McClain, Poacher, Brian Fitzgerald.

Writers: John Pye, Colin Brown, Ken Rock, Barry Reeves.

Producer: Mike Craig.

Doddy's Green Radio Show

R2, Monday, 29 May 1989, 1305–1400

KD, Peter Goodwright, David Ross, Colin Edwynn, Sybie Jones, 'Professor' Stanley Unwin, Brian Fitzgerald (musical director).

Songs: Jeremy Browne.

Writers: Eddie Braben, Geoffrey Atkinson, John Pye, John Brown, Richard Jones, Barry Reeves, Norman Beedle, Ken Rock, Nigel Harrat, Robert Stayrt.

Producer: Mike Craig.

How Tickled I Am

R2, Monday, 28 May 1990, 1305–1400

KD, Peter Goodwright, David Ross, Colin Edwynn, Sybie Jones, Marlene Sidaway.

Writers: Eddie Braben, John Walker, Barry Reeves, Geoffrey Atkinson, John Brown, Richard Jones.

Producer: Mike Craig.

Yule Be Tickled

Tuesday, 25 December 1990, 1300–1330

KD, Peter Goodwright, Colin Edwynn, Sybie Jones, Marlene

Sidaway, David Ross, Michael McClain, the Russell Leite Children.

Producer: Mike Craig.

Guest appearances and spots

Workers' Playtime (from a canteen in Barton, Eccles)

HS, Thursday, 23 December 1954, 1225–1255

Charlie Chester, Carole Carr, KD, The Jimmy Leach Organolian Quartet, Fred Harries (piano).

Producer: Geoffrey Wheeler.

The Show Goes On

LP, Thursday, 31 March 1955, 1930–2000

Morecambe and Wise with the Kordites and the Raymond Woodhead Choir, presenting Max Miller, John Horvelle, KD, Edouin et Rachelle, the BBC Augmented Northern Variety Orchestra conducted by Alyn Ainsworth.

Recorded: 27 March 1955, Hulme Hippodrome, Manchester.

Producers: Geoffrey Wheeler and Ronnie Taylor.

The Show Goes On

LP, Thursday, 21 April 1955, 1930–2000

Morecambe and Wise with the Kordites and the Raymond Woodhead Choir, presenting Fayne and Evans, Rawicz and Landauer, KD, Pearl Carr, Martin Lukins, the BBC Augmented Northern Variety Orchestra conducted by Alyn Ainsworth.

Recorded: 17 April 1955, Hulme Hippodrome, Manchester.
Producers: Geoffrey Wheeler and Ronnie Taylor.

The Show Goes On

LP, Monday, 26 May 1955, 1930–2000
Morecambe and Wise, John Horvelle, Gladys Morgan, Ronald
  Chesney, KD, the Hedley Ward Trio, The Kordites, the
  Raymond Woodhead Choir, the Augmented BBC Northern
  Variety Orchestra conducted by Alyn Ainsworth.
Producers: Geoffrey Wheeler and Ronnie Taylor.

Blackpool Night

LP, Wednesday, 6 July 1955, 2100–2200
Reginald Dixon 'at the Tower Organ', Reggie Dennis, Edna Savage,
  KD ('Crazy Capers'), Tommy Reilly, Monkhouse and Goodwin,
  David Whitfield, Jimmy James and Eli Woods, Littlewoods'
  Girls' Choir, the Augmented BBC Northern Variety Orchestra
  conducted by Alyn Ainsworth, host Jack Watson.
Producer: Eric Miller.

Blackpool Night

LP, Wednesday, 10 August 1955, 2100–2200
Reginald Dixon, KD, Sylvia Campbell, Denis Goodwin, Raymond
  Woodhead and Harry Heyward ('At two pianos'), Morecambe
  and Wise, Dickie Valentine, Vic Oliver, Littlewoods' Girls' Choir,
  the Augmented BBC Northern Variety Orchestra conducted by
  Alyn Ainsworth, host Jack Watson.
Producer: Eric Miller.

Blackpool Night

LP, Wednesday, 14 September 1955, 2100–2200

Reginald Dixon, The Hedley Ward Trio, Denis Goodwin, Edna Savage, KD, Kenny Baker, Peter Cavanagh, John McHugh, Jewel and Warriss, Littlewoods' Girls' Choir, Geraldo and his Concert Orchestra, host Jack Watson.

Producer: Eric Miller.

Northern Variety Parade: Keep 'Em Laughing

HS, Tuesday, 8 August 1956, 1900–1930

Derek Roy, Jimmy Wheeler, Harry Bailey, KD, The Radio Revellers and the Augmented BBC Northern Variety Orchestra conducted by Alyn Ainsworth.

Producer: James Casey.

Blackpool Night

LP, Wednesday, 11 July 1956, 2100–2200

Charlie Chester, Tessie O'Shea, KD, Bill McGuffie, Chic Murray and Maidie, John Hanson, Bill Waddington, Reginald Dixon, The George Mitchell Singers, Augmented BBC Northern Variety Orchestra conducted by Alyn Ainsworth, Jack Watson (host).

Producer: Eric Miller.

Workers' Playtime (from the canteen of a steel works at Dukinfield, Cheshire)

HS, Thursday, 12 July 1956, 1225–1255

KD, Shani Wallis, Hal Garner, The Harmonichords, The Harry Hayward Trio, Randal Herley (host).

Producer: James Casey.

Blackpool Night

LP, Wednesday, 22 August 1956, 2100–2200

Hylda Baker, Shani Wallis, KD, Tom Mennard, John McHugh, Reg Thompson, Jerry Allen and his Trio, Reginald Dixon, The George Mitchell Singers, Jack Watson (host), orchestra conducted by Billy Ternent.

Producer: Eric Miller.

Blackpool Night

LP, Wednesday, 12 September 1956, 2100–2200

Jimmy James, Ronnie Carroll, KD, The Three Monarchs, Mrs. Shufflewick, Margaret West, Len Marten, Reginald Dixon, The George Mitchell Singers, the Augmented BBC Northern Variety Orchestra conducted by Alyn Ainsworth, Jack Watson (host).

Producer: Eric Miller.

Northern Variety Parade: Keep 'Em Laughing

HS, Tuesday, 2 October 1956, 1900–1930

Richard Murdoch, KD, Bob Andrews, the Smith Brothers and the BBC Northern Dance Orchestra.

Producer: James Casey.

Workers' Playtime (from a factory canteen in Gateshead)

HS, Thursday, 11 April 1957, 1225–1255

KD, The Kordites, Bob Andrews, Barbara Law, The Harry Hayward Trio, Randal Herley (host).

Producer: James Casey.

Merseyside Merry-Go-Round

LP, Sunday, 30 June 1957, 2100–2200

Arthur Askey, Ted Ray, Frankie Vaughan, Sheila Sim, Lita Roza, KD, Michael Holliday, Nancy Evans, Frank Pettingell, Deryck Guyler, The Littlewood Songsters, Brian Reece (master of ceremonies), the Jimmy Leach Organolian Quartet, the Augmented BBC Northern Dance Orchestra directed by Alyn Ainsworth.

Producers: James Casey, Vivian Daniels and Ronnie Taylor.

Blackpool Night

LP, Wednesday, 4 September 1957, 2100–2200

Harriott and Evans, Matt Innes, Chic Murray and Maidie, Donald Purchese, KD, Eve Boswell, Jewel and Warriss, Reginald Dixon, The Raymond Woodhead Singers, Jack Watson (host), Billy Ternent and his Orchestra.

Producer: Geoffrey Wheeler.

Northern Variety presents Star Train

LP, Monday, 7 November 1957, 2030–2100

KD, Bruce Trent, Denis Goodwin, The Gaunt Brothers, The Raytones, the BBC Northern Dance Orchestra conducted by Alyn Ainsworth with Jimmy Leach at the electronic organ, Roger Moffat.

Producer: Geoff Lawrence.

Blackpool Night

LP, Wednesday, 16 July 1958, 2030–2130

Norman Evans, Alma Cogan, KD, Rawicz and Landauer, Bill
Waddington, Percy Edwards, The Maple Leaf Four, Reginald
Dixon, The Littlewood Songsters, Jack Watson (host), the BBC
Northern Dance Orchestra conducted by Alyn Ainsworth.
Producer: John Ammonds.

Blackpool Night

LP, Wednesday, 6 August 1958, 2030–2130
Jewel and Warriss, Josef Locke, KD, Camilleri, Bill Waddington,
The Gaunt Brothers, Reginald Dixon, The Littlewood Songsters,
Jack Watson (host), the BBC Northern Dance Orchestra con-
ducted by Alyn Ainsworth.
Producer: John Ammonds.

Midday Music Hall

LP, Monday, 11 August 1958, 1230–1300
The Southlanders, Bob Bennett, Penny Nicholls, KD, Roger
Moffat (host), the BBC Northern Dance Orchestra conducted
by Alyn Ainsworth.
Producer: Eric Miller.

Blackpool Night

LP, Wednesday, 10 September 1958, 2030–2130
KD, Michael Holliday, Harry Bailey, Rawicz and Landauer,
Percy Edwards, The Gaunt Brothers, Reginald Dixon, The
Littlewood Songsters, Jack Watson (host), the BBC Northern
Dance Orchestra conducted by Alyn Ainsworth.
Producer: John Ammonds.

Workers' Playtime (from a factory canteen in Droylsden, Manchester)

LP, Thursday, 9 October 1958, 1230–1300

KD, John McHugh, Hal Roach, The Melfi Kids, The Harry Hayward Trio, Randal Herley (host).

Producer: Bill Scott-Coomber.

Midday Music Hall

LP, Monday, 10 November 1958, 1230–1300

KD, Marion Ryan, Norman Vaughan, The Demijeans, Randal Herley (host), the BBC Northern Dance Orchestra conducted by Alyn Ainsworth.

Producer: James Casey.

Workers' Playtime (from the VHF Exhibition in Liverpool)

LP, Thursday, 19 February 1959, 1230–1300

KD, Jill Day, Bud Bennett, The Taveners, The Harry Hayward Trio, Randal Herley (host).

Producer: Geoff Lawrence.

Midday Music Hall

LP, Monday, 23 February 1959, 1230–1300

KD, Norman Evans, Tommy Reilly, Peter Goodwright, The Daleans, Roger Moffat (host), the BBC Northern Dance Orchestra conducted by Alyn Ainsworth.

Producer: James Casey.

Workers' Playtime (from an engineering factory in Willenhall, Staffordshire)

LP, Thursday, 2 April 1959, 1230–1300

Betty Smith, Graham Stark, Hermene French, KD, Harry Engleman (piano), Vic Mortiboys (string-bass), Bob Mansell (drums).

Producer: Richard Maddock.

Funny Side Up

LP, Tuesday, 13 September 1959, 2000–2030

The Adams Singers, Patricia Lambert, Chic Murray and Maidie, Frank Cook, KD, the Malcolm Lockyer Orchestra, Peter Haigh (host).

Producer: Bill Gates.

Midday Music Hall

LP, Friday, 25 September 1959, 1230–1300

Sid Phillip, Chris Carlsen, Ken Morris and Joan Savage, KD, Mike Hall (host), BBC Variety Orchestra conducted by Paul Fenoulhet.

Producer: John Simmonds.

Flying High from RAF West Malling

LP, Wednesday, 30 September 1959, 1930–2000

KD, Lorie Mann, Frank Cook, The Terry Sisters, James Moody (piano), Bert Weedon (guitar), Tim Bell (double-bass).

Producer: Bill Gates.

Workers' Playtime (from a brewery in Warwickshire)

LP, Tuesday, 13 October 1959, 1230–1300

The Barry Sisters, Paddy Edwards, Benny Lee, KD, Harry Engleman (piano), Vic Mortiboys (string-bass), Bob Mansell (drums).

Producer: Richard Maddock.

Workers' Playtime (from the canteen of a mail order stores in Liverpool)

LP, Thursday, 26 November 1959, 1230–1300

KD, Brendan O'Dowda, Wyn Calvin, The Peter Crawford Trio, The Harry Hayward Trio, Randal Herley (host).

Producer: Geoff Lawrence.

Midday Music Hall

LP, Friday, 11 December 1959, 1230–1300

Maureen Evans, Mrs. Shufflewick, John Vallier, KD, Mike Hall (host), BBC Variety Orchestra conducted by Paul Fenoulhet.

Producer: John Simmonds.

Workers' Playtime (from No. 3 District Police Training Centre, Pannal Ash, Harrogate)

LP, Thursday, 25 February 1960, 1230–1300

KD, Jack Watson, Julie Jones, The Gaunt Brothers, The Harry Hayward Trio, Randal Herley (host).

Producer: Geoff Lawrence.

Workers' Playtime (from a spinning mill near Mansfield, Notts)

LP, Tuesday, 26 April 1960, 1230–1300

Alan Randall, Graham Stark, Carole Carr, KD, Harry Engleman (piano), Vic Mortiboys (string-bass), Bob Mansell (drums).

Producer: Richard Maddock.

Midday Music Hall from the Midlands

LP, Monday, 6 June 1960, 1230–1300

Nicholas Parsons (host), The Coventry Theatre Orchestra conducted by William Pethers, The Tracy Sisters, Vie West, Lorrae Desmond, KD.

Producer: James Pestridge.

London Lights

LP, Wednesday, 8 June 1960, 2030–2130

KD, Una Hale and André Turp, Barbara Leigh and Ian Wallace, The Ray Ellington Quartet, Ann Lancaster ('alias Mabel Crivets – she's a scream'), Janet Waters, The Adams Singers directed by Cliff Adams, the BBC Variety Orchestra conducted by Paul Fenoulhet.

Writers: Gene Crowley, Dick Vosburgh and Brad Ashton.

Producer: Trafford Whitelock.

Midday Music Hall from the BBC Theatre, Bristol

LP, Monday, 15 August 1960, 1230–1300

KD, Janie Marden, Douglas Horner, The Zodiacs, orchestra directed by Lawrence Adam, Derek Jones (host).

Producer: Brian Patten.

Workers' Playtime (from a factory in Rainhill, near Liverpool)

LP, Thursday, 13 October 1960, 1231–1300

KD, Julie Jones, Sonny Day, the Peter Crawford Trio, the Harry Hayward Trio with Brian Fitzgerald at the piano, Randal Herley (host).

Producer: James Casey.

The Northcountryman – Ray Davies interviewing KD

HS(N), Tuesday, 29 November 1960, 1825–1900

Midday Music Hall – special edition from the North of England

LP, Monday, 26 December 1960, 1100–1130

KD, Marion Ryan, Semprini, The Gaunt Brothers, Bob Bain, Pat O'Hare, Bud Bennett, Dennis Newey, The Littlewoods, Roger Moffat (host), the BBC Northern Dance Orchestra directed by Bernard Herrmann.

Producer: Bill Scott-Coomber.

Midday Music Hall from the Midlands

LP, Monday, 6 March 1961, 1231–1300

Nicholas Parsons (host), KD, Coral Tye, Bob Cort, the Terry Sisters, the Coventry Theatre Orchestra conducted by William Pethers.

Producer: James Pestridge.

London Lights

LP, Sunday, 26 March 1961, 1830–1930

Van Johnson with Patricia Lambert, KD, Petula Clark, Joe Church, Alan Loveday (violin) accompanied by Ruth Loveday, Gerry Gibson, Jack Watson (host), Tin Pan Alley Singers, the BBC Variety Orchestra conducted by Paul Fenoulhet.

Writer: Ronnie Hanbury.

Producer: Trafford Whitelock.

In Town Today

HS, Saturday, 20 May 1961, 1230–1255

Workers' Playtime (from a locomotive works canteen at Eastleigh, Hampshire)

LP, Thursday, 17 August 1961, 1231–1300

KD, Barbara Kay, The Four Ramblers, Gwenda Wilkin, Ron Millington (electronic organ), Jack Toogood (guitar), Colin Hawke (bass), Derek Jones (host).

Producer: Brian Patten.

Seaside Night from Bournemouth

LP, Sunday, 3 September 1961, 1830–1900

KD (host), the Beverley Sisters, Joe Henderson, the Three Monarchs, Billy Burden, The Raindrops, Jackie Brown and his Orchestra.

Producer: Eric Miller.

Seaside Night from Bournemouth

LP, Sunday, 10 September 1961, 1830–1900

KD (host), Alma Cogan, Rawicz and Landauer, Mark Wynter,

Joe Church, the Beverley Sisters, Joe Henderson, the Three Monarchs, Billy Burden, The Raindrops, Jackie Brown and his Orchestra.

Producer: Eric Miller

Workers' Playtime (from a factory in Chester)

LP, Thursday, 28 September 1961, 1231–1300

KD, Julie Jones, Norman Vaughan, The Dixielanders, the Harry Hayward Trio, Randal Herley (host).

Producer: James Casey.

London Lights

LP, Sunday, 22 October 1961, 1830–1930

Hughie Green (host), KD, Marie Collier and Ronald Dowd, Mrs. Shufflewick, Stephanie Voss and Ian Wallace, Alan Loveday, Johnny Clive, the Bill Shepherd Singers, the BBC Variety Orchestra conducted by Paul Fenoulhet.

Writers: Gene Crowley, Jimmy Coghill and Bill Smith.

Producer: Trafford Whitelock.

Today in the North

HS(N), Wednesday, 13 December 1961, 2015–2035

Producer: Geoffrey Wheeler.

Music Hall from the North of England

LP, Monday, 1 January 1962, 1231–1300

KD, Anne Shelton, Rawicz and Landauer, Peter Goodwright,

David Macbeth, Tommy Reilly, Peter Robinson, The Barry Sisters, the BBC Northern Dance Orchestra directed by Bernard Herrmann, Roger Moffat (host).

Producer: James Casey.

Workers' Playtime (from a factory in Manchester)

LP, Thursday, 1 February 1962, 1231–1300

KD, Julie Jones, Peter Robinson, Gordon Glenn, the Harry Hayward Trio, Randal Herley (host).

Producer: Geoff Lawrence.

Calendar

HS(N), Friday, 23 February 1962, 1930–2000

Talk with Rev N. Hood about humour in religion.

Parade of the Pops

LP, Wednesday, 21 March 1962, 1231–1300

Bob Miller and The Millermen, Lynn Collins, Vince Hill, Gordon Somers, The Milltones, KD, Joanne, Denny Piercy (host).

Producer: John Kingdon.

Music Hall from the Midlands

LP, Monday, 26 March 1962, 1231–1300

KD, Robert Earl, Freddy Frinton, Dorita y Pepe, Peter Goodwright, Gwen Davies, the Bell-Tones, the Coventry Theatre Orchestra directed by William Pethers.

Producer: James Pestridge.

Music Hall from the North of England

LP, Monday, 25 June 1962, 1231–1300

KD, Dennis Lotis, Joe 'Mr. Piano' Henderson, Bill Waddington, Penny Nicholls, Tom Mennard, The Trad Lads, the BBC Northern Dance Orchestra directed by Bernard Herrmann, Roger Moffat (host).

Producer: James Casey.

Blackpool Night

LP, Sunday, 15 July 1962, 1830–1900

Jack Watson (host), KD, Eddie Calvert, Denis Goodwin, Terry Burton, Reggie Dennis, The C Men, Edmund Hockridge, Reginald Dixon, the BBC Northern Dance Orchestra directed by Bernard Herrmann.

Producer: James Casey.

Workers' Playtime (from a factory in Rainhill, near Liverpool)

LP, Thursday, 26 July 1962, 1231–1300

KD, The Kaye Sisters, Tom Mennard, Martin and David Lukins, the Harry Hayward Trio, Roger Moffat (host).

Producer: Geoff Lawrence.

Blackpool Night

LP, Sunday, 19 August 1962, 1830–1930

Jack Watson (host), Peter Goodwright, Barbara Law, Bill Pertwee, the Freemen, Ken Frith, Edmund Hockridge, Reginald Dixon, the BBC Northern Dance Orchestra directed by Bernard Herrmann.

Producer: James Casey.

Music Hall from the North of England

LP, Monday, 12 November 1962, 1231–1300

KD, Rosemary Squires, Eddie Calvert, Bill Waddington, the Polka Dots, Ken Kirkham, Reg Thompson, the Swinging Blue Jeans, the BBC Northern Dance Orchestra conducted by Bernard Herrmann, Roger Moffat (host).

Producer: Peter Pilbeam.

The North Stars

HS(N), Thursday, 22 November 1962, 2030–2145

Producer: James Casey.

Workers' Playtime from a factory in Manchester

LP, Thursday, 20 December 1962, 1231–1300

KD, Rosemary Squires, Reg Thompson, the Gaunt Brothers, the Harry Hayward Trio, Roger Moffat (host).

Producer: Geoff Lawrence.

Carnival

HS and GOS, Saturday, 22 December 1962, 1445–1545

Alan Freeman, KD, Winifred Atwell, Bernard Braden, Barbara Kelly, Carmita, Edmund Hockridge, Peter Goodwright, the Maori Hi-Five, the Adams Singers, the BBC Variety Orchestra conducted by Paul Fenoulhet.

Producer: Eric Miller.

The North Stars (networked repeat of 22 November 1962)

LP, Monday, 7 January 1963, 1231–1331

Wilfred Pickles (host), KD, Clinton Ford, Jimmy James, Ken Platt, Rosalie Williams, John Lawrenson, Eddie Calvert, Sheila Buxton, David Wilde, Peter Goodwright, the Four Barry Sisters, the BBC Northern Dance Orchestra directed by Bernard Herrmann.

Producer: James Casey.

A Good and Comely Life

HS(N), Tuesday, 26 February 1963, 2030–2130

Interview with John Mapplebeck on working-class humour.

Radio Newsreel

LP, Thursday, 14 March 1963, 1900–1930

Interview with Tom Heaney.

Music Hall from the North of England

LP, Monday, 27 May 1963, 1231–1300

KD, Ronnie Hilton, Julius Nehring, Don Arrol, Barbara Law, Martin Lukins, Reg Thompson, Robin Hall, Jimmie MacGregor, the BBC Northern Dance Orchestra conducted by Bernard Herrmann.

Producer: James Casey.

Desert Island Discs

HS, Saturday, 13 July 1963, 1340–1410

Producer: Monica Chapman.

Yes, it's Great Yarmouth

LP, Wednesday, 17 July 1963, 1931–2030

KD, Eddie Calvert and the C Men, Rosemary Squires, the Barry
  Sisters, Joe Brown and the Bruvvers, The Tornados, Jackie
  Brown and his Orchestra.

Producer: John Simmonds.

Workers' Playtime (from the staff recreation hall of the King's Lynn hospitals)

LP, Tuesday, 30 July 1963, 1231–1300

Alan Randall, Percy Edwards, Rosemary Squires, KD, Harry
  Engleman (piano), Vic Cook (string bass), Bob Mansell (drums).

Producer: Richard Maddock.

Yes, it's Great Yarmouth

LP, Wednesday, 14 August 1963, 1931–2030

KD, Stan Stennett, Edmund Hockridge, the Three Monarchs,
  Helen Shapiro, the Trebletones, Rolf Harris, Dorothy Wayne,
  the Bell-Tones, Jackie Brown and his Orchestra.

Writer: Eddie Braben.

Producer: John Simmonds.

Holiday Highlights

LP, Sunday, 8 September 1963, 1830–1930

Joe Brown and the Bruvvers, the Peter Crawford Trio, Reginald
  Dixon, KD, Jimmy Edwards, Peter Goodwright, Max Jaffa
  with Jack Byfield (piano), Morecambe and Wise, the Polka
  Dots, Cliff Richard and the Shadows, Terry Scott and Hugh

Lloyd, Helen Shapiro with The Trebletones, the Tornados, Jack Watson (host).

Compiler: John Simmonds.

Parade of the Pops

LP, Wednesday, 2 October 1963, 1231–1331

Bob Miller and the Millermen, Alan Lee, the Milltones, Vince Hill, Chad and Jeremy, KD, Denny Piercy (host).

Producer: John Kingdon.

Workers' Playtime (from a factory in Hull)

LP, Thursday, 21 November 1963, 1231–1300

KD, The Barry Sisters, Tom Mennard, Martin Lukins, The Harry Hayward Trio, Roger Moffat (host).

Producer: James Casey.

Music Hall from the North of England

LP, Monday, 2 December 1963, 1231–1300

KD, Rawicz and Landauer, Paul Andrews, Jack Storey, The Raindrops, Norman George, Bobby Dennis, Martin and David Lukins, the BBC Northern Dance Orchestra conducted by Bernard Herrmann, Roger Moffat (host).

Producer: Geoff Lawrence.

Voice of the North

HS(N), Tuesday, 10 December 1963, 1810–1832

Interview with Bob Mosley about proposal to establish Department of Giggleology at Liverpool University.

Workers' Playtime (from a garments factory at Hucknall, Nottinghamshire)

LP, Thursday, 9 January 1964, 1231–1300
The Barry Sisters, Tommy Reilly, Gary Miller, KD, Harry Engleman (piano), Vic Cook (string bass), Bob Mansell (drums).
Producer: Richard Maddock.

Playing at God – 'the way in which we handle power'

HS, Sunday, 12 January 1964, 1945–2025
Stafford Beer, Jim Clark, KD, Charles Forte, a GP, Ray Dunbobbin, David Mahlowe, Brenda Ann Hall, Struan Rodger, John Morris.
Producer: Reverend Raymond A. Short.

The Public Ear

LP, Sunday, 26 January 1964, 1500–1600
Producer: John Fawcett Wilson.

Today

HS(N), Tuesday, 28 January 1964, 0715–0840
Interview about 'Merseyside Maniacs' on football trains.

Workers' Playtime (from Whitwood Mining and Technical College, Castleford)

LP, Thursday, 30 January 1964, 1231–1300
KD, Julie Jones, Wyn Calvin, Bert Weedon, the Harry Hayward Trio, Roger Moffat (host).
Producer: James Casey.

Music Hall from the North of England

LP, Monday, 17 February 1964, 1231–1300

KD, David Hughes, Mrs Mills, Jimmy Gay, Barbara Kay, Rod King, Jack Chadwick, Peter Robinson, the Four Ramblers, the BBC Northern Dance Orchestra conducted by Bernard Herrmann.

Producer: John Wilcox.

Music Hall from the North of England

LP, Monday, 6 April 1964, 1231–1300

KD, Ian Wallace, Joe 'Mr Piano' Henderson, Billy Dainty, Julie Jones, Gordon Glenn, Les Dawson, the Morgan-James Duo, the BBC Northern Dance Orchestra conducted by Bernard Herrmann.

Producer: John Wilcox.

Housewives' Choice

LP, Monday, 13 April–Friday, 17 April, 0900–0955

Host: KD.

Workers' Playtime (from a heavy chemical works at Avonmouth)

LP, Tuesday, 5 May 1964, 1231–1300

KD, Rosemary Squires, Tommy Reilly, the Barry Sisters, Ron Millington (electronic organ), Jack Toogood (guitar), Colin Hawke (double bass), Derek Jones (host).

Producer: Brian Patten.

Blackpool Night

LP, Sunday, 16 August 1964, 1830–1930
Jack Watson (host), KD, Susan Maughan, Denis Goodwin, Joe 'Mr Piano' Henderson, David Macbeth, Peter Robinson, the Square Pegs, Reginald Dixon, the BBC Northern Dance Orchestra conducted by Bob Miller.
Producer: James Casey.

Voice of the North

HS(N), Thursday, 27 August 1964, 1810–1825
Interview with John Watmough about joke poachers.

Blackpool Night

LP, Sunday, 6 September 1964, 1830–1930
Jack Watson (host), KD, Rosemary Squires, Les Dawson, Clive Lythgoe, Pat O'Hare, Reg Thompson, the Morgan-James Duo, Reginald Dixon, the BBC Northern Dance Orchestra conducted by Bob Miller.
Producer: James Casey.

Variety on Tour at a factory in Hebden Bridge, Yorkshire

LP, Tuesday, 13 October 1964, 1231–1300
KD, the Dalmours, Bert Gaunt, the Kestrels, the Harry Hayward Trio, Roger Moffat (host).
Producer: James Casey.

Startime

LP, Monday, 19 October 1964, 1231–1331

Roger Moffat (host), KD, The Barry Sisters, Norman George, Les Dawson, Myrna Rose, Mike Yarwood, The Brooks, the BBC Northern Dance Orchestra conducted by Bernard Herrmann.

Producer: James Casey.

Variety on Tour at No. 2 Flying Training School, RAF Syerston, near Newark

LP, Tuesday, 27 October 1964, 1231–1300

KD, Lita Roza, Don Lang, the Barry Sisters, Harry Engleman (piano), Vic Cook (double-bass), Bob Mansell (drums).

Producer: Richard Maddock.

Forces Gala Night Twenty-First Anniversary

LP, Sunday, 8 November 1964, 1800–1930

David Jacobs (host), Harry Secombe, Jon Pertwee, Larry Adler, Charlie Chester, Jimmy Edwards, Edmund Hockridge, Vera Lynn, Spike Milligan, Richard Murdoch, Harry Secombe, Anne Shelton, Eric Barker, Bill Crozier, Pearl Hackney, Kenneth Horne, Susan Maughan, Jon Pertwee, Semprini, Tommy Trinder, Judith Chalmers, KD, McDonald Hobley, Cliff Michelmore, Jean Metcalfe, Matt Monro, Ted Ray, Peter Sellers, Alan Wheatley, the New Radio Orchestra conducted by Paul Fenoulhet.

Writer: Gale Pedrick.

Producer: Bill Worsley.

Parade of the Pops from the Town Hall, Walsall, 'heralds BBC-2'

LP, Wednesday, 25 November 1964, 1231–1300

Bob Miller and the Millermen, Dougie Arthur, June Lesley, Allan Lee, the Milltones, Vince Hill, the Bob Rogers Five, Gordon Somers, KD, Denny Piercy (host).

Producer: John Kingdon.

Startime

LP, Monday, 1 February 1965, 1300–1400

Roger Moffat (host), KD, the Barry Sisters, George Meaton, Peter Goodwright, Joanne Michelle, Jimmie Ryder, the Lorne Gibson Trio, the BBC Northern Dance Orchestra conducted by Bernard Herrmann.

Producer: Geoff Lawrence.

Housewives' Choice

LP, Monday, 2 August–Friday, 6 August 1965, 0900–0955

KD (host).

Doddy's Fun Fair

LP, Monday, 30 August 1965, 1700–1800

KD (host).

Producer: Teddy Warrick.

Carnival

LP, Tuesday, 9 November 1965, 2315–2345

KD, Maggie Fitzgibbon, the Blue Notes, Princess Patience, the Carnival Orchestra conducted by Paul Fenoulhet.

Producer: Bryant Marriott.

Home for the Day

HS, 19 December 1965, 1130–1210

Marjorie Anderson (presenter), includes item on the deadly sin of sloth with BA Mason, KD, Charlotte Mitchell, Al Capp and Malcolm Muggeridge.

It Takes All Sorts

HS, Tuesday, 25 January 1966, 1120–1140

Philip Radcliffe (interviewer), KD.

Liverpool Parade from the stage of the Royal Court Theatre

LP, Monday, 30 May 1966, 1400–1500

Ted Ray (host), KD, Gerry and the Pacemakers, Ray Fell, Julie Jones, Mike Burton, the Morgan-James Duo, the BBC Northern Dance Orchestra directed by Bernard Herrmann.

Producer: James Casey.

Going Places

LP, Monday, 13 June 1966, 1300–1350

David Symonds (host), KD, Viera, Pepe Jaramillo, the Nigel Brooks Singers, the Radio Orchestra conducted by Geoff Love.

Producer: Michael Shrimpton.

Blackpool Night

LP, Saturday, 18 June 1966, 1930–2030

Geoffrey Wheeler (host), Jimmy Clitheroe, The Bachelors, Mrs Mills, Freddy Davies, Bert Weedon, Myrna Rose, Joe Kenyon,

KD, Reginald Dixon, the BBC Northern Dance Orchestra conducted by Bernard Herrmann.

Producer: Geoff Lawrence.

Blackpool Night

LP, Saturday, 2 July 1966, 1930–2030

Geoffrey Wheeler (host), KD, Winifred Atwell, the Rockin' Berries, Ray Fell, Barbara Law, John Anthony, the Reggie Dennis Four, Reginald Dixon, the BBC Northern Dance Orchestra conducted by Bernard Herrmann.

Producer: Geoff Lawrence.

Blackpool Night

LP, Saturday, 23 July 1966, 1930–2030

Geoffrey Wheeler (host), Val Doonican, Frank Berry, Mrs Mills, George Meaton, Gordon Glenn, the Merrymen, Bert Gaunt, Reginald Dixon, the BBC Northern Dance Orchestra conducted by Bernard Herrmann.

Producer: Geoff Lawrence.

Blackpool Night

LP, Sunday, 20 August 1966, 1930–2030

Geoffrey Wheeler (host), KD, Mrs Mills, Rosemary Squires, Freddy Davies, Bruce Trent, Paul Templar, Ken Goodwin, Reginald Dixon, the BBC Northern Dance Orchestra conducted by Bernard Herrmann.

Producer: Geoff Lawrence.

Housewives' Choice

LP, Monday, 5 December–Friday, 9 December 1966, 0834–0955
KD (host).

Pop North

LP, Thursday, 22 December 1966, 1300–1400
Ray Moore (host), Bernard Herrmann and the Northern Dance
    Orchestra, Johnny de Little, the Mal Craig Three, the Trad Lads,
    Sandra Stevens, KD, Wayne Fontana, the Rockin' Vickers.
Producer: John Wilcox.

Forces Jamboree

LP, Saturday, 24 December 1966, 1915–2015
Ted Ray (host), Janie Marden, the Barron Knights, Max Jaffa,
    Peter Jones, Georgie Fame, Larry Adler, KD, the Adams Singers
    directed by Cliff Adams, the Radio Show Band conducted by
    Paul Fenoulhet.
Producer: Bill Worsley.

Pop North

LP, Thursday, 2 February 1967, 1300–1400
Ray Moore (host), Bernard Herrmann and the Northern Dance
    Orchestra, Johnny de Little, the Mal Craig Three, the Trad Lads,
    Sandra Stevens, KD, the Peddlers.
Producer: John Wilcox.

The North Stars

LP, Saturday, 18 March 1967, 2005–2100

Gay Byrne (host), KD, Susan Maughan, Joe Henderson, Ray Fell, the Alan Price Set, Tom Mennard, the BBC Northern Dance Orchestra directed by Bernard Herrmann.

Producer: James Casey.

Home This Afternoon

HS, Monday, 25 September 1967, 1645–1725

Features item with John Ellison interviewing KD.

Follow the Stars

R2, Wednesday, 7 October 1967, 2015–2115

KD (host), the Grumbleweeds, Chris Carlsen, Eddie Calvert, Rosemary Squires, Mr Acker Bilk, Terry Scott, orchestra conducted by Brian Fahey.

Producer: Bill Worsley.

Cotton's Christmas Knees-Up

R2, Monday, 25 December 1967, 1700–1800

Billy Cotton (host), Alan Breeze, Kathie Kay, Rita Williams and the Bandits, KD, Mrs Mills, Fred Emney, Ken Haynes, Alan Haynes.

Writer: Eddie Gurney.

Producer: Richard Willcox.

Home This Afternoon

R4, Tuesday, 26 December 1967, 1645–1725

Magazine programme, includes KD talking to Wyn Calvin about the subject of his song 'Happiness'.

Pop North

R2, Thursday, 28 December 1967, 1300–1400

Dave Lee Travis (host), Bernard Herrmann and the Northern Dance Orchestra, Terry Webster, the Mal Craig Three, Mireille Gray, Dave Blakeney, KD, the Montanas.

Producer: John Wilcox.

Follow the Stars

R2, Saturday, 4 May 1968, 2015–2115

KD, Sheila Buxton, Wout Steenhis, the Karlins, Mike Burton, Roslynn and her harp, the Lorne Gibson Trio, the BBC Northern Dance Orchestra conducted by Bernard Herrmann.

Producer: Geoff Lawrence.

The Blackpool Show

R2, Saturday, 3 August 1968, 1935–2050

KD (host), Josef Locke, Les Dawson, Julius Nehring, Johnny Stafford, Mike Newman, Friday, Brown, Reginald Dixon, the BBC Northern Dance Orchestra conducted by Bernard Herrmann.

Producer: Geoff Lawrence.

The Blackpool Show

R2, Saturday, 10 August 1968, 1935–2050

KD (host), Eve Boswell, Joe 'Mr Piano' Henderson, Mike Yarwood, Norman George, Bert Gaunt, Steve Montgomery, Reginald Dixon, the BBC Northern Dance Orchestra conducted by Brian Fitzgerald.

Producer: Geoff Lawrence.

The Blackpool Show

R2, Saturday, 17 August 1968, 1935–2050

KD (host), Vince Hill, Tommy Reilly, Jimmy Marshall, David and Marianne Dalmour, Dave Gray, Norman Teal, Reginald Dixon, the BBC Northern Dance Orchestra conducted by Brian Fitzgerald.

Producer: Geoff Lawrence.

The Blackpool Show

R2, Saturday, 24 August 1968, 1935–2050

KD (host), Tessie O'Shea, Ray Fell, Chester Harriott, Sheila Buxton, Johnny Ball, John Anthony, Reginald Dixon, the BBC Northern Dance Orchestra conducted by Brian Fitzgerald.

Producer: Geoff Lawrence.

The Blackpool Show

R2, Saturday, 31 August 1968, 1935–2050

KD (host), Norman Vaughan, Clinton Ford, Alan Randall, Reg Thompson, Terry Burton, Roslynn and her harp, Reginald

Dixon, the BBC Northern Dance Orchestra conducted by Brian Fitzgerald.
Producer: Geoff Lawrence.

The Blackpool Show

R2, Saturday, 21 September 1968, 1935–2050
KD (host), Freddy 'Parrot Face' Davies, Solomon King, Julius Nehring, Spencer's Washboard Kings, Reginald Dixon, the BBC Northern Dance Orchestra conducted by Bernard Herrmann.
Producer: Geoff Lawrence.

Home This Afternoon

R4, Monday, 14 October 1968, 1645–1725
Magazine programme featuring 'Let's Laugh: Michael Meech looks into the subject of laughter with Professor John Cohen and KD'.

The Jokers

R4, Thursday, 10 July 1969, 0945–1015
Producer: Geoff Lawrence.

Doddy's Christmas Crackers

R2, Thursday, 25 December 1969, 1400–1430
KD, Vince Hill, Mrs Mills, Clodagh Rodgers, the augmented BBC Northern Dance Orchestra conducted by Brian Fitzgerald.
Producer: Geoff Lawrence.

Be My Guest

R4, Monday, 23 February 1970, 2015–2045
KD talks to David Hamilton.
Producer: Denis Lewell.

The Entertainers: The Sage of Knotty Ash

R4, Tuesday, 10 August 1971, 1930–2015
Frank Dixon on KD.
Producer: Herbert Smith.

Scan

R4, Thursday, 18 November 1971, 2045–2130
Interview with Michael Billington.
Producer: Rosemary Hart.

The Best of British Laughs

R4, Sunday, 12 December 1971, 1900–1930
Barry Took talks to KD.
Producer: John Browell.

There was an Englishman, an Irishman and a Scotsman

R4, Monday, 12 June 1972, 2000–2030
Frank Muir on Liverpudlian comedy.
Producers: David Hatch and Simon Brett.

Woman's Hour (from the Theatre Complex at the Liverpool Show)

R2, Sunday, 13 July 1972, 1403–1502
Introduced by Judith Chalmers.

Ken Dodd with Janie Marden and Brian Fahey and the New Scottish Radio Orchestra

R2, Thursday, 26 October 1972, 2030–2115
Producer: Andy Park.

Celebration: Commemorating 50 years of concert parties

R4, Wednesday, 28 August 1974, 1930–2015
Producer: Trafford Whitelock.

Woman's Hour introduced from Manchester by June Knox-Mawer

R4, Friday, 27 December 1974, 1345–1445
Including 'Getting Over Christmas: some lighthearted remedies for
post-holiday blues from Mike Yarwood, KD and Fritz Spiegl'.

Woman's Hour introduced by Sue MacGregor

R4, Monday, 29 March 1976, 1345–1445

The Northern Comic

R3, Saturday, 15 May 1976, 2255–2340
Who is he, why is he? Jim Casey in conversation with KD.
Producer: James Casey.

The Ken Dodd Collection

R2, Monday, 6 June 1977, 1230–1330
Producer: Chris Morgan.

Variety Club

R2, Tuesday, 7 June 1977, 2302–0000
Martin Dale (host), KD, Duggie Brown, Alan Randall, Cool Breeze,
 the Variety Club Showband conducted by Brian Fitzgerald.
Devised by Mike Craig.
Producer: James Casey.

Pete Murray's Open House from Courtaulds' Sports and Social Club, Aintree

R2, Friday, 24 February 1978, 1230–1430
Pete Murray, KD, The Spinners, Alan Randall.
Producer: Angela Bond.

On the Town

R4, 11 March 1978, 2215–2300
Portrait of a City – Liverpool by Roger McGough.
Producer: David Rayvern Allen.

Variety Club

R2, Tuesday, 31 October 1978, 2202–2302
Martin Dale (host), KD, Nigel Hopkins, Turnstule, Chester Harriott,
 Sandy Powell, the Variety Club Showband conducted by Brian
 Fitzgerald.
Producer: Mike Craig.

Laughter in the Air

R2, Tuesday, 13 March 1979, 2202–2302

Smile Darn Ya Smile – 'Barry Took considers the pleas and persuasions of radio comedians including KD.'
Producer: Martin Fisher.

Variety Club

R2, Tuesday, 31 July 1979, 2202–2302
Martin Dale (host), KD, Karen Kay, Los Zafiros, Syd Francis, Chester Harriott, the Variety Club Showband conducted by Brian Fitzgerald.
Producer: Mike Craig.

It's a Funny Business

R2, Saturday, 27 December 1980, 1302–1330
Mike Craig interviews KD about his career.
Producer: Mike Craig.

Be My Guest

R2, Wednesday, 7 January 1981, 2230–2300
Producer: Phyllis Robinson.

Jimmy Jewel's Seaside Show

R4, Monday, 31 August 1981, 1045–1140
'A Bank Holiday breeze on the airwaves as Jimmy Jewel considers the seaside summer show', featuring a contribution from KD.
Producer: Danny Greenstone.

Funny You Should Ask

R2, Monday, 7 June 1982, 2200–2230
Panel game with Peter Jones (host), KD, Betty Driver, Ken Platt.
Questions set by Michael Pointon.
Producer: Ron McDonnell.

What's So Funny About Liverpool? 'A celebration of the Scouse sense of humour'

R2, Monday, 13 September 1982, 2200–2300
Producer: Peter Everett.

Workers' Playtime from a factory in Bolton

R2, Thursday, 7 October 1982, 1230–1300
KD, Rosemary Squires. Bert Weedon, Johnny More, the Harry
  Hayward Trio, Peter Wheeler (host).

Stuart Hall (KD guesting after midnight)

R2, Monday, 25 April 1983, 2230–0100

The Week's Good Cause

R4, Sunday, 31 July 1983, 0850–0900
KD talks about St Mary's Hospice in Birmingham.

Funny You Should Ask

R2, Wednesday, 17 August 1983, 2200–2230

Peter Jones (host), KD, Betty Driver, Ken Platt.
Producer: Ron McDonnell.

Funny You Should Ask

R2, Wednesday, 7 September 1983, 2200–2230
Peter Jones (host), KD, Betty Driver, Ken Platt.
Producer: Ron McDonnell.

Midweek

R4, Wednesday, 7 November 1984, 0905–1000
Birthday guest KD talking to Michael Billington.
Producer: Pippa Burston.

Good Morning Sunday

R2, Sunday, 30 December 1984, 0730–0900
Paul McDowell (host), KD.
Producer: Julia Brosnan.

Cup Final

R2, Saturday, 10 May 1986

Kaleidoscope – Laughing Matters with Tony Staveacre

R4, Friday, 17 July 1987, 2145–2215
Producer: Mary Price.

In the Psychiatrist's Chair

R4, Wednesday, 19 August 1987, 0905–0940
Dr Anthony Clare in conversation with the comedian KD.
Producer: Michael Ember.

Sounds of the Sixties

R2, 12 December 1987, 0900–1000
Producer: Stuart Hobday.

Good Morning Sunday

R2, Sunday, 20 March 1988, 0730–0905
Producer: Stephen Lynas.

Junkin's Jokers

R2, Saturday, 3 November 1990, 1730–1800
John Junkin, KD
Producer: Jon Magnusson.

Television

Starring vehicles

The Ken Dodd Show

Special:

BBC TV, Saturday, 25 July 1959, 2020–2110

KD, the Joe Slack Trio, the Four Kents, Kenny Baker, Rosemary Squires, Nino Frediani and Sister, the Leslie Roberts Silhouettes, Betty Alberge, Leonard Williams, John Broadbent, Tony Melody. Producer: Albert Stevenson.

Series 1:

BBC TV, Saturdays, approximately monthly, 9 January–10 December 1960

Shows 1 and 2 from the Hippodrome, Ardwick, 3–7 from the Grand Continental Theatre, Bolton, 8 and 9 from the Playhouse, Hulme.

Producers: Albert Stevenson (shows 1–5), Barney Colehan (shows 6–9).

Writers: KD and Eddie Braben, with Frank Roscoe and James Casey (show 1), Arthur Lay and Bill Kelly (show 2).

Regulars: KD, the BBC Northern Dance Orchestra.

9 January, 1950–2040: Dennis Spicer, Reco and May, The Rain-drops, The Leslie Roberts Silhouettes, Judith Chalmers, Leonard

Williams, Peter Goodwright, The Raymond Woodhead Group, Alyn Ainsworth (musical director).

6 February, 1950–2040: The Manettis, Johnny Laycock and Bee, Elaine Delmar, The Two Heinkis, The Leslie Roberts Silhouettes, Peter Goodwright, The Littlewood Songsters, Victor Gilling, Alyn Ainsworth (musical director).

5 March, 1950–2040: Rosemary Squires, The Three Tarragonis, Clinton Ford, The Merseysippi Jazz Band, The Littlewood Songsters, Leonard Williams, Horace Mashford, Victor Gilling, Alyn Ainsworth (musical director).

2 April, 2005–2050: Wilson Keppel and Betty, Don Lang and his Frantic Five, Barbara Law, The Trio Rayros, The Littlewood Songsters, The Leslie Roberts Silhouettes, Leonard Williams, Peter Goodwright, Rex Rashley, Horace Mashford, Victor Gilling, Alyn Ainsworth (musical director).

30 April, 1920–2010: Dennis Spicer, Janie Marden, Elizabeth and Collins, The Leslie Roberts Silhouettes, Valli Newby, Christina Mayo, Mildred Dyson, Victor Gilling, Leonard Williams, Peter Goodwright, John McHugh, Rex Rashley, Alec McKenzie, Dennis Winn, Alyn Ainsworth (musical director).

28 May 1960, 1930–2020: no listings available

25 June 1960, 1950–2040: Jill Day, Harry Corbett and Sooty, Pan Yue Jen Troupe, Freddie Mills, George Baron, The Littlewood Songsters, The Larry Gordon Dancers, Victor Gilling, Ken Barnes, Valli Newby, Barbara Simpson, Fred Godfrey, Terry Day, Alex McKenzie, Brett Williams, Billy Tweedle, Hilda Fairclough.

12 November 1960, 2105–2150: The Trio Andaluz, Joyce Blackham, Brian Andro, The Littlewood Songsters, The Larry Gordon Dancers, Joan Hurley, Ken Barnes, Valerie Brooks, Fred Godfrey, Victor Gilling, Rex Rashley, Ken Baker, Midge Cowan, Bernard Herrmann (musical director).

10 December 1960, 2035–2120: Eddie Calvert, The Wiseguys and Bobby Adrian, The Modern Jazz Dancers, The Littlewood Songsters, The Larry Gordon Dancers and Ken Barnes, Joan Hurley, Leonard Williams, Fred Godfrey, Rex Rashley, Hilda Fairclough (Miss United Kingdom), The Harrison Singers, Tommy Watt (musical director).

Series 2:

BBC TV, Saturdays, approximately monthly, 29 April–9 December 1961
Regulars: KD, the Augmented BBC Northern Dance Orchestra.
Writers: KD and Eddie Braben.
Producer: Barney Colehan.

29 April 1961, 1945–2030: The Blue Diamonds, Joe 'Mr Piano' Henderson, The Littlewoods, The Larry Gordon Dancers and Leonard Williams, Ken Barnes, Rex Rashley, Joan Hurley, Jim Couton, Sonny Day, Fred Godfrey, Victor Gilling, Tommy Watt (musical director).

27 May 1961, 1945–2030: Audrey Arno, Crazy Otto, Alex Macintosh, The Littlewoods and Leonard Williams, Ken Barnes, Rex Rashley, Joan Hurley, Sonny Day, Senta Yamada, Victor Gilling, Patricia Jagger, Winifred Brown, Fred Godfrey, William Kerfoot,

Ginger Chilton, Eddie Falcon, Gerry Marcus, Jimmy Thompson, Bud Casey, Tommy Watt (musical director).

17 June 1961, 1945–2030: The Niberco Brothers, Dennis Spicer, Ken Barnes, Joan Hurley, Rex Rashley, Alec Bregonzi, Michael Guest, Alice Esmie-Bell, John Caesier, Patrick Scanlan, Katie Cashfield, Dawn Escott, Alec Foster, George Crowther, Neil Robinson, John Simpson, Douglas Chadwick and Pauline Chadwick, The Bryan Ryman Dancers. Tommy Watt (musical director).

18 November 1961, 1915–2000: Rawicz and Landauer, Lita Roza, Rob Murray, Victor Gilling, Fred Godfrey, Denis Kazbek, Joan Boardman, Billy Dodd, Eddie Braben, Joan Humble, Kathleen Elkerton, Members of the St. Helens Rugby League Football Team, The Savoy Dancers, Bernard Herrmann (musical director).

9 December 1961, 1915–2000 (from the Pavilion Theatre, Winter Gardens, Blackpool): Mona Baptiste, The Frank Medini Trio, Rene and Lorentz, Denny Bettis, Leonard Williams, Jim Couton, Fred Godfrey, Rex Boyd, Anthony Hartwell, Ken Baker, Billy Dodd, Joyce Adcock, The Denny Bettis Dancers, Bernard Herrmann (musical director).

Series 3:

BBC TV, Saturdays, approximately monthly, 19 May–8 December 1962
Regulars: KD, the BBC Northern Dance Orchestra directed by Bernard Herrmann.
Writers: KD and Eddie Braben.
Producer: Barney Colehan.

19 May 1962, 1930–2015: Hazel Scott, Les Franky Babusio, Denny Bettis and Joe Gladwin, Joan Hurley, Ken Barnes, Rex Rashley, Fred Godfrey, Victor Gilling, Sonny Day, Frank Farrer, Billy Dodd, Bruno, The Denny Bettis Dancers.

2 June 1962, 1930–2015: Eddie Calvert and the C Men, Jula de Palma, Mirko de Yorke, Denny Bettis and Joan Hurley, Joyce Adcock, Anastasia, Sonny Day, Carl von Wurden, Barbara Sibley, Billy Dodd, Isobel Bennett, Bobby Breen, The Denny Bettis Dancers.

27 October 1962, 1915–2000: The Kaye Sisters, John Slater, Martin Lukins and his Accordion Orchestra, Krystyna and Linda Saville, Alan Clarke, the Leo Kharibian Dancers.

10 November 1962, 2101–2145: Edmund Hockridge, John Laurie, The Raindrops, the Leo Kharibian Dancers.

8 December 1962, 1915–2000: Rosemary Squires, The Mike Sammes Singers, John Laurie, Patricia Hayes, The Lazybones, Ken Barnes, Rex Rashley, Sonny Day, Fred Godfrey, Rex Boyd, Arthur Johnson, Gerald Campion, the Leo Kharibian Dancers.

Specials:

BBC TV, Saturday, 8 June 1963, 2015–2100
KD with Alma Cogan, John Laurie, Sandros, Susan Lane, Patricia Hayes, Joan Hurley, the Savoy Dancers.
Writers: KD and Eddie Braben.
Producer: Barney Colehan.

BBC2, Sunday, 31 October 1965, 1930–2030

KD with Julie Rogers, The Fortunes, David Mahlowe, Annette Searle, Gerry Lube, Peter Sheldon, Tony Newbury, John Clifford, Fred Powell, The Malcolm Goddard Dancers, The Michael Sammes Singers, Graham Stark, Patricia Hayes, John Laurie.

Producer: Bill Lyon-Shaw.

Director: Michael Hurll.

BBC1, Saturday, 25 December 1965, 2130–2230

KD, Sandie Shaw, Graham Stark, John Laurie, Neville King, Irving Davies, David Mahlowe, Patricia Hayes, The Irving Davies Dancers, The Michael Sammes Singers.

Writers: KD and Eddie Braben.

Producer: Michael Hurll.

Series 4:

BBC1, Sundays, 24 July–11 September 1966 (from the Opera House, Blackpool)

Regulars: KD, Roger Stevenson and his Diddymen, the Bluebell Girls, the Augmented BBC Northern Dance Orchestra directed by Bernard Herrmann (shows 1–3 and 6–8), orchestra conducted by Peter Knight (shows 4 and 5).

Writers: KD and Eddie Braben, with Ray Galton and Alan Simpson on show 1.

Producer: Duncan Wood.

24 July 1966, 2015–2100: Wilfrid Brambell and Harry H. Corbett, Salena Jones, Graham Stark, the Shepherd Singers.

31 July 1966, 2015–2100: Cilla Black, Neville King, the Barron Knights, Graham Stark, the Shepherd Singers.

7 August 1966, 2015–2100: Dickie Henderson, Hope and Keen, Graham Stark, Judy Collins, Jack Douglas.

14 August 1966, 2015–2100: Gene Detroy, Marquis and the Chimps, Vince Hill, the Mastersingers.

21 August 1966, 2015–2100: Kenneth McKellar, Winifred Atwell, Johnny Hackett, Graham Stark.

28 August 1966, 2015–2100: Petula Clark, Arthur Worsley, Eddie Calvert.

4 September 1966, 2015–2100: Shani Wallis, Ted Ray, Cardew Robinson.

11 September 1966, 2015–2100: Dusty Springfield, Gene Detroy, Marquis and the Chimps, Graham Stark, the Merrymen, Jack Douglas, David Mahlowe.

Specials

BBC1, Sunday, 25 December 1966, 2000–2045
KD, the Bachelors, Graham Stark, John Laurie, Patricia Hayes, Rita Webb, David Mahlowe, Roger Stevenson and his Diddymen with Penny Nairn, Wally Lamb, Jeanette Rossini, Jimmy Mac, orchestra directed by Bernard Herrmann, the Lissa Gray Singers.
Writers: KD and Eddie Braben.
Producer: Michael Hurll.

BBC1, Monday, 25 December 1967, 2040–2140
The Ken Dodd Christmas Show – KD, the Seekers, Graham Stark,

Patricia Hayes, John Laurie, Silvan, the Tiller Girls, the Mike Sammes Singers, orchestra directed by Peter Knight.

Writers: KD and Eddie Braben.

Producer: Michael Hurll.

Doddy for Christmas

BBC1, Wednesday, 25 December 1968, 2045–2145

KD, Graham Stark, Patricia Hayes, Dermot Kelly, Señor Wences, the New Faces, Judith Chalmers, Norman Caley, Jennifer Lowe, Doddy's Diddymen staged by Peggy O'Farrell, Children of Rybank School, Peter Barbour's Beanstalks, Henry Vadden, Watneys Silver Band, Joe Gandy's Circus, The Barking Playleader Drum Majorettes, The Knotty Ash State Dancers, Phil Fazakerley Kernott, Arthur Johnson, Collins and Lopez, Cuthbert Braben the Icky, the Firebobby Singers, Little Jimmy from Pegrams, Ken's Cutie-Girls, orchestra directed by Ken Jones.

Writers: KD and Eddie Braben.

Producer: Michael Hurll.

The Ken Dodd Show

Saturday, 21 June 1969, 1900–2000, BBC1

KD, Arthur Mullard, Dermot Kelly, Ruth Kettlewell, Talfryn Thomas, David Mahlowe, The Diddymen, Vince Hill, Sandy Powell, Luis Alberto del Paraná and Los Paraguayos, The Herculeans, Nigel Hopkins, the Mike Sammes Singers, Peter Knight and the Orchestra.

Writer: KD.

Producer: Michael Hurll.

Doddy's Music Box

Series 1:

ABC for the ITV network, Saturdays, 1745–1830, 7 January–11 March 1967

Regulars: KD, David Hamilton.

Writers: KD and Eddie Braben.

Producer: Peter Frazer-Jones (Philip Jones on show 1 with PFJ directing).

7 January 1967: Tom Jones, Julie Rogers, Peter and Gordon, The Gale Brothers.

14 January 1967: Sandie Shaw, The Three People, Gerry Stevens, Wayne Fontana.

21 January 1967: Adam Faith, The Bitter End Singers, Samantha Leigh, Oscar.

28 January 1967: Clinton Ford, Cat Stevens, Vince Hill, Jackie Trent.

4 February 1967: Herman's Hermits, Joe Henderson, Toni Eden, Normie Rowe.

11 February 1967: Freddie and The Dreamers, Julie Felix, Robbie Royal, Paul Jones.

18 February 1967: Dave Dee Beaky Dozy Mick and Titch, Donald Peers, The Settlers, James Royal.

25 February 1967: Dusty Springfield, Billy Fury, Paul and Barry Ryan, The Searchers.

4 March 1967: Russ Conway, Rosemary Squires, Dick Francis, Two and A Half.

11 March 1967: The Hollies, Johnny Hackett, Keith, Barbara Law.

Series 2:

ABC for the ITV network, Saturdays, 1815–1900, 20 January–9 March 1968

20 January 1968: The Bachelors, The Tremeloes, Salena Jones, Solomon King.

27 January 1968: Herman's Hermits, Julie Rogers, Billy Fury, The Love Affair.

3 February 1968: Long John Baldry, Clinton Ford, The Moody Blues.

10 February 1968: Manfred Mann, Esther and Abi Ofarim, Anita Harris, Fanny Cradock.

17 February 1968: The Dave Clark Five, Paul and Barry Ryan, Friday, Brown, Frankie Vaughan.

24 February 1968: Sandie Shaw, Vince Everett.

2 March 1968: Adam Faith, Vince Hill, Anita Harris, Nigel Hopkins, Graham Stark, Rita Webb, Arthur Mullard.

9 March 1968: Matt Monro, The Scaffold, Lena Martell.

Ken Dodd and the Diddymen

KD, Roger Stevenson (puppeteer), Sydney Arnold, Jerold Wells.
Writer: Bob Block.
Producer: Stan Parkinson.

Series 1:

BBC1, Sundays, 1755–1805, 5 January–9 February 1969 – 6 x 10m

Easter special – Sunday, 6 April 1969, 1755–1805, BBC1: 'In order to provide the children with free chocolate Easter bunnies Ken and the Diddymen decide to tap the vast underground reserves

of hot natural chocolate which have recently been discovered beneath Diddyland.'
Sunday, 31 August 1969, 1755–1805, BBC1

Series 2:

BBC1, Sundays, 12 October–9 November 1969 – 5 x 10m
Special – Sunday, 21 December 1969, 1755–1805, BBC1: 'A plumptious Christmas Party organized by the Diddy Male Voice Choir with Sydney Arnold, Cyril Varley and Bryan Thanner. Before the party the Diddymen take KD carol-singing. But there are problems whenever they hit a top note.' Director: Ken Wrench.

Series 3:

BBC1, Sundays, 1755–1805, 1 March–12 April 1970 – 6 x 10m
KD, Colin Edwynn in show 1.
Writer: Bob Block.
Producer: Stan Parkinson.
Director: Ken Wrench.

Series 4:

BBC1, Sundays, various times
29 November 1970: Return of the Prodigal Diddyman.
6 December 1970: The Stowaways – Director: Ken Wrench.
20 December 1970: The Abominable Snowman.
Saturday, 26 December: His Doddyness the Mayor – Director: Ken Wrench.
27 December 1970: Harry Cott Superman – Director: Ken Wrench.
3 January 1971: Doddy the Peacemaker – Director: Ken Wrench.
10 January 1971: Diddyland Television – Director: Ken Wrench.

Series 5:

BBC1, Sundays, various times
8 August 1971: Safari to Darkest Diddyland.
15 August 1971: The Haunted Treacle Mines.
22 August 1971: The Recording.
29 August 1971: The Spy Smashers (with Colin Edwynn) – Director: Ken Wrench.
12 September 1971: The Horticultural Contest.
3 October 1971: Looking After Doddy.

Series 6:

BBC1, Sundays, various times
9 January 1972: How Harry Cott Saved the World.
16 January 1972: A Star is Born – Director: Andrew Snell.
23 January 1972: The Plague of the Diddy Fireflies.
30 January 1972: The Crime Wave.
20 February 1972: Shipwrecked, with Reuben Martin.
27 February 1972: The Great Jumping Bean Disaster (with Peter Wheeler and Paula Tilbrook).
5 March 1972: Doddy the Peacemaker – Director: Ken Wrench.

We Want to Sing

Occasional series for BBC1 – 'Ken Dodd joins 300 Diddy boys and girls in a plumptious absolutely discomknockerferatingly tattifilarious tickling tonic guaranteed to make you full of gertitude and disgracefully contrapuntal aided and abetted by the Northern Dance Orchestra conducted by Bernard Herrmann.'
Producer: Nick Hunter.
Director: Hazel Lewthwaite.

Guests:

Friday, 30 July 1971, 1845–1915 – The Settlers.

Saturday, 25 December 1971, 1250–1315 – The Settlers.

Saturday, 1 April 1972, 1705–1735 – Middle of the Road.

Sunday, 25 June 1972, 1500–1530 – Middle of the Road.

Saturday, 24 February 1973, 1705–1735 – Middle of the Road.

Monday, 10 December 1973, 1530–1600 – Middle of the Road.

Saturday, 20 July 1974, 1715–1745 – The Karlins, Alan Moorhouse replaces Herrmann.

Funny You Should Say That

ATV for the ITV network, Saturdays, mostly 1745–1815, 8 April–13 May 1972 – 6 x 30m

KD, Talfryn Thomas, David Hamilton, Barbara Mullaney, Bill Dean, Jack Parnell and his Orchestra.

Writers: Norman Beedle, David McKellar, Wally Malston, Malcolm Cameron, Stuart Campbell, Maurice Bird, David McKay.

Producer: Bill Hitchcock.

Additional guest casts: 8 April 1972 – Jonathan Cecil, Margaret Nolan, Jeremy Lloyd, Jennifer Lowe; 15 April 1972 – Pat Coombs, Gladys Morgan.

Schooldays: Times Remembered

BBC2, Wednesday, 30 May 1973, 2045–2100

KD talking to Bob Wellings.

Producer: Catherine Boyd.

Doddy's Christmas Forces Show

BBC1, Monday, 24 December 1973, 2020–2120

'A film made entirely on location in the Indian Ocean, Cyprus, Gibraltar and Ulster'

KD, Neville King, Jan Hunt, Mark Raffles and members of the Armed Forces, The Forces Sweethearts (Wendy Baldock, Alison Basham, Marie Betts, Marilyn Brown, Suzanne Danielle, Tricia Doran, Lynn Hayworth, Alison Minto, Lamona Snow, Suzie Toogood), the Stan Clarke Seven.

Producer: Michael Hurll.

Ken Dodd's World of Laughter

Series 1:

BBC1, Fridays, 2015, 22 November 1974–3 January 1975 – 6 x 45m.

KD, The Young Generation, Miriam Margolyes, Michael McClain, Jo Manning Wilson, Windsor Davies, Bill Tidy, Talfryn Thomas (shows 4–6), John Bouchier (show 1), Army Gymnastic Display Team (show 2), Trevor Brooking (show 2), Martin Chivers (show 2), Chris Finnegan (show 2), Phil 'Fazakerley' Kernott (show 2), Chantal and Dumont (show 3), Percy Edwards (show 3), Barking Playleader Majorettes (show 3), Romford Drum and Trumpet Corps (show 3), Al Carthy (show 4), Johnny Hart (show 4), Lee Brennan (show 5), Jean Rosaire and Goldie the Wonderhorse (show 5), Ronnie Hazlehurst and his Orchestra.

Script editor: Peter Robinson.

Producer: Michael Hurll.

Series 2:

BBC1, Thursdays, 1945, 30 October–4 December 1975 – 6 x 45m.
KD, Chris Emmett, Hilda Fenemore, Michael McClain, Talfryn
    Thomas, Jo Manning Wilson, Vicki Michelle (show 6), Ronnie
    Hazlehurst and his Orchestra.
Writers: KD, Norman Beedle, Dave Dutton, David McKellar.
Producer: Michael Hurll.

Series 3:

BBC1, Fridays, 1925, 29 October 1976–10 December 1976 – 7
    x 45m.
KD, Chris Emmett, Faith Brown, Hilda Fenemore, Michael McClain,
    The Wurzels (show 2), Enrico (show 3), Roy Rivers (show 3),
    Stromboli (show 3), Talfryn Thomas (show 4), Bob 'Tray'
    Blackman (show 4), Alison Ruffell (show 5), The Patton Brothers
    (show 6), acts from Gerry Cottle's Circus (show 7).
Writers: KD, Dave Dutton, Norman Beedle, Roy Dixon, Ken Wallis,
    Barry Roberts.
Executive producer: Michael Hurll.
Producer: James Moir.

The Ken Dodd New Year's Eve Special

BBC1, Wednesday, 31 December 1975, 1950–2040
KD, Rolf Harris, New Edition, Ronnie Hazlehurst and his
    Orchestra.
Producer: Michael Hurll.

Seaside Special – The Ken Dodd Blackpool Centenary Show

BBC1, Saturday, 19 June 1976, 2030–2130

KD, Tim Brooke-Taylor, Graeme Garden, Bill Oddie, Mollie Sugden, Frank Thornton, John Inman, Wendy Richard, Nicholas Smith, Charlie Cairoli and Company, Johnny Hart, Tony Blackburn, Dave Lee Travis, The Daredevils, New Edition, Ronnie Hazlehurst and his Orchestra.

Producer: Michael Hurll.

The Ken Dodd Show

Thames for the ITV network, Thursday, 28 December 1978, 2000–2100

KD, Graham Stark, Hilda Fenemore, Talfryn Thomas, Jo Manning Wilson, Michael McClain, The Mike Sammes Singers, Alan Braden (musical director)

Writers: KD, Frank Hughes and Norman Beedle.

Producer: Dennis Kirkland.

The Ken Dodd Laughter Show

Thames for the ITV network, Mondays, 1900, 8 January–12 February 1979 – 6 x 25m

KD, Talfryn Thomas (shows 1–4 and 6), The Ladybirds, Hilda Fenemore (shows 1 and 4), Rita Webb (shows 2, 5 and 6), Charles Craig (show 2), Derek Deadman (shows 3 and 5), Michael McClain (show 3), Hank Walters and his Dusty Road Ramblers (show 4), Pat Ashton (show 5), Jo Manning Wilson (show 6).

Writers: KD, Norman Beedle, Frank Hughes.

Producer/director: Dennis Kirkland.

Doddy!

BBC1, Friday, 1 January 1982, 1855–1935

KD, George Carl with The Diddy Kids, Doddy's Daisy Chain, Ken Jones (musical director), the Mike Sammes Singers.

Director: Geoffrey Posner.

Producer: John Fisher.

Ken Dodd's Showbiz

BBC1, Saturdays, 1905, 13 March–17 April 1982 – 6 x 35m

KD, Touch of Class, Ken Jones (musical director), the Mike Sammes Singers, Mac Ronay (show 1), Compagnie Philippe Genty (show 1), Norm Nielsen (show 2), the Ghezzi Troupe (show 2), Neville King (show 3), Rao (show 3), Alfredo (show 4), Philippe Genty and his Military Parade (show 4), the Diddy Kids (show 4), Professor Stanley Unwin (show 4), Rolf Knic Jr (show 5), Gaston and Pipo (show 5), Clarence Nash with Donald Duck (show 5), Robert Dhery and company (show 6), Otto Wessely (show 6), KD's Diddymen (show 6), Arthur Askey (show 6).

Director: Brian Penders (show 1), John Bishop (shows 2–6).

Producer: John Fisher.

A Question of Entertainment

BBC1, Sundays, 1915–1945, 24 April–21 August 1988 – 17 x 30m

Tom O'Connor (host), KD, Larry Grayson (team captains).

Executive producer: Alan Walsh.

Producer/director: John Rooney.

Ken Dodd at the London Palladium

Thames for the ITV Network, Tuesday, 25 December 1990, 1815–
 1930
KD, Brian Rogers Dancers, Roby Gasser.
Director: Paul Kirrage.
Producer: John Fisher.

Guest appearances and spots

The Good Old Days

BBC TV, Friday, 11 March 1955, 2115–2215
Robin Hunter (chairman), Margery Manners, Joe Black, Norman
 Grant and Niki Grant, Barbara Hicks, KD, Joan Rhodes, Hylda
 Baker, orchestra conducted by Alyn Ainsworth.
Producer: Barney Colehan.

It's a Great Life

BBC TV, Saturday, 16 April 1955, 2130–2230
Ralph Reader (host), Mrs Shufflewick, Fay Dewitt, Maria Pavlou,
 Charles Stewart, Tanya Duray, KD, Six Flying De Pauls, Johnny
 Denis and his Ranchers, The Sherman Fisher Girls, the George
 Mitchell Singers, orchestra conducted by Eric Robinson.
Producer: Bryan Sears.

Let's Have Fun

BBC TV, Thursday, 23 May 1955, 2215–2245

Jimmy Clitheroe, Joy Harris, The Kordites, KD, Kenny Baker, Morecambe and Wise, Peter Webster.
Producer: Barney Colehan.

Red Riding Hood – excerpts from the Lyceum, Sheffield

BBC TV, Monday, 26 December 1955, 1930–2015
KD, Mrs Shufflewick, Little Walter and his musical daughters, Tibor Alexander's Wonder Dogs, Izna Roselli's singers and dancers, Mary Harkness, Barbara Haydn, Eric Williams, Joan Ross, Colin Bean, Billy Blue, Jack Falcon, Jimmy Green, Eddie Falcon, Eileen Falcon.
Writer: John Beaumont.
Television production: Ronnie Taylor.

The Cosmopolitan

BBC TV, Wednesday, 29 February 1956, 2030–2130
Alex d'Arcy (host), Irene Hilda, Rima Rudina, Les Marionettes Lafaye, Jimmy Lover, Mall Davis, Sheila Clarke, KD.
Producers: Harry Carlisle and Christian Simpson.

Let's Have Fun – an excerpt of the show from the Central Pier, Blackpool

BBC TV, Friday, 8 June 1956, 2100–2130
Jimmy James, KD, Jimmy Clitheroe, Dennis Spicer, Joy Harris, Joseph Ward, Roy Castle, The Orchid Room Lovelies, Corinne.
Producer: Barney Colehan.

Northern Showground from the Playhouse Theatre, Manchester

BBC TV, Sunday, 29 July 1956, 1945–2030

Richard Murdoch (host), Lita Roza, KD, The Chocolateers, Joe Lynch, Tutte Lemkow, Sara Luzita, The Kordites, the Hindley-Taylor Singers, the BBC Northern Variety Orchestra conducted by Alyn Ainsworth.

Producer: Ronnie Taylor.

Director: Frederick Knapman.

Six Five Special

BBC TV, Saturday, 18 May 1957, 1805–1850

Josephine Douglas, Pete Murray, Terry Dene and his Deneagers, the Delta Four, KD, Don Lang and his Frantic Five, Harry Walton and his Dixieland Jazzmen.

Producer: Jack Good.

Blackpool Show Parade presents Rocking with Laughter (an excerpt from Tom Arnold and Jack Taylor's 1957 Summer Revue at the Hippodrome, Blackpool)

BBC TV, Friday, 5 July 1957, 2115–2200

KD, Jill Day, Stan Stennett, The Marcellis, The Two Pirates, Gordon Needham, Michael and Shirley Davis, The Royal Sextet, The Twelve Rockettes.

Producer: Barney Colehan.

Stars at Blackpool from the Spanish Hall at the Winter Gardens

BBC TV, Monday, 23 September 1957, 2115–2200

Brian Reece (host), The Three Deuces, Kenny Baker, The Boliana Ivanko Quartet, Karen Greer, Morecambe and Wise, The Tanner

Sisters, Anne Shelton, KD, the BBC Northern Dance Orchestra conducted by Alyn Ainsworth.
Producer: Barney Colehan.

The Good Old Days

BBC TV, Wednesday, 16 October 1957, 2215–2300
Leonard Sachs (chairman), The Three Buffoons, Jimmy Gay, Betty Driver, Freddie Frinton, The Munks Twins (Nancy and Molly), KD.
Producer: Barney Colehan.

Ticket for Friday – Let's Have Fun from the Central Pier, Blackpool

BBC TV, Friday, 30 May 1958, 1930–2000
Jack Watson (host), KD, Don Lang, Yvonne Michel and Erik, Brenda Barry and The Zio Angels, Josef Locke.
Producer: Barney Colehan.

The Good Old Days

BBC TV, Thursday, 20 November 1958, 2230–2315
Leonard Sachs (chairman), KD, Terry Scott, Leon Cortez assisted by Freddy Liston and Rose Alba, Kitty Gillow, The Magical Claudine with Old Stephens the Butler, The Gay Edwardians.
Producer: Barney Colehan.

Great Yarmouth: an excerpt from Tom Arnold's Tops Again at the Britannia Theatre

BBC TV, Friday, 28 August 1959, 1930–2000
KD, Kenneth Earle and Malcolm Vaughan (at the piano Michael

Austin), The Three Barry Sisters, The Iris Roy Trio, Shelagh Miller, Sylvia Lee, The Jean Belmont Dancers.
Producer: Barrie Edgar.

Sing Along With Joe

ABC, Sunday, 4 February 1962, 1720–1750
'Joe (Mr Piano) Henderson visits a biscuit factory in Liverpool for the fourth section final of the Miss Industry of 1962 and Find a New Voice contests and invites you to sing along with Jim Dale, Barbara Law, Don Rennie, The Raindrops and the voice of Bob Danvers-Walker.'
Producer: Ben Churchill.

Thank Your Lucky Stars

ABC for the ITV network, Saturday, 24 March 1962, 1750–1830
Brian Matthew (host), KD, Humphrey Lyttelton and his Band, Bert Weedon, Jimmy Justice, Patti Brooks, Frankie Townsend, Peter Wynne, Cliff Richard, Steve Race.
Producer: Philip Jones.

Point North

BBC TV (North), Wednesday, 15 January 1964, 1935
Item on Dodd at the Royal Court.

Look North

BBC TV (North), 22 April 1965, 1805–1826
Interview about Palladium success.

Lucky Stars – Summer Spin

ABC for the ITV network, Saturday, 28 August 1965, 1750–1835

Jim Dale (host), KD, Cliff Bennett and The Rebel Rousers, Vince Hill, The Primitives, Val McKenna, Adam, Mike and Tim, Sylvan, The Sorrows.

Director: Keith Beckett.

Thank Your Lucky Stars

ABC for the ITV network, Saturday, 2 October 1965, 1750–1835

Jim Dale, KD, Petula Clark, The Fortunes, Lance Percival, Bo Diddley (with Jerome Green and The Duchess), Alan David, Jan Panter, Yardbirds – Evil Hearted You, The Lionel Blair Dancers.

Director: Keith Beckett.

Royal Variety Performance

ATV for the ITV network, Sunday, 14 November 1965, 1925–2225

Arthur Haynes, Dusty Springfield, Arthur Mullard, The Dave Clark Five, Shirley Bassey, Peter, Paul and Mary, Spike Milligan, KD, Max Bygraves, Neville King, Peter Cook, Dudley Moore, Tony Bennett, Jack Benny, Johnny Halliday, Tony Fayne, Leslie Noyes, Michael Henry, Hope and Keen, Frank Ifield, The Kaye Sisters, Roddy Maude-Roxby, Bill Kerr, The Alberts, Peter Sellers, Audrey Bayley, The Shepherd Singers, Sylvie Vartan, Eddie Vartan and his Band, Lilly Yokoi, The London Palladium Boys and Girls, The London Palladium Orchestra directed by Billy Ternent.

Director: Bill Ward.

Thank Your Lucky Stars

ABC for the ITV network, Saturday, 11 December 1965, 1750–1835

Jim Dale, KD, Manfred Mann, Ketty Lester, Kenny Lynch, Wayne Fontana, Janie Jones.

Director: Keith Beckett.

Top of the Pops

BBC1, Saturday, 25 December 1965, 2235–2350

Featuring the No.1 records of the year by The Beatles, The Byrds, KD, Georgie Fame and the Blue Flames, The Hollies, Tom Jones, The Kinks, The Moody Blues, Elvis Presley, The Righteous Brothers, The Rolling Stones, The Seekers, Sandie Shaw, Sonny and Cher, Jackie Trent, Unit Four Plus Two, The Walker Brothers, with Jimmy Savile, David Jacobs, Alan Freeman, Pete Murray (hosts).

Producer: Johnnie Stewart.

Crossroads

ATV for the ITV network, Wednesday, 16 March 1966, 1835–1900

Playing himself as a motel guest.

Thank Your Lucky Stars

ABC for the ITV network, Saturday, 4 June 1966, 1750–1835

Jim Dale, KD, Freddie and The Dreamers, Chris Andrews, Shirley Abacair, The Luvvers, Tony Hazzard, Toni Caroll, Don Spencer.

Director: Peter Frazer-Jones.

The Good Old Days – special 100th edition

BBC1, Wednesday, 24 January 1968, 2000–2050

KD, Ray Alan and Lord Charles, Vince Hill, Eira Heath, Doreen
Hermitage, Rita Morris, Kathleen West, Wendy Wayne, Freddie
Frinton, Leonard Sachs (host), Bernard Herrmann (musical
director).

Producer: Barney Colehan.

Royal Variety Performance

ATV for the ITV network, Sunday, 19 November 1967

KD, Sandie Shaw, Dickie Henderson, Tommy Cooper, Lulu, Harry
Secombe, Rolf Harris, Vikki Carr, Bob Hope, The Rockin'
Berries, The Bluebell Girls, Val Doonican, Dougie Squires' Boys
and Girls, Tom Jones, Mireille Mathieu, The Rumanian National
Dance Company and Orchestra, Tanya, The London Palladium
Orchestra directed by Billy Ternent, The Bel Cantos.

Executive producer: Bill Ward.

Director: Albert Locke.

At Last It's Christmas

Granada, Tuesday, 24 December 1968, 1805–1830

Chris Kelly (host), Kenny Lynch, KD, Keith Dewhurst, Freddie
Garrity, Richard Stilgoe, Derek Hilton, Jean Hart, Jeremy Taylor,
Ray Gosling, John McGregor, Alan Towers, Bob Greaves.

Producers: Christopher Kelly/Bryan Shiner.

The Golden Shot

ATV, Sunday, 27 July 1969, 1645–1730

Nursery rhymes and fairy tales: Bob Monkhouse (host), Anne

Aston, Carol Dilworth, Len Lowe, KD, Anita Harris, Johnny Patrick (musical director).

Writer: Wally Malston.

Producer: John Pullen.

Omnibus – George Robey

BBC1, Sunday, 28 September 1969, 2200–2250

Lady Robey, Arthur Askey, John Baxter, Ivor Brown, Sir Neville Cardus, Charlie Chester, KD, Edward Glibbery, Hetty King, Evelyn Laye, Harry Loman, Yehudi Menuhin, Henry Oscar, Wee Georgie Wood, with narration by Cyril Fletcher and Charles Leno.

Producer: John Ingram.

Doddy's Christmas Bizarre

LWT for the ITV network, Friday, 26 December 1969, 1930–2030

KD, Billy Eckstine, David Hamilton, Rudy Cardenas, Talfryn Thomas, The Diddymen.

Script editor: Barry Cryer.

Producer: David Bell.

The Golden Shot

ATV for the ITV network, Sunday, 18 January 1970, 1645–1730

Pantomime parade: Bob Monkhouse, KD, Anita Harris, Johnny Patrick (musical director).

Writer: Wally Malston.

Producer: Edward Joffe.

The Golden Shot

ATV for the ITV network, Sunday, 12 July 1970, 1645–1730
The Crazy Show: Bob Monkhouse, Anne Aston, Sheila Steafel, Alan Bailey, KD.
Writer: Wally Malston
Producer: Mike Lloyd.

Disney Time

BBC1, Monday, 31 August 1970, 1845–1930
Producer: Richard Evans.

Junior Showtime

YTV for the ITV network, Tuesday, 3 November 1970, 1655–1720
KD, Gott Sisters, Diane Hunt, Caroline Brearley, Nigel Brearley.
Producer: Jess Yates.
Director: David Millard.

The Golden Shot

ATV for the ITV network, Sunday, 8 November 1970, 1645–1735
Funny folk: Bob Monkhouse (host), Anne Aston, Yutte Stensgaard, John Baker, KD, Terry Wogan, Eva Demarczyk, The Scaffold, Johnny Patrick (musical director).
Writer: Wally Malston.
Producer: Mike Lloyd.

The Rolf Harris Show

BBC1, Saturday, 21 November 1970, 1930–2025

Rolf Harris, The Young Generation, KD, Bruce Forsyth, Iwan
    Rebroff with Bibi Johns, Alyn Ainsworth and his Orchestra.
Writer: Eric Merriman.
Production: Stewart Morris.

Junior Showtime

YTV for the ITV network, Tuesday, 15 December 1970, 1655–1720
KD, Deborah Price, Mark Price, David Grayson, Lynda Jenkins,
    Kathryn Apanowicz.
Producer: Jess Yates.
Director: David Millard.

Robinson Crusoe

BBC1, Friday, 25 December 1970, 1710–1840
KD, the Diddymen choreographed by Peggy O'Farrell, the
    Maljohns, Roy Gunson Dancers, the Bowles Bevan Singers, Burt
    Rhodes (musical director).
Writer: Phil Park.
Producer: Terry Hughes.

The Golden Shot

ATV for the ITV network, Sunday, 27 December 1970, 1645–1735
Show business: Bob Monkhouse (host), Anne Aston, Yutte Stens-
    gaard, Alan Bailey, Anita Harris, KD, Freddie Davies, Vince Hill,
    Johnny Patrick (musical director).
Writer: Wally Malston.
Producer: Mike Lloyd.

Gala Performance: Liverpool by Liverpool

Granada for the ITV network, Sunday, 27 June 1971, 1955–2125

Peter Adamson, KD, Robert Flemyng, Adrian Henri, Paula Hinton, Jacqui and Bridie, Bill Kenwright, Gerry Marsden, John McCabe, Roger McGough, The New Boys, Jennifer Paull, Patricia Routledge, The Scaffold, The Spinners, Marion Studholme, Jimmy Tarbuck, Frankie Vaughan, Everyman Repertory Company, Liverpool Playhouse Company, Band of The Liverpool and Bootle Constabulary, Merseyside Youth Orchestra, Northern Dance Theatre Company.

Producers: William Chappell and John Hamp.

Director: Eric Harrison.

Lift Off

Granada for the ITV network, 17 August 1971, 1655–1720

Ayshea Brough, Wally Whyton, Ollie Beak, The Feet, KD, The Tremeloes.

Producer: Muriel Young.

Director: Dave Warwick.

The Golden Shot

ATV for the ITV network, Sunday, 29 August 1971, 1645–1735

Unusual occupations: Bob Monkhouse (host), Anne Aston, Jenny Lee-Wright, Alan Bailey, KD, Lena Martell, Johnny Patrick (musical director).

Writer: Wally Malston.

Producer: Mike Lloyd.

The Golden Shot – 200th edition – live from Warwick Castle

ATV for the ITV network, Sunday, 31 October 1971, 1640–1735

Bob Monkhouse (host), Anne Aston, Chelsea Brown, Alan Bailey, Clodagh Rodgers, Scott Walker, Yutte Stensgaard, Hugh Boyle, Derek Dougan, Rachel Heyhoe-Flint [as Rachel Heyhoe], Ann Jones, Patrick Allen, Moira Anderson, Petula Clark, Leslie Crowther, KD, Kenny Lynch, David Tomlinson, Johnny Patrick (musical director).

Writer: Wally Malston.

Producer: Mike Lloyd.

The Golden Shot

ATV for the ITV network, Sunday, 5 December 1971, 1645–1735

Poetry and prose: Bob Monkhouse (host), Anne Aston, Ayshea Brough, John Baker, KD, Cyril Fletcher, Manitas De Plata, Johnny Patrick (musical director).

Writer: Wally Malston.

Producer: Mike Lloyd.

Lift Off

Granada for the ITV network, Wednesday, 5 January 1972, 1655–1720

Ayshea Brough, Wally Whyton, Ollie Beak, The Feet, KD, Gilbert O'Sullivan, Mac and Katie Kissoon.

Producer: Muriel Young.

Director: David Warwick.

The Golden Shot

ATV for the ITV network, Sunday, 26 March 1972, 1645–1735

Norman Vaughan (host), Anne Aston, Dana, Stéphane Grappelli, KD, Jenny Hanley, Johnny Patrick (musical director).
Writers: Spike Mullins and Charles Hart.
Producer: Les Cocks.
Director: Paul Stewart Laing.

The Golden Shot

ATV for the ITV network, Sunday, 9 April 1972, 1640–1735
Norman Vaughan (host), Anne Aston, KD, Steve and Bonnie, Johnny Patrick (musical director).
Writers: Spike Mullins and Charles Hart.
Producer: Les Cocks.
Director: Paul Stewart Laing.

Omnibus: Whatever Turns You On or Variations on a Noisy Theme

BBC1, Sunday, 7 May 1972, 2225–2310
Michael Aspel, James Blades, Johnnie Johnston, Susan Stranks, Eleanor Summerfield, John Timpson, Ken Russell, KD, John Dankworth, Cleo Laine, Dr Kevin Murphy, Duncan Steele, Juliette Alvin, Michael Hordern (narrator).
Writer and producer: Herbert Chappell.

Lift Off with Ayshea

Granada for the ITV network, Wednesday, 17 May 1972, 1655–1720
Ayshea Brough, KD, Bruce Ruffin, Rock Candy.
Producer: Muriel Young.
Director: David Warwick.

Ryan and Ronnie

BBC1, Wednesday, 23 August 1972, 1855–1925
Ryan Davies, Ronnie Williams, Myfanwy Talog, Bryn Williams,
    KD, Benny Litchfield (musical director).
Script editor: Bob Hedley.
Producer: David Richards.

Royal Variety Performance from the London Palladium

BBC1, Sunday, 5 November 1972, 1925–2215
Carol Channing, Los Diablos del Bombo, KD, Dickie Henderson,
    Rod Hull and Emu, Jackson 5, Elton John, Jack Jones, Danny La
    Rue, Liberace, Warren Mitchell, Dandy Nichols, Anthony Booth,
    Una Stubbs, Trio Hoganas, Mike Yarwood, Tom Fleming.
Producer: Michael Hurll.

The Golden Shot

ATV, Sunday, 12 November 1972, 1620–1715
Norman Vaughan (host), Anne Aston, KD, Vicky Leandros.
Writers: Spike Mullins and Charles Hart.
Producer: Les Cocks.
Director: Paul Stewart Laing.

Lift Off with Ayshea

Granada, Wednesday, 29 November 1972, 1625–1650
Ayshea Brough, KD, Muffin, Gaynor Jones.
Producer: Muriel Young.
Director: David Warwick.

The Gang Show – highlights of the 40th Anniversary Gang Show (televised from the stage of the Odeon, Temple Fortune, in the presence of HM The Queen and HRH The Duke of Edinburgh)

BBC1, Saturday, 23 December 1972, 1700–1745

KD (host), Dick Emery, Brian Johnston, David Lodge, Graham Stark.

Writer and producer: Ralph Reader.

Television presentation: Michael Hurll.

The Good Old Days

BBC1, Monday, 25 December 1972, 2300–2350

Leonard Sachs (chairman), KD, Neville King, Lyn Kennington, Alfredo, Louisa Jane White, The Trio Hoganas, Trevor Little, members of the Players' Theatre London, Bernard Herrmann (musical director).

Producer: Barney Colehan.

Pebble Mill at One

BBC1, Wednesday, 6 June 1973, 1300–1400

KD talking to Tom Coyne.

Editor: Terry Dobson.

Look Who's Talking

Border, 26 July 1973

Producer: Derek Batey.

Pebble Mill at One

BBC1, Tuesdays, 2 October–13 November 1973, 1300–1345
'Ken Dodd's Anthology of Humour' ran as a regular item for seven
weeks.

That Stuart Hall Show

BBC1, Friday, 21 December 1973, 1500–1530
Thora Hird, KD, Bill Tidy, Mike Harding, Dave June and Sam,
Brian Fitzgerald, Neil Wayne.
Producer: Douglas Boyd.

Look Who's Talking

Border, 26 December 1973
Producer: Derek Batey.

Lift Off with Ayshea

Granada for the ITV network, Wednesday, 2 January 1974, 1625–
1650
Ayshea Brough, KD, Dana, Magic Bus.
Producer: Muriel Young.
Director: David Warwick.

The Golden Shot

ATV for the ITV network, Sunday, 13 January 1974, 1640–1735
Charlie Williams (host), Jill Stanford, KD, Tony Rome, Tessie
O'Shea.
Writers: Alec Myles and Les Lilley.
Producer: Dicky Leeman.

The Good Old Days

BBC1, Friday, 1 March 1974, 2015–2100

Leonard Sachs (chairman), KD, Lyn Kennington, Jan Hunt, Panto
    Chantal and Dumont, members of the Players' Theatre – Jacquie
    Toye, Clifton Todd, Loraine Hart, Mike Fields, Dudley Stevens,
    Colin Richmond, Bernard Herrmann (musical director).

Producer: Barney Colehan.

The Golden Shot

ATV for the ITV network, Sunday, 24 March 1974, 1640–1730

Charlie Williams (host), Lee Patrick, KD, Carl Wayne, Brotherhood
    of Man, Frankie Holmes.

Writers: Alec Myles and Les Lilley.

Producer: Dicky Leeman.

Cup Final Grandstand

BBC1, Saturday, 4 May 1974, 1115–1715

Including at 12.35, Cup Final It's a Knockout – Liverpool vs
    Newcastle.

The Good Old Days

BBC1, 17 January 1975, 1945–2030

Leonard Sachs (chairman), KD, Barry Kent, Lyn Kennington, John
    Bouchier, Saxburger, members of the Players' Theatre, Bernard
    Herrmann (musical director).

Producer: Barney Colehan.

Seaside Special – from the BBC1 Big Top at Blackpool

BBC1, Saturday, 5 July 1975, 2015–2100

KD with The Diddymen, Dana, Wild Honey, David Hamilton, New Edition, Ronnie Hazlehurst and his Orchestra.

Producer: Michael Hurll.

The Good Old Days

BBC1, Thursday, 4 March 1976, 2125–2210

Leonard Sachs (chairman), KD, Sheila Steafel, Valerie Masterson, Johnny Hart, The Tornados, members of the Players' Theatre – Jacquie Toye, Norman Warwick, Jenny Wren, Clifton Todd, Loraine Hart, Dudley Stevens, Doreen Hermitage (choreographer), Bernard Herrmann (musical director).

Producer: Barney Colehan.

For My Next Trick

BBC1, Saturday, 31 July 1976, 1730–1800

Faith Brown, Paul Daniels, Terry Seabrook, John Wade, Les Diaboliques, Johnny Hart, KD.

Producer: Peter Ridsdale Scott.

Director: Keith Phillips.

The Big Time

BBC1, Thursday, 9 December 1976, 2125–2215

'Tony Peers, a comedian at Butlin's Holiday Camp is given the chance to appear in BBC TV's Seaside Special – if he can make his act good enough.'

Director: Ian Sharp.

Producer: Esther Rantzen.

A Jubilee of Music

BBC1, Friday, 31 December 1976, 2230–2345

Vera Lynn, Acker Bilk, Max Bygraves, Petula Clark, KD, Val Doonican, Rolf Harris, Kathy Kirby, Lulu, Matt Monro, Cliff Richard, Helen Shapiro, Norman Wisdom, The Young Generation, Alyn Ainsworth and his Orchestra.

Producer: Stewart Morris.

The Good Old Days

BBC1, Thursday, 6 January 1977, 2125–2210

Leonard Sachs (chairman), KD, Beatrice Aston, John Bouchier, Bill Drysdale, Christine Cartwright, Leo Bassi, members of the Players' Theatre – Loraine Hart, Dudley Stevens, Jenny Wren, Clifton Todd, Maria St. Clare, Norman Warwick.

It's No Joke

BBC2, Thursday, 31 March 1977, 2320–closedown

Barry Took, Alan Coren, Gwyn Thomas, Dr Anthony Buffery view highlights from proceedings at the International Humour Conference at Cardiff University including Professor KD of Knotty Ash University and wonder can humour be put under the microscope?

Producer: Derek Trimby.

Everyman: What's So Funny About Religion Anyway?

BBC1, Sunday, 1 May 1977, 2215–2315

John Pitman talks to KD, Frank Carson, Kenneth Williams, Eric Morecambe, Spike Milligan.

Producer: Jim Murray.

Be My Guest

Granada for the ITV network, Saturday, 16 July 1977, 1925–2025
Duggie Brown, Brotherhood of Man, KD, Sacha Distel, Ronnie
    Dukes, Ricki Lee, Good Vibrations.
Producer: Rod Taylor.
Director: Nicholas Ferguson.

Ken Dodd's Christmas Laughter Show

BBC1 North West only, Tuesday, 13 December 1977, 1840–1910

The Good Old Days

BBC1, Thursday, 29 March 1979, 2125–2215
Leonard Sachs (chairman), KD, Valerie Masterson, The King's
    Singers, Doreen Hermitage, Bill Drysdale, Chrissie Cartwright,
    The Duo Lanka, Albert Aldred, members of the Players' Theatre
    – Jenny Till, Penny Rigden, Suzanne Roberts, Pauline Antony,
    Norman Warwick, David Machin, Peter Sutherland, Christopher
    Molloy, Barney Colehan (musical director).
Producer: Barney Colehan.

The Good Old Days

BBC1, Tuesday, 10 January 1978, 2010–2100
Leonard Sachs (chairman), KD, Jan Hunt, Maryetta and Vernon
    Midgley, Doreen Hermitage and Julia Sutton, José Luis Moreno,
    The Hurricanes, Inga-Lise, Dora Bryan, members of the Players'
    Theatre – Jenny Wren, Camilla Blair, Jenny Till, Julie Morgan,
    Diane Jane Argyle, Dudley Stevens, Penny Rigden, Norman
    Warwick, Debbie Goodman, Deryk Parkin, Emma Bryant,

Christopher Wren, Carol Busby, Bernard Herrmann (musical director).

Producer: Barney Colehan.

The Good Old Days

BBC1, Tuesday, 14 March 1978, 2010–2100

Leonard Sachs (chairman), KD, Kenneth McKellar, Jan Hunt, Francis Van Dyke, Soo-Bee Lee, Pat Mooney, Bartschelly, members of the Players' Theatre: Jenny Wren, Dudley Stevens, Jenny Till, Norman Warwick, Diane Jane Argyle, Deryk Parkin, Penny Rigden, Christopher Wren.

Producer: Barney Colehan.

Look Who's Talking

Border for the ITV network, 30 March 1978

Producer: Derek Batey.

Director: Anna K Moore.

Seaside Special

BBC1, Saturday, 28 July 1979, 2025–2115

KD, The Brother Lees, Tony Brutus, The Angels and The Diddymen, Peter Powell, Geoff Richer's First Edition, Ronnie Hazlehurst and his Orchestra, Maggie Stredder and her Singers.

Producer: Michael Hurll.

Parkinson

BBC1, Saturday, 15 March 1980, 2230–2330

Producer: John Fisher.

Director: Bruce Milliard.

The Good Old Days

BBC1, Wednesday, 25 June 1980, 2125–2215

Leonard Sachs (chairman), KD, Teresa Cahill, Pat Mooney, Lynda Gloria, Eleanor McCready, The Chuckle Brothers, members of the Players' Theatre – Jenny Till, Penny Rigden, Pauline Antony, Nicola Kimber, Peter Sutherland, Christopher Molloy, Peter Loury, Martin Knight, Bernard Herrmann (musical director).

Producer: Barney Colehan.

Des O'Connor Tonight

BBC1, Monday, 15 December 1980, 2010–2100

Des O'Connor (host), KD, Norman Collier, Mimi Hines, Colin Keyes (musical director).

Writer: Neil Shand.

Executive Producer: James Moir.

Producer: Brian Penders.

Boxing Night at the Mill

BBC1, Friday, 26 December 1980, 2310–closedown

Bob Langley (host), KD, Susan Hampshire, Peter Davison, Wall Street Crash, Kenny Ball and his Jazzmen.

Director: Roy Norton.

Producer: Roy Ronnie.

Parkinson

BBC1, Saturday, 5 December 1981, 2250–2350

Director: Bruce Milliard.

Producers: Graham Lindsay and Gill Stribling-Wright.

Executive producer: John Fisher.

Batley

BBC1, Wednesday, 24 February 1982, 2010–2100

Michael Parkinson (narrator), Shirley Bassey, James Corrigan, Cilla Black, Cannon and Ball, Bernie Clifton, Con Cluskey, Paul Daniels, KD, Gracie Fields, The Grumbleweeds, Vince Hill, Engelbert Humperdinck, Eartha Kitt, Danny La Rue, Lulu, Vera Lynn, Johnny Mathis, Eric Morecambe, Gene Pitney, Cliff Richard, Neil Sedaka, Derek Smith, Alvin Stardust, Freddie Starr, Frankie Vaughan, Charlie Williams, Mike Yarwood.

Producer: Rod Taylor.

In at the Deep End

BBC1, Tuesday, 14 September 1982, 1945–2035

Paul Heiney becomes a stand-up comedian, advised and encouraged by the top names in comedy including Jimmy Perry, KD, Danny La Rue, Little and Large, Beryl Reid and Marti Caine.

Producer: Nick Handel.

Blankety Blank

BBC1, Saturday, 25 September 1982, 1915–1950

Terry Wogan, Judith Chalmers, Leslie Crowther, Sandra Dickinson, KD, Liza Goddard, Jonathan King.

Director: Dave Perrottet.

Producer: Marcus Plantin.

Blankety Blank

BBC1, Saturday, 27 November 1982, 1855–1930

Terry Wogan, Pat Coombs, KD, Stu Francis, Nerys Hughes, Roy Kinnear, Tessa Wyatt.

Director: Dave Perrottet.
Producer: Marcus Plantin.

Des O'Connor Tonight

BBC2, Monday, 6 December 1982, 2010–2100
Des O'Connor (host), KD, Jack Jones, Kelly Monteith, Colin Keyes
(musical director).
Programme associate: Neil Shand.
Producer/director: Brian Penders.

Jim'll Fix It

BBC1, Saturday, 25 December 1982, 1720–1800
Producer: Roger Ordish.

Des O'Connor Tonight

Thames for the ITV network, Tuesday, 20 December 1983, 2000–
2100
Des O'Connor (host), KD, Grace Kennedy, Nelson Sardelli, Colin
Keyes (musical director).
Script: Eric Davidson.
Producer/director: Brian Penders.

The Early Beatles

Granada for the ITV network, Sunday, 1 January 1984, 1740–1840
Producer: John Hamp.
Director: Philip Casson.

Under the Blackpool Tower

BBC1, Sunday, 1 January 1984, 1300–1345
KD, Norman Barrett, James Clubb, The Simets, The Rastellis.
Producer: Ian Christie.

321: Victorian Music Hall

Yorkshire for the ITV network, Saturday, 1 September 1984, 2000–2100
Ted Rogers (host), KD, Chris Emmett, Mike Newman, Caroline Munro, Sheila Steafel, Harold Taylor, Nicky Hinkley, The Brian Rogers Connection, Robert Hartley (musical director).
Writers: John Bartlett, Eric Davidson and Wally Malston.
Producer: Terry Henebery.
Director: Graham Wetherell.

The Dog Show

BBC2, Monday, 17 September 1984, 1730–1800
Dennis McCarthy (presenter), KD.
Producer: Mike Derby.

Pebble Mill at One

BBC1, Tuesday, 27 November 1984, 1300–1345

Blankety Blank

BBC1, Tuesday, 25 December 1984, 1730–1805
Les Dawson (host), Lorraine Chase, Suzanne Danielle, KD, Russell Harty, Ruth Madoc, Derek Nimmo.
Director: David Taylor.
Producer: John Bishop.

The Railway Carriage Game

BBC1, Wednesday 9 January 1985, 1730–1758

Gyles Brandreth (host), Lennie Bennett, Stan Boardman, Floella Benjamin, Faith Brown, Jimmy Cricket, KD.

Director: John Rooney.

Producer: Peter Ridsdale Scott.

The Railway Carriage Game

BBC1, Wednesday, 13 February 1985, 1730–1758

Gyles Brandreth (host), Lennie Bennett, Stan Boardman, Floella Benjamin, Pat Coombs, KD, John Inman.

Director: John Rooney.

Producer: Peter Ridsdale Scott.

Blankety Blank

BBC1, Friday, 20 December 1985, 1940–2015

Les Dawson (host), KD, Cherry Gillespie, Anita Harris, Roland Rat Superstar, Wendy Richard, Freddie Trueman.

Director: Bruce Millar.

Producer: Stanley Appel.

English File: The Power of Language – Power to Move

BBC2, Saturday, 17 January 1986, 1430–1450

KD talks about making people laugh and Linda Thompson sings a love song.

Producer: Edward Hayward.

Looks Familiar

Thames for Channel 4, Friday, 20 June 1986, 2015–2100
Denis Norden, Janet Brown, KD, Frankie Howerd.
Producer: David Clark.

Looks Familiar

Thames for Channel 4, Friday, 8 August 1986, 2015–2100
Denis Norden, Judith Chalmers, KD, Bob Holness.
Producer: David Clark.

By Royal Command

BBC1, Friday, 28 November 1986, 2130–2235
The story and stories, triumphs and heartaches, laughter and tears
of the Royal Variety Performances since they began in 1912.
Producer: Rod Taylor.

Royal Variety Performance, from the Theatre Royal, Drury Lane

BBC1, Saturday, 29 November 1986, 1915–2220
Victor Borge, Rory Bremner, Max Bygraves, Marti Caine, Frank
Carson, Cyd Charisse, Petula Clark, Lesley Collier, Ronnie
Corbett, Tyne Daly, Paul Daniels, Michael Davis, KD, Val
Doonican, Noel Edmonds, Margot Fonteyn, Sharon Gless,
Stéphane Grappelli, Simon Howe, Huddersfield Choral Society,
David Jason, Stephen Jefferies, Aled Jones, Penelope Keith,
Margaret Kelly, Kit and the Widow, Lulu, Nicholas Lyndhurst,
Vera Lynn, Ruth Madoc, Valerie Masterson, Buster Merryfield,
Bob Monkhouse, Nana Mouskouri, Paul Nicholas, Michael
Parkinson, Nicholas Parsons, Peking Opera, Carolyn Pickles,

Su Pollard, Alan Randall, Angela Rippon, Leonard Sachs, Mike Smith, Peggy Spencer, Latin American Formation Team, Peter Ustinov, Marti Webb, Terry Wogan, Victoria Wood, the companies of 42nd Street and Charlie Girl, the Royal Variety Dancers, Pipes and Drums Of The 1st Battalion The King's Own Scottish Borderers, Sue Lawley (presenter), Ronnie Hazlehurst (musical director).

Director: Brian Whitehouse.

Stage Director and Associate Producer: Norman Maen.

Producer: Yvonne Littlewood.

Twist the Cat's Whisker

BBC2, Tuesday, 23 December 1986, 1520–1550

Tom O'Connor (presenter), Ray Alan, KD, Alan Freeman, Sir Charles Groves, Stuart Hall, Sooty, The Spinners, Harry Worth, Godfrey Talbot.

Writer/producer: Barry Bevins.

321

YTV for the ITV network, Saturday, 19 September 1987, 1945–2045

Ted Rogers (host), KD, Shane Richie, the Minitones, Helen Gelzer, Felix Bowness.

Producer/director: Philip Casson.

Doctor Who – Delta and the Bannermen

BBC1, Monday, 2 November 1987, 1935–2000

Sylvester McCoy, Bonnie Langford, KD.

Writer: Malcolm Kholl.
Producer: John Nathan-Turner.
Director: Chris Clough.

The Animals Holiday Roadshow

BBC1, Monday, 28 December 1987, 1205–1245

Dr Desmond Morris, Sarah Kennedy, Brian Blessed, Michael Fish, KD, Robert Kilroy-Silk, Rick Wakeman, Andrew Sachs, Rustie Lee.

Director: Kate Kinninmont.
Producer: Lan Christie.
Editor: David Martin.

Children's Royal Variety Performance

BBC1, Monday, 2 May 1988

Anneka Rice (television host), David Tomlinson (stage host), Johnny Ball, Michael Barrymore, Jeremy Beadle, Kate Bellamy, Floella Benjamin, Christopher Biggins, Harry Blackstone, Lionel Blair, Bob Bramson, Bros, Roy Castle, Chas 'n' Dave, Don Crann, Christopher, David Copperfield, Jimmy Cricket, Mark Curry, Dana, Letitia Dean, Dooby Duck and Company, KD and the Diddymen, Eddie 'The Eagle' Edwards, Fenella Fielding, Yvette Fielding, Les Frères Taquins, Gordon The Gopher, Derek Griffiths, Keith Harris, Jim Henson's Muppets, Peter Howitt, Gloria Hunniford, Gorden Kaye, Caron Keating, Matthew Kelly, Bonnie Langford, Jessica Martin, Sylvester McCoy, Mickey Mouse, Jane Marie Osborne, Vanessa Paradis, Nicholas Parsons, The Royal Ballet, Royal Shakespeare Company (featuring John Bowe, Jim Carter, Paul Greenwood,

Imelda Staunton), Phillip Schofield, Carmen Silvera, Wayne
Sleep, Great Soprendo, The State Trumpeters, Jimmy Tamley,
Michelle Thorneycroft, Vienna Boys Choir, Norman Wisdom,
Peggy O'Farrell Stage School, Russell-Leite School, Babette
Langford's Young Set.
Producer: John Fisher.
Director: Brian Whitehouse.

Michael Barrymore's Saturday Night Out

BBC1, Saturday, 6 August 1988, 1925–2010
Michael Barrymore, KD, Martin P. Daniels, Gorden Kaye, Su
Pollard, Micky Zany, Don Hunt (musical director).
Writers: Geoff Atkinson, Kim Fuller, Michael Barrymore.
Producer/director: Kevin Bishop.

Des O'Connor Tonight

Thames, Wednesday, 14 December 1988, 2000–2100
Des O'Connor (host), KD, Kim Wilde, Geoffrey Durham [as The
Great Soprendo], Peter O'Brien, Elaine Smith, Colin Keyes
(musical director).
Writers: Neil Shand, Eddie Braben, Eric Davidson.
Producer/director: Brian Penders.

A Night of Comic Relief 2

BBC1, Friday, 10 March 1989, 1930–0230

Noel Edmonds Saturday Roadshow ('live from a dig on the site of an old Roman hypermarket')

BBC1, Saturday, 14 October 1989, 1740–1825
Noel Edmonds (host), KD, Desmond Lynam.
Writers: Charlie Adams, Martin Booth, John Machin, Stuart Silver, Alan Whiting, Malcolm Robertson.
Producer/director: Michael Leggo.

Give Us a Clue

Thames for the ITV network, Tuesday, 19 December 1989, 1500–1525
Michael Parkinson, Gillian Taylforth, Anthea Turner, Eamonn Holmes, KD, Liza Goddard, Roger Kitter, Paula Wilcox.
Producer: David Clark.
Director: Paul Kirrage.

Des O'Connor Tonight

Thames for the ITV network, Wednesday, 27 December 1989, 2000–2100
Des O'Connor (host), KD, Dionne Warwick, Colin Keyes (musical director).
Writers: Neil Shand, Barry Cryer, Eddie Braben, Eric Davidson.

Bruce Forsyth's Generation Game

BBC1, Friday, 28 September 1990, 2005–2100
Bruce Forsyth (host), Clive James, KD, Royal Navy Training School, The Fabulous Singlettes.
Producer: David Taylor.
Director: Sylvie Boden.

Stage work

24 November 1952 – Tivoli, New Brighton

Meet the Stars

Harry Bailey, Three Cassandras, Pat Hatton and Peggy, Charles and Jupp, Sheila Heffernan, Don Ellis, Ida Shirley, KD, James Ruddy.

11 December 1952 – Shakespeare, Liverpool

The Back Entry Diddlers

Ronald Owen, Eve and John (or Pat and Peter Lee), Jimmy Charters and Co, Gabrielle, Rhythmettes, Harry Castelli, Ken Dodds [sic], Martin Crosbie and Thelma, etc.

1 March 1953 (one-nighter) – Floral Pavilion, New Brighton

Mick Mulligan and his Band, George Melly, Jo Lennard, KD, Basil Guest (impressionist), James Ruddy (tenor), Dorothy Griffiths (vocalist), etc.

6 April 1953 – Floral Pavilion, New Brighton

Easter weekend: Harry Gold and his Pieces of Eight, Jon Clark, Geraldine Scott. Dick Emery, Tom O'Neill, KD.

3 August 1953 – Shakespeare, Liverpool

Grand Holiday Variety

The Four Aces, The Larry Macari Quintette, Ken Dodds [sic], Sandra Wells, Professor Sparks and Thelmina, Hazel and Anthony Ross, Chow Ding, Nat Hope, Gandy Brothers.

19 October 1953 – Hippodrome, Hulme

Lovely to Look At

Phil Strickland, Jack Hayes, Harry Dawson, Sheila Poyser, Paul and Peta Page, Mavis Whyte and KD.

25 January 1954 – Palace, Reading

Malcolm Mitchell Trio, Norman and Niki Grant, The Bashful Boys, Ronnie Dukes, Fredericka's Cats and Dogs, Milton Woodward and Millicent Cooper, KD, Walton and Dorraine.

19 April 1954 – Shakespeare, Liverpool

Tanner Sisters, Norman and Niki Grant, Wilfred Briton and his West End Lovelies, Ravel, KD, Don Arrol and Johnny Lane, Sandow Sisters, Tex James's Ponies and Dogs.

7 June 1954 – Pavilion, Liverpool

Beauty on Duty

Dan Young, KD, Sam Linfield and his Scouts, Syd Jackson, Olga Sanderson, Tommy Dee, Tony Merry, Dick Collins, Fred Renwick.

21 June 1954 – *Grand, Bolton*

Great Cingalee and Co, Lorraine, Aerial Kenways, Lyn and Len Paule, Delly Kin, Derry and Johnstone, Ruby and Charles Wlaat, KD.

9 August 1954 – *Hippodrome, Wigan*

Folies Parisiennes

Jimmy Mac and Frank, Ragoldi Bros, Burke and Kovac, Accordionaires, Jan Harding, Al Shaw, Miss Blandish and her Orchid Models, Jean Raymond's Monte Carlo Bikini Girls, KD, etc.

16 August 1954 – *Derby Castle, Douglas*

Two Pirates, KD, Dumarte and Denzer, Augustos Family, Les Galentos, etc.

13 September 1954 – *Floral Pavilion, Wallasey*

KD, Mavis Whyte, Ramoni Bros, Eddy Bayes, Hilda Heath, Charles and Jupp, Eric D'Arcy, The Great Richard.

20 September 1954 – *Empire, Nottingham*

Brian Andro, Tony Brent, Syd and Paul Kaye, Kenny Baker, Trio Botandos, KD, Marie de Vere's Debutantes.

27 September 1954 – *Empire, Leeds*

Kenny Baker, Gary Miller, Valento and Dorothy, Charles Warren and Jean, Suzette Tarri, Ruby Murray, KD, Marie de Vere's Debutantes.

4 October 1954 – Empire, Sunderland

Kenny Baker, Jimmy James and Co., Pharos and Marina, KD, Ruby Murray, Corzon Trio, Rex and Bessie, Trio Botandos.

18 October 1954 – Queen's, Blackpool

Frankie Vaughan, KD, Paul Dalton, Manley and Austin, Joe Crosbie, David Demott, Bob Nelson, Derry and Johnstone, Hal and Winnie Mack, etc.

1 November 1954 – Hippodrome, Ardwick

Kenny Baker, Jill Day, KD, Skyliners, Jeffrey Lenner, Baker and Douglas, Kelroys, Joan and Earnest, Valento and Dorothy.

22 November 1954 – Palace, Hull

Lupino Lane, George Truzzi, KD, Syret and Cecil, Vadios Brothers, Flack and Lucas, Merry Martins, Calienta and Lolita, Three Buffoons.

26 December 1954 (pantomime) – Pavilion, Liverpool

Aladdin

KD, Marie Joy, Joan Price, Philip Becker, Erik Leifson, Lamarr Bros and Suzette, Benson Dulay and Co., Pan Yue Yen Troupe, etc.

31 January 1955 – Royal Court, Warrington

KD, Thelmina, Two Matanzas, Ringle Brothers, Hollander and Hart, Hilda Heath, Colin Robins, Shirley Sisters.

21 February 1955 – Grand, Bolton

Johnny Brandon and Co., KD, Kentones, Ansons, Ken Swan and McGhee, Eva May Wong, Marie De Vere's Debutantes.

14 March 1955 – Palace, Hull

Kentones, Max Bacon, KD, Harriott and Evans, Two Yolandas, Terry Wilson, Bea and Zelda Marvi, Hilda Heath.

21 March 1955 – Empire, Edinburgh

Eddie Calvert, Herbert De Vere's Girls, The Kordites, Curzon Trio, KD, Jackie, Eddie Parker, Leslie Randall, Jeffrey Lenner.

4 April 1955 – Empire, Nottingham

Eddie Calvert, Nelson Brothers, The Kordites, Jackie, Eddie Parker, Jeffrey Lenner, KD, Marie De Vere's Girls.

18 April 1955 – Carlton, Norwich

Eddie Calvert, The Kordites, Edorics, Mike and Bernie Winters, Quaino, KD, Bob and Marion Konyot, Richman and Jackson.

25 April 1955 – Empire, Finsbury Park

Eddie Calvert, Kordas, The Kordites, Paulette and Renee, KD,

Two Boris, Jeffrey Lenner, Herbert De Vere's Girls, Don Arrol, Norman Meadows.

2 May 1955 – Empire, Liverpool

Eddie Calvert, Riki Linaana and Diane, KD, Raf and Julian, The Kordites, Marie De Vere Girls, Wilson, Keppel and Betty, Jeffrey Lenner, 36 Voices of Variety.

09 May 1955 – Empire, Sunderland

Eddie Calvert, Kordas, KD, The Kordites, Eddie Parker, Jeffrey Lenner, Marie De Vere Girls.

16 May 1955 – Hippodrome, Derby

Eddie Parker, KD, Wilson, Keppel and Betty, Camilleri, Nordics, Ken Barnes and Jean, Valdettes, Earle and Vaughan.

21 May 1955 (summer season) – Central Pier, Blackpool

Let's Have Fun
Morecambe and Wise, KD, Kenny Baker, Jimmy Clitheroe, The Kordites, Joy Harris.

24 October 1955 – Hippodrome, Ardwick

Let's Have Fun
Kenny Baker, KD, Jimmy Clitheroe, Dennis Spicer, The Kordites, Joan Davis Lovelies, Joy Harris, Harry Norway, Peter and Sam Cherry.

31 October 1955 – Empire, Chiswick

Let's Have Fun

Kenny Baker, Joan Turner, The Kordites, Dave Gray, Eva May
Wong, Joan Davis Lovelies, Joy Harris.

14 November 1955 – Opera House, Belfast

Let's Have Fun

KD, Kenny Baker, The Kordites, Dennis Spicer, etc.

21 November 1955 – Empire, Nottingham

Let's Have Fun

Kenny Baker, KD, The Kordites, Jimmy Clitheroe, Dave Gray,
Joan Davis Lovelies, Joy Harris, Romanos.

28 November 1955 – Empire, Sunderland

Let's Have Fun

Kenny Baker, KD, The Kordites, Jimmy Clitheroe, Reg Russell and
Susie, Dave Gray, Joan Davis Lovelies, Joy Harris.

5 December 1955 – Empire, Glasgow

Tony Brent, Averil and Aurel, Jimmy James and Co., Beryl and
Bobo, Kenny Baker, Raf and Julian.

17 December 1955 (pantomime) – Lyceum, Sheffield

Red Riding Hood

11 March 1956 – Palace, Hull

The Blackpool Show
KD, The Kordites, Dennis Spicer, Devine and King, etc.

1 April 1956 – Hippodrome, Ardwick

The Star Show
KD, Joan Turner, Devine and King, Singing Scholars, Westway Girls, Vadios Brothers, Jim Dale, Winston Foxwell.

22 April 1956 – Hippodrome, Brighton

Joan Turner, The Westway Girls, Jimmy James and Co., The Botandos, KD, Devine and King, Dennis Spicer, Eddie Parker.

7 May 1956 – Empire, Liverpool

KD, The Westway Girls, Jimmy James and Co, Winston Foxwell, Joan Turner, The Botandos, Don Lang, The Kordites.

18 May 1956 (summer season) – Central Pier Blackpool

Let's Have Fun
Jimmy James and Co, Jimmy Clitheroe, KD, Roy Castle, Dennis Spicer, Joy Harris, Joseph Ward, Orchid Room Lovelies.

30 October 1956 (six weeks) – Hippodrome, Coventry

The Birthday Show
Jewel and Warriss, Tommy Cooper, Jill Day, Arthur Worsley, KD, Camilleri and Latona, Graham and Chadel.

22 December 1956 (pantomime) – Empire, Liverpool

Cinderella

Beverley Sisters, KD, Terry Bartlett and Colin Ross, Jack and
Manny Francois, Valerie Miller, etc.

10 March 1957 – Gaumont, Cheltenham

Petula Clark, KD, Mrs Shufflewick, The Kordites, Joe 'Mr Piano'
Henderson, Dunn and Grant, Gordon and Bunny Jay, Val and
Laurie Aubrey.

1 April 1957 – Hippodrome, Birmingham

KD, Two Elites, Petula Clark, Die Naukos, Three Deuces, Jeff
Lenner, Joe 'Mr Piano' Henderson, Brian Andro.

8 April 1957 – Empire, Newcastle

Petula Clark, Three Martinis, KD, Brian Andro, Three Deuces,
Donald B Stuart, Joe 'Mr Piano' Henderson, Jimmy Edmundson.

15 April 1957 – Empire, Glasgow

Petula Clark, Three Martinis, KD, Brian Andro, Mike and Bernie
Winters, Three Deuces, Joe 'Mr Piano' Henderson.

22 April 1957 – Hippodrome, Brighton

Petula Clark, Brian Andro, KD, Patricia and Neil del Rina, The
The Kordites, Donald B Stuart, Joe 'Mr Piano' Henderson,
Jeffrey Lenner.

6 May 1957 – Empire, Sheffield

KD, Roy Rivers, Joan Turner, Marie de Vere Trio, Dennis Spicer, Brian Andro, Three Deuces, Jeffrey Lenner

20 May 1957 – Palace, Manchester

KD, Brian Andro, Petula Clark, Jeffrey Lenner, Robert Earl, Del Rinas, Dennis Spicer, Joe 'Mr Piano' Henderson, Trio Rayroc.

27 May 1957 Hippodrome Bristol

Off the Record
Eddie Calvert, KD, Gerry Brereton, Jim Couton, Eddie Rose and Marion, Brian Andro, Paul Dalton, Gillian and June.

1 June 1957 (summer season) – Hippodrome, Blackpool

Rocking with Laughter

11 October 1957 – Royal, Barnsley

Lea Howard, KD, Ansons, Joe Baker and Jack Douglas, Alexander's Dogs, Maureen Kershaw, Windy Blow and the Renee Veamore Girls.

20 October 1957 – Royalty, Chester

Ken Dodd Show

2 November 1957 – Hippodrome, Dudley

Pat Kirkwood, KD, Charlie Cairoli and Paul, Hedley Ward Trio, Boyer and Ravel, Four Furres, Patricia d'Or.

4 November 1957 – Palace, Hull

KD, Jimmy Jackson and his Trio, Winston Foxwell, Georgette, Barbara Law, Barry Anthony, Roy Earl.

17 December 1957 (pantomime) – Palace, Manchester
Aladdin

Norman Evans, Eve Boswell, KD, Arthur Richards, Tilibs Brothers, Leon and Eunice Bartell, Leonard Henry, Joy Zandra, Anne Wilson.

24 March 1958 – Empire, Middlesbrough

KD, Carl Barriteau, Liss Lennon, Duo Russmar, King and Day, Nicky and Charles Carta, Candy Sisters.

31 March 1958 – Empire, Leeds

KD, Al Fuller and Janetta, The Kordites, Tilib Bros, Nick and Charly Carta, Mike Coyne, Liss Lennon.

7 April 1958 – Hippodrome, Brighton

KD, Holt and Gillis, Russ Hamilton, Tilib Brothers, Janie Marden, Terry Scanlon, Mike Coyne, Gilbert.

21 April 1958 – Hippodrome, Bristol

KD, Russ Hamilton, Dennis Spicer, James Green, Barbara Law, Granville Taylor and Valerie, Tilibs Brothers, Rey and Ronjy.

12 May 1958 (summer season) – Central Pier, Blackpool

Let's Have Fun

KD, Don Lang, Yvonne Michel and Erik, Brenda Barry, The Zio Angels, Wally Harper, Mike Coyne, Liss Lennon, Mere Marshall, Victor Gilling, Rita Shearer with guest star, Josef Locke.

13 October 1958 – Hippodrome, Ardwick

KD, The Raindrops, Max and Harry Nesbitt, Jeff Lenner, Paul King, Eddie Ash, Lama Orchid Dancers.

27 October 1958 – Alhambra, Bradford

KD, Two Carols, Dennis Spicer, Two Clifts, The Raindrops, Donna Douglas, Kelwins.

03 November 1958 – Empire, Sheffield

KD, Orchid Dancers, Max Geldray, El Granadas, Don Rennie, Roy Earl, Johnny Lister, Donna Douglas.

10 November 1958 – Empire, Finsbury Park

Eddie Calvert, Blue Orchid Dancers, KD, Georgette, Don Rennie, Trio Rayros, Erikson.

24 December 1958 (pantomime) – Empire, Liverpool
Aladdin

KD, Aileen Cochrane, Jack Storey, Grace O'Connor, Fisher Morgan, David Davenport, Pan Yue Yen Troupe.

13 April 1959 – Empire, Glasgow

KD, Norman and Niki Grant, Rosemary Squires, Russell's Chimps, Kenny Baker, Robert Earl, Jim Cuny and Marion, Dev Shawn.

27 April 1959 – Empire, Leeds

KD, Two Caroles, Kenny Baker, Jim Cuny and Marion, Joe 'Mr Piano' Henderson, Dev Shawn, Billy Russell's Baby Chimps.

25 May 1959 – Royalty, Chester
Ken Dodd Show

8 June 1959 – Hippodrome, Coventry
It's Great to be Young

KD, Rosemary Squires, Kenny Baker, Dev Shawn, Dunja Twins and 'Cool for Cats'.

26 June 1959 (summer season) – Britannia Pier, Great Yarmouth
Tops Again

KD, Earle and Vaughan, the Barry Sisters, Joan and Arnaut, the Iris Roy Trio, Shelagh Miller, Sylvia Lee, Michael Austin, Jean Belmont Dancers.

19 October 1959 – Hippodrome, Ardwick

KD, The Raindrops, Dennis Spicer with James Green, Dinah Kay, Reco and May, Rochelle Trio, Rexanos.

2 November 1959 – Empire, Newcastle

KD, Al Fuller and Janette, Mandy and Sandy, Dinah Kaye, Trio Vedette, Jimmy Edmundson, Reco and May.

23 November 1959 – Royal, Hanley

KD, Elaine Delmar, Bridie Devon, Gilbert, Mike Coyne, Davies and Lee, Dene Four.

23 December 1959 (pantomime) – Alhambra, Bradford

Jack and the Beanstalk

KD, Tony Heaton, Lisbeth Lennon, Carol Payne, Manetti Twins, Rex Rashley, The Astaire Brothers and Gulliver Giants, Trevor Evans, Brigid Cadman, Laidler Sunbeams, Corps de Ballet.

18 April 1960 (six weeks) – Hippodrome, Coventry

Spring Show

KD, Shirley Bassey, Three Monarchs, The Raindrops, Freddie Sales, Les Mathurins, Les Frank Medini, Six Debonnaires, Sixteen Debutantes.

1 June 1960 (summer season) – Pavilion, Torquay

Star Time

KD, Lauri Lupino Lane and George Truzzi, The Raindrops, Janie

Marden, Emerson and Jayne, Linda Bywaters, George Mitchell Singers, Eight Starettes.

23 October 1960 – Palace, Manchester

Star Time (four weeks)

KD, the Peters Sisters, Eddie Calvert, Lauri Lupino Lane and George Truzzi, Joe 'Mr Piano' Henderson, Freddie Sales, Dior Dancers, Three Merkys, 16 Debutantes, 8 Debonnaires.

21 November 1960 – Empire, Liverpool

Star Time (two weeks)

KD, the Peters Sisters, Eddie Calvert, Lauri Lupino Lane and George Truzzi, Joe 'Mr Piano' Henderson, Freddie Sales, Dior Dancers, Three Merkys, 16 Debutantes, 8 Debonnaires.

19 December 1960 – Hippodrome, Coventry

The Pied Piper of Hamelin

KD, Beryl Reid, Janie Marden, Ken Roberts, Stanley Platts, Joyanne Delancey, Vivien Grant, Kenneth Gilbert, Wilfred Grove, Jonathan Fryer, Lynda Bywaters, the Roselli Singers, Corps de Ballet, the Three Merkys.

Notes

Introduction

1 'Comic Ken Dodd, whose fame rivalled the Beatles, dies at 90', Associated Press, 12 March 2018.
2 @sanditoksvig, Twitter, 12 March 2018.
3 'Sir Ken Dodd's widow Lady Anne pays moving tribute', *Liverpool Echo* (online edition), 12 March 2018.
4 @GaryDelaney, Twitter, 12 March 2018.
5 Author's interview with Ashtar Al Khirsan, 15 May 2019.
6 Tom Price (BBC Radio Wales, tx: 21 August 2015).
7 *Behind the Laughter* (BBC1, tx: 13 October 2003).
8 Michael Billington, 'Funny Ha Ha', *The Guardian*, 7 April 1973, p. 8.
9 *An Audience with Ken Dodd* (LWT, tx: 3 December 1994).
10 *Behind the Laughter* (BBC1, tx: 13 October 2003).
11 Author's interview with Ashtar Al Khirsan, 15 May 2019.

Chapter 1 – Portrait of the artist as a Diddyman

1 *Liverpool Echo*, 8 November 1927, p. 1.
2 *Liverpool Echo*, 5 November 1925, p. 11.
3 Contemporary account, quoted in *Knotty Ash, Old Swan and West Derby* by Gordon Radley (A&R Publications, Liverpool, 1986), p. 9.
4 *Knotty Ash, Old Swan and West Derby* by Gordon Radley (A&R Publications, Liverpool, 1986), p. 27.
5 'He Doesn't Exist – Officially', *Liverpool Echo*, 1 May 1931, p. 10.
6 Ibid.
7 Derek White, 'The hermit(s) of Knotty Ash who ate squirrels for dinner', *Liverpool Echo*, 27 January 1979, p. 8.

8   *Desert Island Discs*, (BBC Radio 4, tx: 3 June 1990).

9   *Desert Island Discs*, (BBC Home Service, tx: 13 July 1963).

10 *Desert Island Discs*, (BBC Radio 4, tx: 3 June 1990).

11 Nick Garbutt, 'Arrears for souvenirs', *Sunday Tribune* (Dublin), 23 July 1989, p. 12.

12 Anthony Clare, *In the Psychiatrist's Chair* (Heinemann, London, 1992), p. 57.

13 *Desert Island Discs*, (BBC Home Service, tx: 13 July 1963).

14 *Desert Island Discs*, (BBC Radio 4, tx: 3 June 1990).

15 Ibid.

16 '"I ran my own concerts at 7!" says Ken Dodd', *Liverpool Echo*, 27 June 1956, p. 6.

17 Ibid.

18 *Desert Island Discs*, (BBC Home Service, tx: 13 July 1963).

19 *Times Remembered: Schooldays* (BBC2, tx: 30 May 1973).

20 *Desert Island Discs*, (BBC Radio 4, tx: 3 June 1990).

21 Ibid.

22 '"I ran my own concerts at 7!" says Ken Dodd', *Liverpool Echo*, 27 June 1956, p. 6.

23 *Desert Island Discs* (BBC Radio 4, tx: 3 June 1990).

24 *Times Remembered: Schooldays* (BBC2, tx: 30 May 1973).

25 Anthony Clare, *In the Psychiatrist's Chair* (Heinemann, London, 1992), p. 57.

26 *Desert Island Discs* (BBC Radio 4, tx: 3 June 1990).

27 *Times Remembered: Ken Dodd's Schooldays* (BBC1, tx: 30 May 1973).

28 *Desert Island Discs* (BBC Home Service, tx: 13 July 1963).

29 *Times Remembered: Ken Dodd's Schooldays* (BBC1, tx: 30 May 1973).

30 '"I ran my own concerts at 7!" says Ken Dodd', *Liverpool Echo*, 27 June 1956, p. 6.

31 *Arena: Ken Dodd's Happiness* (BBC2, tx: 24 December 2007).

32 *Liverpool Echo*, 20 November 1941, p. 1.

33 '"I ran my own concerts at 7!" says Ken Dodd, *Liverpool Echo*, 27 June 1956, p. 6.

34 Ibid.

35 *Loose Ends* (BBC Radio 4, tx: 5 June 2004).

36 '"I ran my own concerts at 7!" says Ken Dodd', *Liverpool Echo*, 27 June 1956, p. 6.

37 Ibid.

38 *Ken Dodd's Showbiz* (BBC1, tx: 20 March 1982).
39 Ibid.
40 'To Entertain You', *Liverpool Echo*, 16 December 1952, p. 4.
41 *Desert Island Discs* (BBC Radio 4, tx: 3 June 1990).

Chapter 2 – The road to Mandalay and fame

1 'Ball of the Year', *The Stage*, 23 March 1989, p. 13.
2 *The Art of Artists* (BBC Radio 2, tx: 7 March 2016).
3 Author's interview with Peter Pilbeam, 14 April 2019.
4 *Manchester Guardian*, 2 November 1954, p. 3.
5 *Manchester Evening News*, quoted in advertisement for Dodd in *The Stage*.
6 'A meteoric career', *Hull Daily Mail*, 22 July 1925, p. 3.
7 Author's interview with John Fisher, 11 May 2006.
8 Gordon Burn, 'Variety in this country will never ever die', *Radio Times*, 4–10 November 1972, p. 7.
9 'Christmas Shows', *Liverpool Echo*, 28 December 1954, p. 2.
10 'Doddy – the Panto hero', *The Stage*, 23 June 1983, p. 4.
11 *How Tickled I've Been* (BBC Radio 4, tx: 25 December 2007).
12 Author's interview with Peter Pilbeam, 14 April 2019.
13 'Lines from Lancs', *The Stage*, 4 August 1955, p. 5.
14 'Lines from Lancs', The Stage, 16 June 1955, p. 4.
15 Author's interview with Stanley Baxter, 31 May 2006.
16 'Scottish Flavour', *The Stage*, 15 December 1955, p. 4.
17 'Ken Dodd Is Tops', *The Stage*, 3 November 1955, p. 5.
18 Ibid.
19 *Sunday Sunday* (LWT, tx: 20 October 1985).
20 Bob Monkhouse, *Over the Limit* (Century, London, 1998), p. 312.
21 Ibid, p. 313.
22 Ibid.
23 Ibid.
24 Ibid, p. 314.
25 *Desert Island Discs* (BBC Home Service, tx: 13 July 1963).
26 *Night Waves* (BBC Radio 3, tx: 30 October 2012).
27 Brighton's meat is Wigan's poison', *The Guardian*, 23 April 1960, p. 3.
28 *Desert Island Discs* (BBC Home Service, 13 July 1963).
29 'Brighton's meat is Wigan's poison', *The Guardian*, 23 April 1960, p. 3.

30 *My Favourite Hymns* (Granada, tx: 10 October 2004).

31 *Everyman: What's So Funny About Religion Anyway?* (BBC1, tx: 1 May 1977),

32 *An Audience with Ken Dodd* (LWT, tx: 3 December 1994).

33 Memo from Grahame Miller, acting head of north region programmes to WL Streeton, head of programme contracts, 5 December 1958 (BBC Written Archives – Artist file N18/2484/1 Ken Dodd 1953–1960).

34 Memo from W. L. Streeton, head of programme contracts to Grahame Miller, acting head of North Region programmes, 28 November 1958 (BBC Written Archives – Artist file N18/2484/1 Ken Dodd 1953–1960).

35 Denis Norden, Sybil Harper, Norma Gilbert, *Coming To You Live* (Methuen, London, 1986), p. 131.

36 Author's correspondence with Paul Kay, 27 October 2009.

37 *Celebration* (Granada, tx: 17 September 1992).

38 Eddie Braben, *The Book What I Wrote* (Hodder and Stoughton, London, 2004), p. 8.

39 Ibid, p. 6.

40 'Braben's City: To market – and I hated it...', *Liverpool Echo*, 27 October 1982, p. 6.

41 Ibid.

42 Eddie Braben, *The Book What I Wrote* (Hodder and Stoughton, London, 2004), p. 26.

43 Author's interview with Judith Chalmers, 16 April 2019.

44 Letter from Geoff Lawrence to Ken Dodd, 1 March 1960 (BBC Written Archives – Artist file N18/2484/1 Ken Dodd 1953–1960).

45 Letter from Tom Sloan to Dave Forrester, 4 November 1963, (BBC Written Archives – file TVART3 – Ken Dodd – File 2 – 1963–1970).

46 Programme reviews, *The Stage*, 7 June 1962, p. 11.

47 Ibid.

48 Memo from P. Thurstan Holland, assistant head of North Regional programmes, to B.W. Cave-Browne-Cave-Grahame, head of North Regional programmes, 17 July 1961 (BBC Written Archives – Artist file N18/2484/2 Ken Dodd 1961–1965).

49 Memo from Barney Colehan to assistant head of North Regional programmes, 2 November 1961, (BBC Written Archives – Artist file N18/2484/2 Ken Dodd 1961–1965).

50 Author's interview with Peter Pilbeam, 14 April 2019.

51 Author's interview with Dave Dutton, 18 October 2018.

52 *Behind the Laughter* (BBC1, tx: 13 October 2003).

53 Ibid.

54 Anthony Clare, *In the Psychiatrist's Chair* (Heinemann, London, 1992), p. 42.

55 Ibid.

56 Author's correspondence with Angela Wilson, 15 December 2018.

Chapter 3 – The Liverpool explosion

1 *Cotswold Roundabout* number 6, 1964, Cotswold Tape Recording Society, held by Gloucestershire Archives.

2 Ibid.

3 Author's interview with Johnnie Hamp, 17 October 2018.

4 *Late Scene Extra* (Granada: tx: 27 November 1963).

5 'Christmas Shows', *The Stage*, 2 January 1964, pp. 26–27.

6 'What the critics say', *Liverpool Echo*, 7 January 1964, p. 2.

7 'All Doddie wanted was a Beatle sound', *Liverpool Echo*, 12 December 1963, p. 9.

8 Memo from Jim Davidson, assistant head of light entertainment (sound) to Eric Miller, 7 September 1961 (BBC Written Archives – file R19/1622/1, Light Entertainment file 1 – Ken Dodd Programmes 1958–1965).

9 Memo from Grahame Miller, head of North Regional programmes to Con Mahoney, assistant head of light entertainment (sound), 23 July 1963 (BBC Written Archives – file R19/1622/1, Light Entertainment file 1 – Ken Dodd Programmes 1958–1965).

10 Memo from Grahame Miller, head of North Regional programmes to Con Mahoney, assistant head of light entertainment (sound), 1 August 1963 (BBC Written Archives – file R19/1622/1, Light Entertainment file 1 – Ken Dodd Programmes 1958–1965).

11 *It's Great To Be Young* (BBC Light Programme, tx: 18 November 1960).

12 *Star Parade* (BBC Light Programme, tx: 18 April 1963).

13 Eddie Braben, *The Book What I Wrote* (Hodder and Stoughton, London, 2004), p. 30.

14 Author's interview with David McKellar, 25 January 2019.

15 Author's interview with Judith Chalmers, 16 April 2019.

16 Author's interview with Judith Chalmers, 16 April 2019.

17 *The Ken Dodd Show* (BBC Light Programme, tx: 2 May 1965).

18 Ibid.

19 *The Ken Dodd Show* (BBC Light Programme, tx: 4 July 1965).

20 Memo from Con Mahoney, assistant head of light entertainment (sound), to Roy Rich, head of light entertainment (sound), 28 February 1966 (BBC Written Archives – file R19/2038/1, Light Entertainment file – Ken Dodd Programmes).

21 Memo from Roy Rich, head of light entertainment (sound) to all producers, 16 November 1965 (BBC Written Archives – file R19/1622/1, Light Entertainment File 1, Ken Dodd 1958–1965).

22 Author's interview with Johnnie Hamp, 17 October 2018.

23 'No rationing for Mr Dodd', *The Times*, 21 April 1965, p. 13.

24 Clifford Davis, 'A great show', *Daily Mirror*, 21 April 1965, p. 18.

25 'Dotty Ken "Discovered at Last"', *Daily Express*, 21 April 1965, p. 6.

26 *Arena: Ken Dodd's Happiness* (BBC2, tx: 24 December 2007).

27 *Arena: Ken Dodd's Happiness* (BBC2, tx: 24 December 2007).

28 'Palladium: Stories of the Stars', *Reading Evening Post*, 9 October 1978, p. 8.

29 *Ed Doolan interviews Ken Dodd* (BBC7, tx: 1 January 2006).

30 'Doddy and the discs', *The Observer*, 11 December 1966, p. 23.

31 Ibid.

32 'Doddy and the Diddymen' (Columbia SEG7866).

33 'Pop singles', *Melody Maker*, 28 August 1965, p. 12.

34 *Ed Doolan interviews Ken Dodd* (BBC7, tx: 1 January 2006).

35 Ibid.

36 Tom Price (BBC Radio Wales, tx: 21 August 2015).

37 Letter from Tom Sloan to Dave Forrester, 22 June 1965 (BBC Written Archives – file TVART3 – Ken Dodd – File 2 – 1963–1970).

38 'Telecrit', *Liverpool Echo*, 1 November 1965, p. 2.

39 'Zany World of Ken Dodd wins the laughs', *The Times*, 9 November 1965, p. 15.

40 'From tea to Royal cocoa-time', *The Guardian*, 9 November 1965, p. 18.

41 *The Ken Dodd Show*, studio recording for BBC1, 25 December 1965.

42 Ibid.

43 Ibid.
44 *The Ken Dodd Show* (BBC1, tx: 24 July 1966)

Chapter 4 – Doddy at the top

1   'Diddyness is Dodd shaped', *TV Times*, Anglia edition, 7 January 1967, p. 9.
2   Author's interview with David Hamilton, 26 January 2019.
3   Ibid.
4   Ibid.
5   Ibid.
6   Ibid.
7   George Melly, 'Television', *The Observer*, 3 March 1968, p. 31.
8   Marjorie Norris, 'It's Ken at his best', *The Stage*, 26 January 1967, p. 14.
9   Ibid.
10 Author's interview with David Hamilton, 26 January 2019.
11 Ibid.
12 Author's interview with Andy Eastwood, 13 May 2019.
13 Author's interview with David Hamilton, 26 January 2019.
14 Ibid.
15 Author's interview with Anthony Wall, 25 April 2019.
16 Anthony Clare, *In the Psychiatrist's Chair* (Heinemann, London, 1992), pp. 46–47.
17 *My Favourite Hymns* (Granada, tx: 10 October 2004).
18 *How Tickled I've Been* (BBC Radio 4, tx: 25 December 2007).
19 'Ken Dodd gets his best scriptwriter ever for his next big part', *The Stage*, 9 September 1971, p. 1.
20 *Scan* (BBC Radio 4, tx: 18 November 1971).
21 'A triumph for Doddy in *Twelfth Night*', *Liverpool Echo*, 11 November 1971, p. 11.
22 *This Is Your Life* (Thames, tx: 7 May 1990).
23 'Court to reopen for Christmas', *Liverpool Echo*, 13 July 1970, p1.
24 Simon Hoggart, 'Ken Dodd may take Diddy Men to Kendoon', *The Guardian*, 20 February 1969.
25 'Ken Dodd explains his celebration of laughter', *The Stage*, 28 December 1972, p. 1.
26 *Scan* (BBC Radio 4, tx: 18 November 1971).

27 *The Art of Artists* (BBC Radio 2, tx: 7 March 2016).

28 'Funny ha-ha', *The Guardian*, 7 April 1973, p. 8.

29 Ibid.

30 Merete Bates, 'Ken Dodd's Ha Ha in Liverpool', *The Guardian*, 4 April 1973, p. 10.

31 Michael Billington, 'Funny ha-ha', *The Guardian*, 7 April 1973, p. 8.

32 *Night Waves*, BBC Radio 3, tx: 30 October 2012.

33 Author's interview with Andy Eastwood, 13 May 2019.

34 Stephen Dixon, 'Ken Dodd', *The Guardian*, 20 December 1977, p. 8.

35 *Ken Dodd's Comical Market* (BBC Radio 2, tx: 31 December 1972).

36 Author's interview with Peter Pilbeam, 14 April 2019.

37 Author's interview with Dave Dutton, 18 October 2018.

38 Ibid.

39 Michael Billington, *How Tickled I Am* (Elm Tree Books, London, 1977), p. 62.

40 Ibid, p. 61.

41 Author's interview with anonymous, 29 September 2004.

42 *Cotswold Roundabout* number 6, 1964, Cotswold Tape Recording Society, held by Gloucestershire Archives.

43 'Doddy back in limelight', *Liverpool Echo*, 12 April 1990, p. 38.

44 Ken Dodd, Dave Dutton and Hal Dootson, *Ken Dodd's Butty Book* (Macmillan, London, 1977), p. 16.

45 Ibid, p. 27.

46 Author's interview with Tony MacDonnell, 28 January 2019.

47 'Grief stricken Ken: I won't quit', *Liverpool Echo*, 2 July 1977, p. 15.

Chapter 5 – Back to the boards

1   *The Ken Dodd Laughter Show* (Show 1, Thames: tx: 8 January 1979).

2   *The Ken Dodd Laughter Show* (Show 2, Thames, tx: 15 January 1979 – Eric Morbid is a reference to Eric Morley, a director of the ballrooms and gambling firm Mecca and the creator of the *Miss World* contest).

3   Jeremy Myerson, 'Seen at the Palladium', *The Stage*, 30 October 1980, p. 8.

4   'Doddy bides his time: Transatlantic tickle ahead', *Liverpool Echo*, 21 October 1980, p. 7.

5   'Doddy not so tickled by Diddynappers', *Liverpool Echo*, 7 January 1982, p. 3.
6   Author's correspondence with Tim Worthington, 14 May 2019.
7   Author's interview with John Fisher, 11 May 2006.
8   Author's interview with Lesley Taylor, 20 February 2019.
9   Peter Fiddick, 'Ken Dodd's Showbiz', *The Guardian*, 15 March 1982, p. 11.
10   'Arthur Askey who is 75 today talks to Hugh Hebert', *The Guardian*, 6 June 1975, p. 10.
11   *Jim'll Fix It* (BBC1, tx: 25 December 1982).
12   Author's correspondence with Roger Ordish, 19 December 2018.
13   Michael Grade interview, BBC online, 25 April 2004.
14   'Doctor Who takes on the Street', *Daily Mirror*, 20 August 1987, p. 9.
15   'Doddy heads the Who queue', *Liverpool Echo*, 19 June 1987, p. 4.
16   Author's interview with Chris Clough, 5 February 2019.
17   *But First This* (BBC1, 1987).
18   Ibid.

Chapter 6 – The trial of Kenneth Arthur Dodd

1   'Ken Dodd on tax fraud charge', *Daily Mirror*, 7 June 1988, p. 2.
2   'I have done no wrong, says tax-row Doddy', *Daily Express*, 8 June 1988, p. 2.
3   *Roland Rat: The Series* (BBC1, tx: 16 May 1988).
4   Dodd 'paid £825,000 in move to settle tax debts', *Daily Express*, 11 August 1988, p. 7.
5   Ibid.
6   'Piggott sobs as Queen strips him of his OBE', *Daily Mirror*, 7 June 1988, p. 1.
7   'Queen strips Lester's OBE', *Daily Express*, 7 June 1988, p. 1.
8   Memo from Richard Ryder to Margaret Thatcher, 4 October 1979 (Margaret Thatcher archive).
9   Denis Thatcher's handwritten annotation on a copy of a letter from private secretary Caroline Stephens to Ken Dodd, 4 August 1980 (Margaret Thatcher archive).
10   Letter from Margaret Thatcher to Ken Dodd, 31 October 1980 (Margaret Thatcher archive).

11 Letter from Margaret Thatcher to Ken Dodd, 20 October 1981 (Margaret Thatcher archive).

12 'Seasonal Shows', *The Stage*, 12 January 1989, p. 40.

13 'Chop for Mersey comics', *Liverpool Echo*, 14 March 1989, p. 3.

14 'Doddy indulges in a little horseplay', *Liverpool Echo*, 6 February 1989, p. 4.

15 Author's interview with Johnnie Hamp, 17 October 2018.

16 'Diddy Doddy's hair-raising war on litter', *Liverpool Echo*, 9 May 1989, p. 5.

17 'The deceitful side of Ken Dodd – QC', *Liverpool Echo,* 19 June 1989, p13.

18 Doddy shunned superstar life, *Liverpool Echo*, 21 June 1989, p. 17.

19 'The deceitful side of Ken Dodd – QC', *Liverpool Echo*, 19 June 1989, p. 3.

20 Author's interview with Dave Dutton, 18 October 2018 (Mabel Dutton eventually took against Dodd, drawing vampire teeth on a publicity still and burning out the eyes on a Diddyman doll with her cigarette).

21 'Excuse me while I take you apart: George Carman QC, ultimate inquisitor', *The Independent*, 19 September 1992.

22 Ibid.

23 'Carman vs Carman', *The Guardian*, 26 January 2002, p. B9

24 'Wonderland of Doddy's accountant, by trial QC', *Liverpool Echo*, 26 June 1989, p. 11.

25 Ibid.

26 Ibid.

27 'Taxmen "forced accountant" in Ken Dodd probe', *Liverpool Echo*, 27 June 1989, p. 8.

28 'Dodd tells of "Monty Python" accountants', *Liverpool Echo*, 10 July 1989, p. 5.

29 Author's interview with David McKellar, 25 January 2019

30 Author's correspondence with Tim Worthington, 14 May 2019.

31 'Dodd "misled by adverts"', *Liverpool Echo*, 29 June 1989, p. 11.

32 Advertisement, *Belfast Telegraph*, 16 November 1970, p. 9.

33 'Furtive – you are joking!', *Liverpool Echo*, 8 July 1989, p. 4.

34 'Doddy's diddling plan – by his agent', *Liverpool Echo*, 4 July 1989, pp. 1 and 9.

35 Author's interview with David Hamilton, January 2019.

36 Anthony Clare, *In the Psychiatrist's Chair* (Heinemann, London, 1992), p. 55.
37 Ibid.
38 Ibid. p. 47.
39 Roy Hudd, *A Fart in a Colander* (Michael O'Mara Books, London, 2010), p. 108.
40 'Judge tells of Dodd's work and dedication', *Liverpool Echo*, 19 July 1989, p11.
41 'Public tickled pink for Dodd', Daily Express Opinion, *Daily Express*, 22 July 1989, p. 8.
42 'Beyond our Ken', Mirror Comment, *Daily Mirror*, 22 July 1989, p. 2.
43 The mad, sad, mean and lonely world of a Diddyman', *Daily Mirror*, 22 July 1989, pp. 8–9.
44 John Sweeney, 'Honest fool who bared his soul', *The Observer*, 23 July 1989, p. 15.
45 *Night Waves* (BBC Radio 3, tx: 30 October 2012).

Chapter 7 – The last of the variety comics

1   'Doddy is hot property', *The Stage*, 27 July 1989, p. 3.
2   Author's interview with Andy Eastwood, 13 May 2019.
3   Author's interview with Ashtar Al Khirsan, 15 May 2019.
4   Author's interview with Andy Eastwood, 13 May 2019.
5   *Night Waves* (BBC Radio 3, tx: 30 October 2012).
6   'Ken Dodd's stalker locked up', *Liverpool Echo* (online edition), 21 November 2003 (The *Daily Telegraph*'s report of the hearing claimed that Tagg said this in 'a high-pitched mock Diddyman voice'.)
7   Fred Norris, 'Turn again Doddy! Now he may go country-style', *Liverpool Echo*, 13 December 1980, p. 4.
8   Author's correspondence with Gary Bainbridge, 31 May 2019.
9   Author's interview with David Hamilton, 27 January 2019.
10 *The Dog Show* (BBC1, tx: 17 September 1984).
11 *Ed Doolan Interviews Ken Dodd* (BBC7, tx: 6 January 2006).
12 *Night Waves* (BBC Radio 3: tx: 30 October 2012).
13 Author's interview with Andy Eastwood, 13 May 2019.
14 *This Is Your Life* (Thames, tx: 7 May 1990).
15 Author's interview with Andy Eastwood, 13 May 2019.
16 Ibid.

Chapter 8 – Dodd not go gentle...

1   Author's interview with Anthony Wall, 25 April 2019.
2   Author's interview with Ashtar Al Khirsan, 15 May 2019.
3   *Arena: Ken Dodd's Happiness* (BBC2, tx: 24 December 2007).
4   Author's interview with Andy Hollingworth, 19 May 2019.
5   Author's interview with Anthony Wall, 25 April 2019.
6   Pat Elston, 'Now Ken Dodd can keep his promise and marry the girl who helped him get to the top!', *The People*, 24 October 1965, p. 6.
7   Author's correspondence with Jeff Stevenson, 13 May 2019.
8   *The Museum of Curiosity* (BBC Radio 4, tx: 26 January 2016).
9   Author's interview with Ashtar Al Khirsan, 15 May 2019.
10 Author's interview with John Lloyd, 21 January 2019.
11 Author's interview with Ashtar Al Khirsan, 15 May 2019.
12 'This is what it's like to watch a Ken Dodd show', *Liverpool Echo* (online edition), 12 March 2018.
13 'I've been to a very dark place, but tearful Doddy vows "I'm coming out into the sunshine"', *Liverpool Echo*, 26 January 2018, p. 10.
14 'Sir Ken Dodd leaves hospital after 6 weeks – greeted by his Diddy Men', YouTube footage.
15 'Close friend of Ken Dodd from Horwich remembers late comic', *Bolton News*, 12 March 2018.

Chapter 9 – Epilogue

1   Author's interview with Andy Eastwood, 13 May 2019.
2   Ibid.
3   Author's interview with David Hamilton, 27 January 2019.
4   Author's interview with Dave Dutton, 18 October 2018.
5   Pat Elston, 'Now Ken Dodd can keep his promise and marry the girl who helped him get to the top!', *The People*, 24 October 1965, p. 6.
6   Author's interview with Ashtar Al Khirsan, 15 May 2019.
7   Ibid.
8   Author's interview with Andy Eastwood, 13 May 2019.

Bibliography

Michael Billington, *How Tickled I Am: A Celebration of Ken Dodd* (Elm Tree Books, London, 1977).

Eddie Braben, *The Book What I Wrote* (Hodder and Stoughton, London, 2004).

Anthony Clare, *In the Psychiatrist's Chair* (Heinemann, London, 1992).

Mike Craig, *Look Back with Laughter* (four volumes) (Mike Craig, Manchester, 1996–2000).

Ken Dodd, Dave Dutton and Hal Dootson, *Ken Dodd's Butty Book* (Macmillan, London, 1977).

Dave Dutton, *The Fifty Bob Kid: the autobiography of a northern bastard from Factory Street (East) to Coronation Street and beyond* (CreateSpace, Scotts Valley, 2018).

Stephen Griffin, *Ken Dodd: The Biography* (Michael O'Mara Books, London, 2011).

Roy Hudd, *A Fart in a Colander* (Michael O'Mara Books, London, 2010).

Bob Monkhouse, *Over the Limit* (Century, London, 1998).

Denis Norden, Sybil Harper and Norma Gilbert, *Coming to You Live* (Methuen, London, 1986).

Gordon Radley, *Knotty Ash, Old Swan and West Derby* (A&R Publications, Liverpool, 1986).

Acknowledgments

Ken Dodd knew the value of good material. For much of the material in these pages, I have two groups of people to thank.

Firstly, the staff of the BBC Written Archives Centre at Caversham, near Reading, and specifically Louise North, the archivist who found every last memo, contract and scribbled note pertaining to Ken Dodd that had been generated within the Corporation during his long career. It is when trying to find information about Dodd's work for other broadcasters that one realises how special and unique the Written Archives are and the BBC is. There is no other resource like it. Everything else has to be pieced together from fragments.

Next, enormous gratitude is also extended to the people who knew and worked with Sir Ken who spared the time to talk to or correspond with me: Ashtar Al Khirsan, Gary Bainbridge, Danny Baker, Judith Chalmers, Chris Clough, Dave Dutton, Andy Eastwood, David Hamilton, Johnnie Hamp, John Lloyd, Tony MacDonnell, David McKellar, Roger Ordish, Peter Pilbeam, Jeff Stevenson, Lesley Taylor, Anthony Wall, Angela Wilson and Tim Worthington.

It's all very well speaking to people, but the results have to be transcribed, a thankless task. Happily, I was able to pass some of the responsibility on to Juliette Jones, who seems to revel in it, as well as having a knowledge of show business that means there's nothing to correct. She does it for a living and I can't recommend her highly enough.

Next, I must shower warmth, love and thanks upon Georgy Jamieson. When not speaking peace unto the listeners of BBC Radio Suffolk, Georgy keeps her comedy anorak zipped up even tighter than mine, and when I said I was beginning work on this book, she introduced me to Andy Hollingworth, whose enthusiasm, kindness and wisdom were vital. Enthusiasm, kindness and wisdom were also forthcoming from Jason Hazeley, whose insights are always precious, whether delivered over text, email or pints.

Every January, the alumni of the BBC light entertainment department meet for a drink or eight, and I'm lucky enough to be invited as a friend of the family. It's always a joy to see Anna Staniland and Tony Newman, and I have to thank them for making several interview suggestions and then introducing me to the people in question at the do. They also run a smashing B&B at their Somerset home (Tythe Barn in Crowcombe). Tell them I sent you.

The research for this book would have been much harder without the assistance of a small secular cult based upon worship of the monocle-wearing entertainer Fred Emney. In particular, Steve Arnold, Graham Barnard, Steve Berry, Shaun Butcher, Al Dupres, Stephen Dutfield, Ian Greaves, George Grimwood, Toby Hadoke, Simon Harries, Andrew Henderson, Gareth Randall, Gary Rodger, Matt Rosser, Peter Thomas, John Williams and Rob Williams went over and above the call of duty in supplying me with hard-to-locate programmes and literature from their archives as well as introducing me to interviewees.

I offer huge thanks and 15% of my love to my agent, David Smith at the Annette Green Agency. Writing is a solitary business, and David has been a great sounding board. At Head of Zeus, it has been a joy to be reunited with Richard Milbank, an editor of sensitivity, insight and knowledge, and a delight to work with Florence Hare. Thanks also to Steve Doherty of Giddy Goat Productions and Sioned Wiliam at Radio 4 for giving me a documentary to fret about while I was writing. Also, thanks to PLR and ALCS for the seemingly random and always welcome windfalls.

For more general kindness, love and support, I must thank Alanna Lauder, Susannah Godman, Anita Kelly and her son Peter, Alex Newton, Alastair Doughty, Sam Taylor, Clair Woodward, Jonny Bruce, Sophie Jones, John Foster, Martin Fenton, Gavin Sutherland, Patrick Humphries and Sue Parr, Adam Cumiskey, Kerry Swash and Allen Painter, Jane Horrell, Rachel Sommerville, Roy Holliday, Chris Ponting, Martin Cooper, Alan and Debbie Swain, Richard and Karla Howes, Stu and Carole Crawshaw, Pam Sorsby and Steve Morgan, Richie Paradise, Pete Cater, Steve White, Alan Wood and Francis Wheen.

Finally, I must embarrass my daughter, Primrose. When she was a tiny thing, she turned to me while I was watching an archive gem for work purposes and asked 'Daddy, why is all of your television grey?' We watch a lot of (not always age-appropriate) comedy together, and when we visited Knotty

Ash in the pouring rain, she didn't moan. Much. Sir Ken Dodd said his father was the funniest person he ever knew. I think Primrose might be the funniest person I'll ever know.

Any errors contained within are the fault of my senior research assistant Lyttelton, and her apprentice Jessamy Beagle.

Aberdare
September 2019

Index

371